Excavating Indiana Jones

ALSO FROM RANDY LAIST
AND McFARLAND

*The Twin Towers in Film: A Cinematic History
of New York's World Trade Center* (2020)

Looking for Lost: *Critical Essays
on the Enigmatic Series* (edited by, 2011)

Excavating Indiana Jones
Essays on the Films and Franchise

Edited by RANDY LAIST

McFarland & Company, Inc., Publishers
Jefferson, North Carolina

ISBN (print) 978-1-4766-7692-0
ISBN (ebook) 978-1-4766-3972-7

LIBRARY OF CONGRESS AND BRITISH LIBRARY
CATALOGUING DATA ARE AVAILABLE

Library of Congress Control Number 2020012661

© 2020 Randy Laist. All rights reserved

No part of this book may be reproduced or transmitted in any form or by any means, electronic or mechanical, including photocopying or recording, or by any information storage and retrieval system, without permission in writing from the publisher.

Front cover images © 2020 Shutterstock

Printed in the United States of America

McFarland & Company, Inc., Publishers
 Box 611, Jefferson, North Carolina 28640
  www.mcfarlandpub.com

Table of Contents

Introduction
    RANDY LAIST   1

History

Situating Indy: American Archaeologists, Global Ambitions and the Interwar Years
    ANDREW W. BELL   13

Fordian Knots: Indiana Jones and the Cinema of John Ford
    BRIAN BREMS   25

"You call this archaeology?" Indiana Jones and Hollywood's View on the Nature of History
    RYAN STAUDE   38

Cultural Politics

Translocations, Cultural Geography and Anthropological Imperialism in *Raiders of the Lost Ark*
    TATIANA PROROKOVA   51

"I said no camels!" Indiana Jones and the Catalogue of Orientalism
    MAT HARDY   64

The Temple of Orientalism
    DEBADITYA MUKHOPADHYAY   76

The Quest for "Alien" Indigenous Knowledge in *Indiana Jones and the Kingdom of the Crystal Skull*
    KASEY JONES-MATRONA   87

Identity

Indiana Jones and the Crusade for Authenticity
    Siobhan Lyons   103

"I came to find my father": Indiana Jones and the Quest for the Lost Father
    Linda Wight   114

Indiana Jones as Educated Swashbuckler
    Jennifer Crumley   126

"It belongs in a museum," or Does It? Indiana Jones, Artifactology and the Afterlives of Objects
    Kerry Dodd   136

Extended Franchise

Raiders of the Lost Longbox: Rediscovering *The Further Adventures of Indiana Jones*
    Joseph S. Walker   151

The Shadow of the Archaeologist: Archetypes of Evil in Marvel's *The Further Adventures of Indiana Jones*
    Brian A. Dixon   164

"We'll always have Iceland, Indy": Indiana Jones and His Adventures in Video Games
    Carl Wilson   178

Indiana Jones and the Theme Park Adventure
    Sabrina Mittermeier   192

About the Contributors   203

Index   207

Introduction

RANDY LAIST

According to the backstory presented in the opening sequence of *Indiana Jones and the Last Crusade,* Indy's adventures in archaeology trace back to a formative boyhood encounter with a gang of treasure-hunters searching for the long-lost Cross of Coronado. The 13-year-old Indy unsuccessfully attempts to retrieve the Cross from the bandits, and he explains his motives by earnestly declaring that the relic "belongs in a museum." When the story cuts to Indy pursuing the same prize 26 years later, he repeats the same axiom—"It belongs in a museum!"—in response to which his rival, exasperated with Indy's single-mindedness, delivers one of the film's most memorable lines: "So do you!"

The Cross of Coronado sequence suggests that Jones's conviction that valuable artifacts belong in a museum is the driving principle behind his relentless pursuit of archeological objects. Although the films portray Jones as inconsistently committed to the imperative that cultural artifacts belong in museums (he eschews this principle at the ends of both *Indiana Jones and the Temple of Doom* and *Indiana Jones and the Kingdom of the Crystal Skull,* and throughout the rest of *Last Crusade,* he demonstrates no interest in acquiring the Grail for his museum), the Cross of Coronado sequence implies that Indiana has been fixated on the "it belongs in a museum" line since his childhood, perhaps because, for both the character and the audience, the slogan provides an easy rationalization for the more ineffable purposes that drive Indy's quests to find lost historical objects. Whereas Indy's pronouncement of his own motives may be unconvincing, however, his rival's snappy retort—that it is actually Indy himself who belongs in a museum—is strikingly apt. Indy's position on artifactual ethics has apparently been frozen in amber since his childhood, along with his entire self-styled identity. As a representation of a certain attitude about what the past is, who it belongs to, and how it exists within a dynamic present, Indy's entire outlook is itself a historical curiosity fit for exhibition and scholarly analysis.

2 Introduction

Moreover, "in this case," as Dr. Elsa Schneider remarks at one point in *Last Crusade*, "it's a literal truth." Shortly after the release of *Last Crusade*, Harrison Ford donated a fedora and leather jacket he'd worn in that film to the Smithsonian National Museum of American History. In 1999, Lucasfilm donated an Indiana Jones whip and the original draft of Lawrence Kasdan's script for *Raiders of the Lost Ark* to the Smithsonian's collection. In that same year, *Raiders* was officially identified as "culturally, historically, or aesthetically significant" by the U.S. Library of Congress and selected for preservation in the National Film Registry. From 2011 to 2016, an exhibition titled *Indiana Jones and the Adventure of Archaeology* toured museums in Canada, Spain, and the U.S., featuring authentic archeological artifacts alongside props from the Indiana Jones films. Clearly, Indiana Jones has become, just as Belloq had implied he might, a museum artifact. More important than any of these discrete instances, however, is the extent to which "Indiana Jones"—not only the character, but also the films, the franchise, the music, the "look," the spin-offs and knock-offs, the viral allusions, and even the very idea of Indiana Jones—has become incorporated into a permanent display in the collective imagination of the moviegoing public. The famous ending of the first Indiana Jones film, the long shot of the Ark of the Covenant being stored in a government warehouse, in addition to implying that the Ark is being resubmerged into oblivion, also implies that *Raiders* itself is being filed away into the mass-audience's subconscious filmic catalogue of cultural touchstones. More brazenly, the final scenes of *Last Crusade* imply that Indiana Jones earns the immortality that attends sainthood; his long ride off into the celluloid sunset conveys the impression that Indiana Jones is joining the constellation of Hollywood demigods who enjoy eternal life in the dreams and fantasies of the movies.

Like any artifact, furthermore, Indiana Jones provides a nexus for an infinitely variable field of interpretive approaches. To a scholar of Hindu symbolism, the three lines on the Sankara Stones represent the three levels of the universe. To the villagers of Mayapore, however, the Sankara Stone in the village shrine is a fertility symbol, and its absence spells childless blight. For Indiana Jones at the beginning of *Temple of Doom*, the stone represents the allure of "fortune and glory," whereas, at the end of the movie, he has reconceptualized it as a sign of authentic power and a cue to humility. For Mola Ram, the stone represents the path to world domination, whereas for the audience, the object is a more or less interchangeable McGuffin. Artifacts are inherently polysemous, suggesting different meanings to different audiences in different times and places. Although museum labels attempt to consolidate and fix the meaning of a particular artifact, their efforts to do so signify an intentionally limited heuristic. For example, the Smithsonian museum label that accompanies Indy's hat explains that "Jones is a reluctant hero who finds himself fighting evil-doers of all sorts while seeking to preserve cultural heritage." The description of Jones as a hero committed to preserving cultural heritage seems to be based chiefly on Jones's twice-stated position in *Last Crusade* that historical artifacts "belong in a museum," and this interpretation of Indiana Jones's life work is certainly one that aligns him with the Smithsonian's own institutional values. As an overview of Indiana Jones's ethos and activities, however, the Smithsonian's label tells only a partial truth, and obscures other salient aspects of the character's identity. Not only do Indy's activities frequently result in the destruction of cultural artifacts rather than their preservation, but the films also provide opportunities for challenging the very idea of what it means to preserve cultural heritage (Whose? For whom?). While the Smithsonian label proposes a reading of Indiana Jones that aligns the franchise with its own values, it might be helpful to heed the warning of Col. Spalko, the Russian agent who attempts to peer into the archaeologist's mind only to conclude, "You're a hard man to read, Dr. Jones."

One of the greatest obstacles to fluently "reading" Indiana Jones is the films' self-presentation as a frivolous spectacle for mass-entertainment. Along with Star Wars, the Indiana Jones franchise was one of the earliest and most successful experiments in what became known as "high concept" filmmaking, an approach to filmmaking that prioritizes the importance of being able to summarize a movie's plot in a single sentence. Displacing the more character-centered approach to filmmaking that inspired the New Hollywood filmmakers (including, earlier in their careers, both Indiana Jones collaborators Steven Spielberg and George Lucas), the high-concept model has remained the dominant Hollywood formula to this day. *Raiders of the Lost Ark* achieves its visceral thrills by obsessively narrowing its focus on a character who is himself narrowly focused on an obsessive quest; the film's frenetic editing, its clipped use of narrative "shorthand" (stereotyped characters, the airplane travel maps), and its stripped-down depiction of its central character all advance the central purpose—the high concept—of the film, resulting in a cinematic experience that both critics and admirers describe in visceral terms. Roger Ebert, who praised the film, wrote that it left him feeling "breathless, dizzy, [and] worn out," while Pauline Kael, though she dismissed the film as a marketing gimmick, could not deny its physical impact: "It's a workout. You feel as if you've been to the desert digs: at the end your mind is a blank, you're parched, you're puffing hard." Chris Strompolos, interviewed in *Raiders: The Story of the Best Fan Film Ever Made*, recalls, "I saw [*Raiders of the Lost Ark*] and it just ripped me in half." In the book *The Serpent and the Rainbow*, which was adapted into an Indiana Jones–style film in 1988, Wade Davis, who himself became widely known as "the Indiana Jones of ethnobotany," reports a memorable account of the visceral impact a screening of *Raiders* had on an audience in rural Haiti: "The climactic scene when the spirits shoot out of

4 Introduction

the ark and the flesh of the Nazis melts down was simply too much for many of the viewers. Pandemonium gripped the theater. Amid shouts of 'Loup garou'—the werewolf—someone screamed a warning to pregnant women, and another cautioned us to tie ribbons around our left arm" (275). The film's emphasis on physical, narrative, and cinematic movement consumes the audience's consciousness and sensorium, encouraging the speculation that the whole spectacle is a blur without substance, a cotton-candy indulgence devoid of depth or meaning. The "high concept" of a two-hour treasure hunt absorbs the receptive faculties and neutralizes the capacity for critical response.

The perception that Indiana Jones films—along with other Spielberg and Lucas productions and large swaths of popular culture in general—are superficial, childish, or regressive has certainly dissuaded audiences, critics, and cultural studies scholars from examining them more closely. At the same time, however, the effectiveness with which Indiana Jones films channel the raw energies of childhood fantasy, wish fulfillment, narrative momentum, and cinematic spectacle distinguish them as profound dramatic enactments of these basic elements of human reality. Harrison Ford remarked that "*Raiders* is really about movies. It's intricately designed as a real tribute to the craft" (qtd. in Schickel). At a formative stage in his career, George Lucas was deeply influenced by the avant-garde filmmaking techniques that were roiling the art of cinema in the late '60s and early '70s, and *Raiders* can be thought of as an experiment in "pure cinema." Not only is the film conceived as a self-conscious homage to the B-movies of yore, and not only is the film dense with intertextual allusions to other films (Omar Calabrese counts "approximately 350 references to other works, from both films and other sources" [173]), but every element of the film is engineered to push the dials of the movie-going experience as high as they will go, combining the components of film scoring, sound effects, visual effects, editing, acting, and camerawork to create the kind of intense experience to which Ebert, Kael, Strompolos, and contemporary audiences responded. Spielberg gives the game away in the opening seconds of *Raiders*, when the Paramount logo dissolves into a diegetic Peruvian mountain: the movie's goal is to dissolve the borderline between the filmic infrastructure represented by the studio logo and the perceptual experience of the moviegoer.

At the same time, the inherent polysemy of objects prevents them from falling into any single interpretation. *Raiders* can be read as an effort to focalize the elements of cinema into a dazzling spectacle (in the way that the headpiece to the Staff of Ra focuses sunlight into a revelatory light show), but psychological, cultural, and political values inevitably inflect the spectacle's meaning. At the same time that he is a paste-board swashbuckler, Indiana Jones is also invested with Campbellian and psychoanalytic character markers that identify him as a subject bearing the kind of "deep psychology" that we would not expect to see in his matinee serial forebearers. The proliferation of father figures around Indiana, his ophidiophobia, his psychoanalytically suggestive whip and hat, and the Jungian elements that comprise his narrative cosmos all point to more complex readings of the character, and the New Hollywood style of *Raiders*'s acting and cinematography lend these characterological elements texture, depth, and even a certain kind of plausibility. Likewise, Indiana Jones stories are inevitably stories about intercultural encounters between white American masculinity and other global populations. One might speculate that part of the reasons behind Indiana Jones's popularity is that these narratives provided a symbolic template for American audiences to conceptualize the dynamics of such encounters during a period when globalization and multiculturalism were beginning to reshape Americans' perception of their relationship with the rest of the world. The Indiana Jones movies have frequently been criticized as racist expressions of Eurocentric imperialism, most famously by Robert Stam and Ella Shohat, who claim that the series is "premised on an imperialized globe, in which archaeology professors can 'rescue' artifacts from the colonized world for the greater benefit of science and civilization" (124). Some scholars have pushed back against this charge, claiming, as James Kendrick does, that "[w]hile the films certainly engage in and, in some respects reinforce conservative values and reactionary colonialist traditions ... they also mitigate and frequently undermine those values" (103), or, as Nigel Morris does, that the "weak modality" (103) of fantasy clearly indicates that the movies' racist representations of non–Westerners should not be taken at face value. In any event, it is clearly the case that Indiana Jones stories raise questions about cultural representation and appropriation, and that these questions influence our understanding of what Indiana Jones "means." In close connection with these issues is the wider question of Indiana Jones's politics. Robin Wood and Andrew Britton, two influential critics of 1980s cinema, both identified the Indiana Jones films as manifestations of the same conservative values that gave rise to the election of Ronald Reagan. In his article "Blissing Out," Britton wrote that Indiana Jones narratives depict a conservative fantasy of "a vanished golden age in which the nation was great and the patriarchal family flourished in happy ignorance of the scourges of abortion and a soaring divorce rate, gay rights and the women's movement" (109). Wood goes a step further, writing that films like *Raiders of the Lost Ark* "are exactly the kinds of films that a potentially fascist culture would be expected to produce and enjoy" (151). More recently, however, Indiana Jones has enjoyed revived popularity on social media as an anti-fascist icon whose flair for punching Nazis has made him a symbol of resistance against ethno-nationalist movements.

    This multiplicity of different Indiana Joneses is arguably "baked in" to the formula of the series itself. Not only is the world of Indiana Jones composed out of a varied buffet of cultural borrowings and their diverse inheritances, but, from the first time we see him in the Peruvian jungle, Indiana Jones is always already an intrinsically serialized character. Any specific instance of his appearance is backgrounded by an impression that what we are seeing is only one manifestation of a figure whose real existence takes place in a timeless realm of countless narrative permutations. This quality has made the character of Indiana Jones amenable to being reimagined in other stories across a wide variety of media including role-playing games, comic books, "Find Your Fate" adventure stories, young adult novels, video games, fan fiction, theme park rides, a radio drama, merchandise, toys and Lego sets, educational materials, academic articles, trading cards, and a television series, *The Young Indiana Jones Chronicles*, which ran from 1992 to 1993. While certain features of Indiana Jones's character and cosmos remain consistent across these different instantiations, each appearance provides opportunities to revisit and reevaluate the meaning of the entire franchise. Audiences have responded to this implicit adaptability by reimagining the films and the franchise in their own ways. Steven Soderbergh has produced a black-and-white recut version of *Raiders of the Lost Ark*, replacing the soundtrack with electronic music to emphasize the virtuosity of the film's staging and cinematography. A YouTube artist has posted a full-length version of *Raiders* that runs backwards, presenting an entrancing spectacle in which spirits are magically sealed inside the Ark, Marion's bar is miraculously rescued from a catastrophic fire, and Indiana Jones politely restores a golden idol to its altar. In one of the most well-known examples of film fandom, a team of Mississippi pre-teens produced a minutely detailed shot-for-shot remake of the film, *Raiders of the Lost Ark: The Adaptation*, which has itself become the subject of two documentaries.

More recently, the Indiana Jones franchise continues to evoke commentary and controversy. In an article titled "Indiana Jones Is a Lesbian," Areyon Jolivette uses the figure of Indiana Jones as a metaphor for her relationship with her own sexuality. In a parody trailer, *Indiana Jones and the Curse of the Orange God*, Indiana Jones is depicted as a figure who fights against the political rise of Donald Trump, while a popular pro–Trump meme reworks a famous scene from *Raiders* by superimposing Trump's head onto Harrison Ford's body as Indy guns down a sword-wielding Arab whose face has been replaced with CNN logo. The Internet has also hosted a robust conversation about the franchise's racial and cultural politics, if often in a superficial or incoherent way. James Charisma begins a 2019 online article by criticizing Indiana Jones's "It belongs in a museum" line as a manifestation of neocolonial entitlement, but the article ultimately concludes that, at the end of all four Indiana Jones movies, the hero "learns to give up his objects of pursuit in deference to the cultures that produced them." The editors of the website that published Charisma's article confuse matters further by slapping on a clickbait title—"'Indiana Jones' Has Aged Terribly"—that belies the article's thesis, which turns out to be that these movies provide timely lessons about respecting the cultural provenance of archeological artifacts. The sensationalized title refers to yet another aspect of the Indiana Jones franchise, its status a signifier of a previous era of Hollywood blockbusters. As other 1980s franchises, notably Rocky, Star Wars, and Ghostbusters, have been remade in ways that reconsider the masculinist or Eurocentric assumptions of the original films, the retrograde representations of indigenous peoples in *Crystal Skull* suggest that the Indiana Jones series remains committed to a scheme of cultural representation that is fixated in historical stereotypes that were long outdated even in the 1980s. We will have to wait until the forthcoming fifth Indiana Jones film to see if the producers will present audiences with a "woke" variation on the Indiana Jones narrative, but there is no question that contesting interpretations of the fictional archaeologist and his adventures will continue to ramify and proliferate. Something makes it inevitable.

* * *

Excavating Indiana Jones is itself a component of this vibrant discourse, and the essays in this collection are intended to advance the ongoing cultural debate about Indiana Jones and what he means. The first section of the book examines the franchise's historical contexts. In "Situating Indy: American Archaeologists, Global Ambitions and the Interwar Years," Andrew W. Bell compares Indy's adventures with the state of American archaeology in the 1930s, concluding that the franchise serves as a surprisingly apt representation of a period when archaeological digs reflected nationalist impulses. In "Fordian Knots: Indiana Jones and the Cinema of John Ford," Brian Brems examines the Indiana Jones films within the context of film history, tracing the decisive influence that John Ford played in Spielberg's visualization of Indiana's exploits. In the final essay of this section, "'You call this archaeology?' Indiana Jones and Hollywood's View on the Nature of History," Ryan Staude considers the manner in which history—as both a phenomenon and a discipline—is represented in the Indiana Jones films, extracting memorable lessons from the series about what the past can and can't teach us.

The next section of the book examines a crucial element of the Indiana Jones mythos, the representation—typically misrepresentation—of non-Western cultures and peoples. In "Translocations, Cultural Geography and Anthropological Imperialism in *Raiders of the Lost Ark*," Tatiana Prorokova presents a critique of the first Indiana Jones film as an extended advertisement for white imperialism, a system epitomized by the expropriation and translocation—the "raiding"—of objects from colonial territories. In "'I said no camels!' Indiana Jones and the Catalogue of Orientalism," Mat Hardy discusses the subtle and not-so-subtle ways that both *Raiders* and *Last Crusade* adapt the tropes of Orientalism in their depiction of the Middle East, perpetuating dehumanizing stereotypes. Debaditya Mukhopadhyay also draws on the discourse of Orientalism in his essay, "The Temple of Orientalism," which catalogues and anatomizes the many overtly racist elements in the second Indiana Jones film. In the final essay of this section, "The Quest for 'Alien' Indigenous Knowledge in *Indiana Jones and the Kingdom of the Crystal Skull*," Kasey Jones-Matrona observes that, although almost 20 years separate the third and fourth Indiana Jones film, the franchise's representations of non–Western cultures and peoples had clearly not become more sensitive or enlightened during that time.

The third section of *Excavating Indiana Jones* examines the identity of Indiana Jones himself, both as a character and as a cultural icon. In "Indiana Jones and the Crusade for Authenticity," Siobhan Lyons argues that Indiana's adventures serve as a metaphor for the film's 1980s audience's nostalgic pursuit of a lost authenticity. In "'I came to find my father': Indiana Jones and the Quest for the Lost Father," Linda Wight considers Indy as a nexus for anxieties about masculine identity during a time of unstable gender roles. Jennifer Crumley traces the evolution of Indiana Jones's character over the course of the four films in "Indiana Jones as Educated Swashbuckler," concluding that it is the character's humanity and complexity that make him such an enduring symbol. Kerry Dodd concludes this section with an essay titled "'It belongs in a museum,' or Does It? Indiana Jones, Artifactology and the Afterlives of Objects," in which he contends that the representations of the prized objects pursued by Indy reveal the background attitudes that characterize our perception of and our relationship with the non-human world.

While Indiana Jones is most well-known as a film character, an important part of the Indiana Jones brand has always been its exportability into other media. One of Indy's first media-hopping incarnations was his adaptation from celluloid frames to comic book panels, and so the section of the book on the "extended franchise" begins with two essays that examine Indy's adventures as a comic book character. In "Raiders of the Lost Longbox: Rediscovering *The Further Adventures of Indiana Jones*," Joseph S. Walker provides an overview of Indy's career as a Marvel character, while in "The Shadow of the Archaeologist: Archetypes of Evil in Marvel's *The Further Adventures of Indiana Jones*," Brian A. Dixon elucidates the manner in which these comic book storylines elaborate a Jungian theme established in the first Indiana Jones film. Carl Wilson turns our attention to Indy's evolution as a video game character in "'We'll always have Iceland, Indy': Indiana Jones and His Adventures in Video Games," and Sabrina Mittermeier examines the manner in which the franchise has been adapted into experiential attractions in "Indiana Jones and the Theme Park Adventure."

These perceptive authors encourage us to revisit our attitudes about this familiar franchise. Whether you think of Indy as a "reluctant hero" or a racist imperialist, a monomythic archetype or a marketing ploy, an icon or a travesty, or as any combination of any of these interpretations, the essays in this book provide arguments that will both enhance and challenge your way of thinking about this indisputably influential cultural figure.

Works Cited

Britton, Andrew. *Britton on Film: The Complete Film Criticism of Andrew Britton*. Detroit: Wayne State University Press, 2009.

Calabrese, Omar. *Neo-Baroque: A Sign of the Times*. Tr. Charles Lambert. Princeton: Princeton University Press, 1992.

Charisma, James. "'Indiana Jones' Has Aged Terribly." Vice.com. June 21, 2019. https://www.vice.com/en_in/article/j5wnay/indiana-jones-has-aged-terribly.

Davis, Wade. *The Serpent and the Rainbow*. New York: Simon & Schuster, 1985.

Ebert, Roger. "*Raiders of the Lost Ark*." Jan. 1, 1981. https://www.rogerebert.com/reviews/raiders-of-the-lost-ark-1981.

Jolivette, Areyon. "Indiana Jones Is a Lesbian." *The Daily Californian*. Aug. 9, 2019. https://www.dailycal.org/2019/06/27/indiana-jones-is-a-lesbian/.

Kael, Pauline. "Whipped." *The New Yorker*. June 7, 1981. https://www.newyorker.com/magazine/1981/06/15/whipped.

Kendrick, James. *Darkness in the Bliss-Out: A Reconsideration of the Films of Steven Spielberg*. New York: Bloomsbury, 2014.

Morris, Nigel. *The Cinema of Steven Spielberg: Empire of Light*. London: Wallflower Press, 2007.

Schickel, Richard. "Cinema: Slam! Bang! A Movie." *Time*. June 15, 1981. http://content.time.com/time/subscriber/article/0,33009,949205-3,00.html.

Shohat, Ella, and Robert Stam. *Unthinking Eurocentrism: Multiculturalism and the Media*. New York: Routledge, 2014.

Smithsonian National Museum of American History. "Hat from *Indiana Jones and the Last Crusade*." Catalogue number 1989.0323.02. https://americanhistory.si.edu/collections/search/object/nmah_1322673.

Wood, Robin. *Hollywood from Vietnam to Reagan ... And Beyond: A Revised and Expanded Edition*. New York: Columbia University Press, 2003.

History

Situating Indy

American Archaeologists, Global Ambitions and the Interwar Years

Andrew W. Bell

Peru. Egypt. China. India. Hatay. Over the course of the original Indiana Jones film trilogy, the franchise's titular character finds himself on the ground in an impressive number of locales—spanning five continents—for an American in the 1930s. None of this seems accidental, either; the intrepid hero demonstrates deep familiarity with the local places, peoples, and histories wherever his adventures take him. This insight comes with the territory. As an archaeologist, Indy possesses unrivalled knowledge of relics and long-forgotten civilizations as well as of the world. Hardly an aloof tourist, Dr. Jones depends on these skills throughout his globe-spanning quests in search of lost antiquities.

Suggesting that the protagonist of these films is fictional is hardly controversial. No real-life archaeologist, American or otherwise, ever came close to racking up frequent-flier miles or cultural knowledge comparable to Indy's. Any attempt to label any single archaeologist as his true-to-life inspiration will always disappoint. Debunking this, not to mention so many other inaccuracies peppered throughout the franchise, however, does little to build an appreciation for the historical moment that the films portray. What, then, can an historical lens add to understanding these films and the world they depict?

In analyzing the Indiana Jones films and their protagonist historically, Justin Jacobs has produced the most convincing treatments. Rather than locating inspiration of the cinematic hero in any one person, Jacobs has identified several traits central to the character's identity: manhood, European ancestry, a connection to empire, a high level of education, and access to substantial financial resources (usually supplied by social and political elites). Collectively, these traits not only define Indiana Jones, they provide Jacobs with a framework for tracing the history of archaeology and exploration—from the excavation of Pompeii in the mid-eighteenth century to the 1969 moon landing—within the larger contexts of scientific advancement, museum construction, and the expansion and decline of Western imperialism ("Episode I"; *Indiana Jones*).

This essay offers something more modest. Rather than employing Jacobs's broad categories, it focuses on three aspects of the films and their archaeologist protagonist: nationality, geography, and time period. Although Indiana Jones's nationality is almost never directly commented upon in the films, it is clear that he is an *American*. Likewise, the extent of his geographic reach is better articulated through the iconic flight-path sequences featured in each film than in any line of dialogue. These transcontinental and transoceanic routes convey Jones's *global* reach. And while the original film trilogy covers only a brief period of time (1935–1938), the character's background and activities suggest that the height of his career spans the years *between the world wars* (1919–1939). Employing these three categories, this essay offers a brief survey of major American archaeological interests and ambitions across the globe in the interwar years in order to situate the *Indiana Jones* films in the historical context they purport to depict.

The years between the world wars were a golden age for archaeologists in general, and for American archaeologists in particular. After decades of limited success overseas, American dreams of commanding a dominant position on the archaeological world stage finally came true. Long-held global ambitions suddenly appeared possible. In the twenty-year period between the First and Second World Wars, Americans led and financed some of the most significant investigations into the ancient past despite various setbacks. Their exploits abroad also solidified their status as some of their nation's foremost experts in the world on the eve of World War II. In that sense, the experience of American archaeologists in the interwar years mirrored the broad outlines of the globe-trotting character introduced to moviegoers half a century later.

* * *

Americans interested in making a name for themselves through the advancement of archaeological knowledge long looked beyond the borders of the United States. Undoubtedly, some—including Thomas Jefferson and scientists commissioned by the Smithsonian Institution—devoted themselves to discerning the nature of burial mounds scattered across the landscape of their young nation (Patterson 18, 28). But during the nineteenth century, a significant number of them took an interest in antiquity elsewhere. John

Lloyd Stephens documented and popularized dozens of Maya sites between the Yucatán and Honduras (R.T. Evans 44–87). Luigi di Cesnola and W.J. Stillman explored ruins in the Mediterranean (Dyson 61–64, 130–132). Edward Robinson and Selah Merrill ventured to the Levant on missions to prove the historical veracity of the Bible (Patterson 26). Yet these efforts often paled in comparison to the work of Europeans like Giovanni Belzoni, Arthur Evans, Flinders Petrie, and Heinrich Schliemann.

Founded in 1879 as the first professional archaeological organization in the United States, the Archaeological Institute of America (AIA) articulated a distinctly global agenda. "The objects of the Institute have no narrow local interest," announced one of its first circulars. In addition to promoting "an acquaintance with the pre-historic antiquities of our own country," the executive committee also aimed to increase American "interest in classical and Biblical studies" (AIA, *First Annual* 8). Within two years, the AIA launched small expeditions to the U.S. Southwest and to the Greek site of Assos in Anatolia. Members of the executive committee also contracted a U.S. consul in Mexico to explore Maya ruins (AIA, *Third Annual* 35). By 1900, the organization had established field schools in Athens, Rome, and Jerusalem (Seymour).

For all of its ambition, this burgeoning community of professional archaeologists only achieved modest results. The Assos expedition only yielded thirteen crates of artifacts for American museums (Keene 94). Plans for a dig at Delphi were foiled by the French (Dyson 73). Only in 1896 did the field school in Athens receive a long-term lease to dig at Corinth (85–87). The field schools in Rome and Jerusalem failed to secure any excavation rights. An expedition to Cyrenaica was terminated prematurely after the Italian invasion of Tripolitania in 1911 (76–82). In fact, the most sensational archaeological triumph by an American between 1879 and World War I—Hiram Bingham's "discovery" of Machu Picchu—occurred without any AIA involvement.

With the outbreak of war in Europe in 1914, American archaeological prospects looked dim. War hindered research the world over. The Ottoman government expelled American archaeologists from the Levant (King 49). The field school in Athens suspended operations in 1916 (Lord 101). Plans for an American field school in China fell apart (Meyer and Brysac 138–139). Investigations into Central America's Maya ruins continued, but only because the Americans working there moonlighted as spies for the Office of Naval Intelligence (Harris and Sadler).

But amid this chaos, some saw signs of hope. A notice in the back of the December 1916 issue of the AIA's *Art and Archaeology* confidently asserted that "after the European war is over the United States will have to take the lead in archaeological excavations and explorations" ("Do You Know?"). In his annual report issued the next year, the organization's president issued a similar statement. "The nations of Europe are now conceding to America a measure of leadership" in the field "unthought of before the present crisis" (Shipley 15). The war had decimated European culture and society; it also diverted funds from archaeological work and brought about the deaths of several eminent experts across the continent. The time was right for American archaeologists to seize the reins of their discipline's research agenda worldwide.

* * *

Interest in ancient civilizations reached new heights in the two decades after the Great War. New sites, such as the Canaanite city of Ugarit and the settlements of the Indus River Valley, came to light. Well-known sites—Chichén Itzá, Great Zimbabwe, Megiddo, the Mogao Caves, Troy—received renewed attention. New research methods encouraged more thorough and detailed investigations than previously carried out at these sites. The thrill of this work extended beyond professional circles, too. Reports of new discoveries, unearthed treasures, and scientific breakthroughs made newspaper headlines. Unlike almost any other discipline, archaeology had mass-appeal. As much as it was a scientific endeavor, archaeology was popular culture.

Americans could not take credit for all of this attention. British archaeologist Howard Carter's discovery of Tutankhamun's Tomb and the vast store of treasures hidden within its chambers launched the exhumation of the ancient past to front-page news. "Chariots and Canopy of Gold and Other Splendors, Undisturbed for 3000 Years" announced the *Boston Daily Globe* on the day after Carter unveiled the deceased pharaoh's burial chamber ("Coffin"). The excitement of this discovery could not be understated. King Tutankhamun rapidly became a yardstick for writing about archaeology. "Relics in King Tut's Tomb Overshadowed by Dr. Spinden's Discovery of Ancient Maya Civilization in Honduras," ran one headline just three months later (Philpott). In 1927, the *Los Angeles Times* declared that the gold artifacts unearthed by Leonard Woolley at Ur "Rival King Tut's" ("Gold").

But despite the excitement surrounding Carter's find in Egypt's Valley of the Kings, Americans had already begun to eclipse their European colleagues in archaeological discovery. One month before Carter opened Tut's final resting place, Americans boasted two dozen expeditions in the Old World alone. This purportedly surpassed the number of expeditions launched that year by all other nations combined ("Americans"). Moreover, this number excluded many American outfits—probably an equal amount—working in the Western Hemisphere. Non-archaeologists took notice. "Americans Now in Lead in Unraveling the Past," declared the *New York Times* (*ibid.*).

Ralph Van Deman Magoffin, the AIA's president throughout the 1920s, sought to maintain this dominant position. He saw widespread interest in the discipline as an "opportunity of a lifetime," a chance "to reassert our quiescent, though acknowledged, primacy in the entire field of archaeology" (Magoffin, "Forty-Third" 14). To that end, Magoffin approved plans for a research commission consisting of leading experts of American, classical, East Asian, Egyptian, and Middle Eastern antiquity in the United States to undertake a worldwide survey of future archaeological prospects. Two years later, he announced that the AIA was in an ideal position "to extend its influence" (Magoffin, "Forty-Fifth" 3). By this, he meant expanding the AIA's geographic reach with new field schools in China, Egypt, India, South America, and Turkey. AIA schools in Athens, Baghdad, Jerusalem, Rome, and Santa Fe already generated American scientific prestige around the world. "How immensely more will this be true," Magoffin mused, "when the globe is encircled by American Schools of Archaeology all bound together with strongest ties of mutual interest by the guiding hand of the Archaeological Institute of America, with its wider vision and its therefore more evenly directed control" (6).

The AIA was far from the only American institution invested in establishing American archaeologists' global primacy in the interwar years. Beginning in 1914, but blossoming in the 1920s, the Carnegie Institution of Washington (CIW) coordinated extensive work on the remnants of Maya civilization in Central America under the direction of Sylvanus Morley and A.V. Kidder (Delpar 58). In 1919, James Henry Breasted oversaw the foundation of the Oriental Institute (OI), an institution that rapidly assumed a dominant role in Middle Eastern fieldwork, at the University of Chicago (the university where Indiana Jones would study under Abner Ravenwood). By 1934, the OI claimed six expeditions in Egypt as well as excavations in Iraq, Palestine, Persia, Syria, and Turkey (*Buried* 1). The University of Pennsylvania Museum, another archaeological powerhouse, sponsored no fewer than fourteen projects—including digs in Cyprus, Guatemala, Iraq, Italy, and Palestine—in 1931 alone (Madeira 42–46). Universities, from the Ivy Leagues to smaller schools like Haverford College and the University of Cincinnati, sponsored their own expeditions as well. For Americans looking to recover traces of bygone civilizations, opportunities abounded.

But ambitions only went so far. Americans quickly discovered that conditions on the ground varied considerably. These conditions determined success. Consider Turkey. Immediately following the First World War, the Greek army captured a sizable portion of Asia Minor. Americans swiftly negotiated excavation and exportation rights at the Anatolian sites of Sardis and Colophon. The Greek government approved both projects. But as Turkish forces recaptured this territory in late 1922, American plans went south. The Colophon team abandoned the site after only a few months. The Turkish government destroyed their headquarters. The Sardis Committee in New York managed to remove fifty-eight boxes of antiquities before the Turks retook the site. Despite pressure from the Turkish government and the State Department, the Committee stubbornly held on to the artifacts for two years (Davis; Goode 31–42). The resultant friction between American archaeologists and the Turkish government tempered American ambitions to dig in Anatolia throughout the rest of the 1920s.

Chinese authorities also managed to assert control over their nation's antiquities in this period. In 1923–24, American archaeologist and art curator Langdon Warner led an expedition to the Mogao Caves, near the western Chinese town of Dunhuang, where he removed a series of Buddhist frescoes and artwork. He planned a larger undertaking in 1925. Disturbed by this act of plunder, Westernized Chinese scholars, tipped off by Warner's Chinese interpreter, worked with local authorities to thwart Warner's plans to remove more pieces of art. They succeeded not only in having Warner leave China empty-handed, but also in applying similar restrictions on future foreign expeditions (Jacobs, *Indiana Jones* 179–181).

Although Turkish and Chinese authorities effectively exercised sovereignty over the cultural resources within their borders during this period, American archaeologists continued to show up and conduct research in accordance with the new regulations. In 1926, Nels Nelson used his archaeological training developed in the U.S. Southwest to examine traces of early human life in southwestern China ("Andrews"). The next year, a Smithsonian archaeologist surveying the Middle Kingdom's archaeological prospects encouraged further American investment in the study of Chinese antiquity. The prospect of recovering artifacts for American institutions hardly mattered to him. "It is no more reasonable ... to expect China to submit to a general exodus of her antiquities than it would be to expect America to allow her revolutionary relics to be excavated and carried off by the Chinese" ("Chinese"). And in 1932, Carl W. Blegen inaugurated the first of several seasons of work at the site of Troy in western Anatolia. Turkey retained the finds, but Blegen received the distinction of overturning the prevailing interpretations of the site's history (Dyson 178).

In addition to nations like Turkey and China staking claims to their archaeological heritage, French authorities also attempted to limit where American archaeologists could dig. Unlike Turkey and China, however, they aimed to influence regions beyond the borders of *l'Hexagone*. In 1923, the French government negotiated archaeological concessions with Afghanistan and Albania that effectively prohibited non–French expeditions in those countries. "These concessions are of a monopolistic and exclusive character and are prejudicial to the freedom of archaeological investigations by other nations," railed Magoffin in a 1923 address. He called on the U.S. State Department to roll back these concessions and to prevent the French from making similar arrangements with other countries (Magoffin, "Forty-Fourth" 13–14). These protests accomplished little.

Yet even active efforts by the French to exclude archaeological competitors only went so far. Consider the Middle East. Having established Syria as a mandate, the French attempted to turn its *de facto* colony into an exclusive archaeological zone. American attempts to conduct investigations in and export antiquities from Syria were blocked time and again ("Balked"; DeNovo 335). In 1927, however, the U.S. consul in Beirut succeeded in convincing the French high commissioner to overturn this policy. Within a year, the first of several joint Franco-American projects commenced at Dura-Europos (DeNovo 335). Additional American-financed digs followed soon after. American archaeological work in Syria flourished as long as the French exercised a tight grip on the mandate.

Unlike the French, the British adopted a much friendlier disposition toward American archaeologists. When the British established the Palestine mandate in 1920, they prioritized archaeological research and international access. Americans quickly initiated a series of projects there. By 1929, the director of the AIA's field school in Jerusalem bragged that most expeditions in the mandate occurred "under English, American, or joint Anglo-American auspices" (Albright 1–2). These included major excavations at the sites of Megiddo, Beisân, Tell Beit Mirsim, and 'Ain Shems. "Americans Lead in Work," the *New York Times* assured its readers in an article describing archaeological discoveries in the Levant ("Ancient").

Mexico and Central America similarly welcomed American archaeologists. Americans evinced a deep fascination with the Maya civilization since the mid-nineteenth century, but Americans only began to undertake sustained fieldwork in the region in the 1910s. In 1924, under the CIW's auspices, Sylvanus Morley began a decade-long project of exploring, excavating, and preserving Chichén Itzá, one of the most impressive sites in the Yucatán Peninsula. To encourage goodwill, Morley suggested that Mexico keep all finds unearthed in the course of digging (Delpar 58). This work attracted far more attention in the United States than any other archaeological program south of the Rio Grande in the period, but it was hardly the only one of note. Other major American-led Maya projects included the CIW's companion project at Uaxactún in Guatemala, several expeditions by Tulane University to Mexico and Guatemala, and the Penn Museum's excavation of Piedras Negras in the 1930s (58–60).

The culmination of American archaeological efforts in these years, however, occurred in southern Europe. In 1931, the American School of Classical Studies scored a major victory that quickly overshadowed its ongoing work at Corinth: the right to excavate the sixteen-acre agora in the center of Athens alongside a team of Greek archaeologists. An American served as the field director for the project (Dyson 179–181). From the outset, onlookers dubbed it "The World's Great Archaeological Project" ("Marvels"). Ideologically, this dig in the cradle of democracy stood in stark contrast to the excavations in Rome intended to glorify Italian fascism (Dyson 181–182). But ideological lines did not determine where Americans worked. In the same year that the Agora project began, the Penn Museum secured the right to excavate at and export finds from Minturnae in Italy, a rare privilege for foreign archaeologists (Dyson 211). While no American archaeologist ever received an autograph from Adolf Hitler, the Italian government decorated Horace Jayne, the Penn Museum's director, for his role in facilitating the project (Bowie 191).

As these and dozens of other cases demonstrate, the American archaeological community seized opportunities to assert global leadership in their field after the Great War. While they never succeeded in uncovering anything to rival Tutankhamun's Tomb, they did manage to achieve an unequalled geographic reach. Local conditions and the political nature of archaeology invariably differed from place to place, but Americans continued to find ways to work in even the most restrictive contexts. Their ambition to make names for themselves in the field had few limits.

* * *

By the late 1930s—the period depicted in the first three *Indiana Jones* films—the number of American-backed archaeological expeditions noticeably declined. As several scholars have pointed out, assertions of cultural sovereignty by nationalist groups played no small role in the demise of American and European archaeologists' free rein over sites across the globe (Goode; Jacobs, *Indiana Jones* 157–190). This interpretation has a great deal of merit, but it fails to account for the continued presence of Americans working in places with restrictive antiquities policies. It also ignores the importance of two other major events—the Great Depression and World War II—in directly shaping the fate of archaeological research.

Americans remained an active presence in archaeology around the world in the late 1930s. In December 1936, for instance, *Fortune* magazine tallied all American-run digs overseas slated for the upcoming year: at least one apiece in Cyprus, Guatemala, Ireland, Mexico, and Palestine; two in Greece, Syria, and Turkey; three in Iraq; and four in Iran. The OI supported three of these expeditions; the Penn Museum sponsored four ("Fifteen Thousand" 132). Four pages later, readers saw these digs mapped out (136). In addition to these eighteen privately funded ventures, the U.S. government allocated hundreds of thousands of dollars for archaeological projects within the United States through the Works Progress Administration (131).

Because nationalists in many places where Americans continued to dig had imposed restrictions on antiquities exportation, the gradual decline of archaeological work deserves another look. Price tags deserve special attention. After all, the costs of archaeological expeditions ran high. In the early 1920s, one source estimated that a single season of digging outside of the United States cost $10,000 ("Americans"). The Megiddo expedition, one of the most expensive undertakings, operated on a $215,000 budget for its first five seasons (A. Evans). As long as money flowed, American archaeologists saw no end to research possibilities. In the 1930s, however, funds dried up. Slowly but surely, archaeologists' ambitions did as well.

The stock market crash of October 1929 marked the beginning of a slow decline in American fieldwork overseas. The bank accounts of archaeology's most prolific sponsors immediately took a hit. Several wealthy Americans, hoping to reverse new taxes implemented under Franklin D. Roosevelt's New Deal, sank their money in the ill-fated 1936 presidential campaign of Alf Landon. One month after Landon's humiliating loss—the most decisive defeat in twentieth-century U.S. presidential elections—*Fortune* magazine predicted that "the year 1937 may turn out to be archaeology's worst" as far as finances and "foreign digging" were concerned ("Americans" 132). Perhaps this explains the yearlong gap between Indy's discovery of the Ark of the Covenant (1936) and his recovery of Coronado's crucifix (1938).

What ultimately brought an end to this period of extending American archaeological work around the world, however, was the Second World War. Plenty of American archaeologists abhorred the ideas of their counterparts in Nazi Germany prior to the war, but, surprisingly, few shared these thoughts publicly in the 1930s. No major contests for priceless antiquities broke out between Americans and Germans. This changed in 1939. In August, the president of the AIA attended the sixth International Archaeological Congress in Berlin to promote scientific and international goodwill. His hopes were dashed when, as he prepared to return home, reports of the German invasion of Poland shook the world (Allen 19). Soon after, he cut all personal and institutional ties to the German archaeological community. The Germans responded in kind (22). After the fall of France, the Nazi regime also pressured the French High Commissioner of the Levant to cancel the OI's concession in Syria (Palmer 660–661).

By 1940, possibilities for engaging in extensive archaeological work overseas were severely limited. Nations across the Mediterranean and the Middle East, either transformed into warzones or affected by the conflict in other ways, prohibited further archaeological research within their borders ("Seek"). Once again, global conflict confined American archaeologists to the Western Hemisphere. But no calls to dominate the field after victory accompanied these renewed restrictions. In fact, some secretly relished this lull in fieldwork. One Canadian archaeologist, for instance, noted that the war "conferred the blessing of an enforced cessation from excavational activities" (Fraser 87). Decades of expeditions, he observed, had left museums "swamped under the flood of material that has been recovered" (ibid). The war finally offered an opportunity to take stock of the vast, unprocessed collections in their possession.

But the war also offered a fitting coda for American archaeologists' global ambitions. Like Dr. Jones, several classical scholars joined the Office of Strategic Services, employing their expertise for the cause of Allied victory in the Mediterranean. The field schools in Athens and Jerusalem functioned as wartime intelligence hubs (Allen 7, 288). Nelson Glueck, a rabbi turned biblical archaeologist, prepared an evacuation route for British forces fighting in Egypt and planned to organize an Arab guerrilla force to fend off possible Axis invaders under the guise of a scientific survey of Transjordan (Fierman). Even before the United States entered the fray, archaeologists working in Peru used their fieldwork as cover for spying on Germans, Japanese, and South Americans sympathetic to the Axis powers (Price 200–219). Others—including Langdon Warner and the AIA's president—advised the U.S. military on protecting cultural monuments from destruction in both the European and Pacific Theaters (Roberts 162). After two decades of dominating archaeological work worldwide, American archaeologists drew upon their extensive experiences abroad to help win a global war.

* * *

In the decades between the world wars, American archaeologists established a global presence unimaginable in the years prior and unmatched by their contemporary competitors. The national and international politics of archaeology so common to the age often limited their freedom to do as they pleased, but rarely closed spaces off to their research agenda. Interested in dominating the study of antiquity, American archaeologists made the world and its past theirs. Although unquestionably fictitious, the *Indiana Jones* films nevertheless capture the American and global character of archaeology in the interwar period. They provide a valuable entrance into considering the history of American global engagement through archaeology in an era too often mischaracterized as an age of isolationism.

Works Cited

Albright, W.F. "Progress in Palestinian Archaeology During the Year 1928." *Bulletin of the American School of Oriental Research*, no. 33, Feb. 1929, pp. 1–10.
Allen, Susan Heuck. *Classical Spies: American Archaeologists with the OSS in World War II Greece.* University of Michigan Press, 2011.
"Americans Now in Lead in Unraveling the Past." *New York Times*, 28 Jan. 1923, sec. 8, p. 3.
"Ancient Palestine Yields Many Relics." *New York Times*, 16 Sept. 1928, p. 58.
"Andrews Outlines Expedition Plans." *New York Times*, 30 Nov. 1926, p. 3.

Archæological Institute of America. *First Annual Report of the Executive Committee, 1879-1880*. Cambridge: John Wilson and Son, 1880.
Archæological Institute of America. *Third Annual Report of the Executive Committee and First Annual Report of the Committee on the American School of Classical Studies at Athens, 1881-82*. Cambridge: John Wilson and Son, 1882.
"Balked in Purchase of Sidon Treasures." *New York Times*, 26 Mar. 1926, p. 10.
Bowie, Theodore, editor. *Langdon Warner Through His Letters*. Indiana University Press, 1966.
Buried History. University of Chicago Press, 1934.
"Chinese Guard Cultural Past." *Los Angeles Times*, 21 Sept. 1927, p. 6.
"Coffin of Pharaoh Tutankhamen Found." *Boston Daily Globe*, 17 Feb. 1923, p. 1.
Davis, Jack L. "A Foreign School of Archaeology and the Politics of Archaeological Practice: Anatolia, 1922." *Journal of Mediterranean Archaeology*, vol. 16, no. 2, Dec. 2003, pp. 145-172.
Delpar, Helen. *Looking South: The Evolution of Latin Americanist Scholarship in the United States, 1850-1957*. University of Alabama Press, 2008.
DeNovo, John A. *American Interests and Policies in the Middle East, 1900-1939*. University of Minnesota Press, 1963.
"Do You Know? Important Facts Stated in the Form of Questions." *Art and Archaeology*, Dec. 1916, back matter.
Dyson, Stephen L. *Ancient Marbles to American Shores: Classical Archaeology in the United States*. University of Pennsylvania Press, 1998.
Evans, Arthur. "John D. Jr. Aids New Research in Armageddon." *Chicago Daily Tribune*, 5 Sept. 1925, p. 11.
Evans, R. Tripp. *Romancing the Maya: Mexican Antiquity in the American Imagination, 1820-1915*. University of Texas Press, 2004.
Fierman, Floyd S. "Rabbi Nelson Glueck: An Archaeologists' Secret Life in the Service of the OSS." *Biblical Archaeology Review*, vol. 12, no. 5, Sept.-Oct. 1986, pp. 18-22.
"Fifteen Thousand Years." *Fortune*, Dec. 1936, pp. 128-137, 162, 164, 166, 168, 171, 172.
Fraser, A.D. "The Future in Archaeology." *Dalhousie Review*, Apr. 1942, pp. 87-92.
"Gold Fills Ur's Tomb." *Los Angeles Times*, 11 Apr. 1927, p. 1.
Goode, James F. *Negotiating for the Past: Archaeology, Nationalism, and Diplomacy in the Middle East, 1919-1941*. University of Texas Press, 2007.
Harris, Charles H., III, and Louis R. Sadler. *The Archaeologist was a Spy*. University of New Mexico Pres, 2003.
Jacobs, Justin. "Episode I: Who Was Indiana Jones?" *YouTube*, Jan. 10, 2017, youtu.be/5Vki LM3q3pM.
Jacobs, Justin M. *Indiana Jones in History: From Pompeii to the Moon*. Pulp Hero Press, 2017.
Keene, Lenore O., editor. "The Assos Journals of Francis H. Bacon." *Archaeology*, vol. 27, no. 2, Apr. 1974, pp. 83-95.
King, Philip J. *American Archaeology in the Mideast: A History of the American Schools of Oriental Research*. American Schools of Oriental Research, 1983.
Lord, Louis E. *A History of the American School of Classical Studies at Athens, 1882-1942: An Intercollegiate Project*. Harvard University Press, 1947.
Madeira, Percy C., Jr. *Men in Search of Man: The First-Seventy-Five Years of the University Museum of the University of Pennsylvania*. University of Pennsylvania Press, 1964.
Magoffin, Ralph Van Deman. "Forty-Fifth Annual Report of the President of the Archaeological Institute of America." *Bulletin of the Archaeological Institute of America*, vol. 15, Dec. 1924, pp. 3-14.
Magoffin, Ralph Van Deman. "Forty-Fourth Annual Report of the President of the Archaeological Institute of America." *Bulletin of the Archaeological Institute of America*, vol. 14, Dec. 1923, pp. 3-18.
Magoffin, Ralph Van Deman. "Forty-Third Annual Report of the President of the Archaeological Institute of America." *Bulletin of the Archaeological Institute of America*, vol. 13, Dec. 1922, pp. 3-15.
"Marvels of the Agora Await American Spade." *New York Times*, 1 Jan. 1928, sec. XX, p. 4.

Meyer, Karl E., and Shareen Blair Brysac. *The China Collectors: America's Century-Long Hunt for Asian Art Treasures*. Palgrave Macmillan, 2015.

Palmer, Ely E. "The Consul General at Beirut (Palmer) to the Secretary of State," 9 Aug. 1940. *Foreign Relations of the United States Diplomatic Papers, 1941, Volume III*. Government Printing Office, 1959, pp. 660–661.

Patterson, Thomas C. *Toward a Social History of Archaeology in the United States*. Harcourt Brace College Publishers, 1995.

Philpott, A.J. "Harvard Man Home with Word of Prehistoric American Ruins." *Boston Sunday Globe*, 13 May 1923, p. 2.

Price, David H. *Anthropological Intelligence: The Deployment and Neglect of American Anthropology in the Second World War*. Duke University Press, 2008.

Roberts, Owen J. *Report of The American Commission for the Protection and Salvage of Artistic and Historic Monuments in War Areas*. Government Printing Office, 1946.

"Seek New Fields in Archaeology." *New York Times*, 27 Dec. 1940, p. 36.

Seymour, Thomas D. "Twenty-First Annual Report of the Council of the Archaeological Institute of America." *American Journal of Archaeology*, vol. 4, supplement, 1900, pp. 1–7.

Shipley, F. W. "Thirty-Eighth Annual Report of the President of the Archaeological Institute of America." *Bulletin of the Archaeological Institute of America*, vol. 8, Dec. 1917, pp. 3–15.

Fordian Knots

Indiana Jones and the Cinema of John Ford

BRIAN BREMS

One of cinema's foremost historians, author Joseph McBride, has written a pair of exhaustively researched biographies of two of the medium's most celebrated directors: John Ford and Steven Spielberg. Reading both volumes yields a number of fascinating insights that speak to the value of comparing their personal and professional lives as well as their cinematic output. Of Ford, McBride writes that he "used filmmaking as his refuge from reality, a way to create a safe, privileged, mythical world that functioned according to his own private rules" (3). Such assessments have likewise been made of Spielberg, who garnered a reputation for much of his career as a fantasist specializing in escapist entertainment, only belatedly earning (and often needing to perpetually defend) the honorific of "serious artist." In Ford's youth, he was "stigmatized for his ethnic [Irish] and religious [Catholic] background," just as Spielberg claims to have been stigmatized on the basis of his own Jewish faith (47). Both men came to Hollywood at an early age, and according to McBride's Ford biography, "seeming even younger than he actually was contributed to Ford's precocious sense of his own mystique" (97). McBride devotes considerable attention in his volume on Spielberg to his self-generated legend, sneaking onto the Universal Studios lot at 14 and going to work on an episode of Rod Serling's television show *Night Gallery* at age 21. Of Spielberg, McBride argues that "[p]erhaps his greatest artistic strength is his seemingly innate ability to conjure up visual images that evoke archetypal emotions and are nonetheless complex for being nonverbal" (17). Similar assessments might just as well be made of Ford's filmography, especially when those films take place in his favorite sun-drenched location, Monument Valley. In the Spielberg book, McBride explicitly draws the parallel even closer between his two subjects, making the case that each filmmaker was innately driven by the environments in which some of their greatest films took place: "It is impossible to imagine John Ford never having seen Monument Valley [...] and it is equally impossible to imagine Steven Spielberg never having grown up in suburbia" (49). The primacy of visual storytelling is another of McBride's comparisons, with the author placing heavy emphasis on the importance of Spielberg "[s]tarting his moviemaking career shooting film without sound [which] was excellent discipline in the art of visual storytelling, comparable to the training received by the great directors who started in silent movies and perfected their craft in the sound era, such as Hitchcock and John Ford" (83).

In Molly Haskell's efficient biography of Spielberg, she recounts his early interest in Ford's cinema, when "he and a friend put together a silent, two-reel Western homage to John Ford's *The Searchers*" and in his early short, *Amblin,*' the two main characters are shot "[i]n the darkness of a cave, where they are framed, John Ford–style, against the bright outdoors" (30, 42–44). Haskell describes much of his cinematic output as "a blender of high and low influences, from the cheesiest television serials to the sublime imagery of John Ford" (74). Spielberg himself encouraged such parallels early in his career when, speaking to David Helpern in 1974, he said "I've learned economy from John Ford. [...] he's taught me how to hold back for an overhead shot, you know, when to go wide, when to go close—don't shoot close-ups every scene or every shot, they don't mean anything. When a close-up is good. I mean, Ford was so judicious about his close-ups and his wide shots" (13). All these years later, according to Sue Matheson,

> Spielberg still regards Ford as his mentor and watches Ford's films before making his own. "I have to look at *The Searchers*," he says. "I just have to almost every time, and there are some other films like *The Informer* that I have to look at and films like *Tobacco Road* which I love." Likening the way that Ford "uses his camera to paint his pictures" to techniques used by "a classic painter," Spielberg finds Ford's static camera and his blocking and framing of scenes a celebration of "the frame, not just what happens inside of it" [xvii].

Spielberg's reputation as a filmmaker has long been intertwined with his awareness of and love for classic Hollywood cinema, and his films often quote and reference the filmmakers he admires. In author Warren Buckland's stylistic analysis of Spielberg's films, he makes the case that "[a]llusion to other films determines Spielberg's stylistic and narrational choices in *Raiders of the Lost Ark*" (132).

While a number of analyses of the Indiana Jones films have focused on these allusions, most of those analyses have confined themselves to the 1930s serials that Lucas and Spielberg have credited in interviews as shaping their narrative and stylistic approach. Others have occasionally referenced Spielberg's admiration for David Lean and his references to *Lawrence of Arabia* (1961) and the influence of George Stevens's 1939 film *Gunga Din* (especially on *Indiana Jones and The Temple of Doom*). Few, however, have traced the legacy of John Ford. The Devil's Tower rock formation so essential to the narrative and visual design of 1977's *Close Encounters of the Third Kind* is a clear invocation of Ford's favorite location, Monument Valley, and Spielberg's refusal to allow Ray Ferrier (Tom Cruise) entry to the home of his reunited family at the end of his 2006 remake of *War of the Worlds* owes an obvious debt to Ford's 1956 film *The Searchers*, wherein John Wayne's Ethan Edwards ends up similarly outcast. The Indiana Jones films most obviously bear Ford's influence, most blatantly in the opening sequence of *Indiana Jones and the Last Crusade*, when young Jones has his first adventure, frustrating the grave-robbing exploits of a band of brigands. This entire sequence takes place against the backdrop of Monument Valley itself, placing the film firmly in dialogue with Ford's oeuvre. Spielberg's wide shots of the column of Boy Scouts a-horseback, Jones among them, recalls the Cavalry Trilogy in particular, made up of *Fort Apache* (1948), *She Wore a Yellow Ribbon* (1949), and *Rio Grande* (1950).

While a more exhaustive analysis of the lineage between the Indiana Jones films and Ford's cinema is a worthwhile project deserving of more attention, for the sake of efficiency, I have elected to focus directly on the shared relationship of Spielberg's quartet with Ford's 1939 landmark Western *Stagecoach*. The historical moment of its production, just before the United States' entry into World War II, lends it "heroic sensation and premythic purity, lost qualities needed in 1939, as the world turned toward global war" (Gallagher 147). While the film is often (wrongly) credited with reigniting Hollywood's interest in Westerns (a number of other big-ticket Westerns were in production at the same time), Barry Keith Grant argues that "*Stagecoach* was the first 'adult western,' for the film achieves a fine balance of the genre's specific visual pleasures" (2). Ford biographer Scott Eyman makes a similar judgment of *Stagecoach*'s generic viability when he speaks of its singularity: "But B Westerns didn't look like *Stagecoach*, B Westerns didn't have casts like *Stagecoach*, and B Westerns didn't have the distinctly egalitarian message of *Stagecoach*—that it is society's outcasts who do the hard work of American civilization" (188). In its reclamation of a previously dismissed genre, *Stagecoach* shares a mission with the Indiana Jones films, which take the widely-dismissed serials—even Lucas and Spielberg were disappointed upon revisiting them before shooting *Raiders*, finding that they didn't quite hold up to their memories—and elevate the story to A-level budgeting and filmmaking technique. This is clear in each of the four films' central action set pieces, each of which quotes *Stagecoach*'s famous Apache assault at length, from general filmmaking approach to individual stunts: the truck chase in *Raiders*;

the mine car chase in *Temple of Doom*; the tank chase in *The Last Crusade*, and the jungle chase in *Kingdom of the Crystal Skull*.

Beyond the circumstances of production, though, there is the project of myth, a Fordian concern throughout much of his career, represented most obviously by the oft-quoted maxim from his 1962 Western *The Man Who Shot Liberty Valance* that "when the legend becomes fact, print the legend." But Ford's interest in myth was underway well before that. Thomas Schatz calls *Stagecoach* "a singular prewar Western with one foot planted in U.S. history and the other in American mythology. The symbiosis of fact and legend is the very essence of the film's enduring appeal and its tremendous influence on the regenerate A-Western form" (42). The film's intersection with questions of history and mythology make it an apt progenitor of Spielberg's Indiana Jones films, rooted as they are in the imagined past (the 1930s for the first three films, and the late 1950s for the as-of-now final installment). In each of the four Indiana Jones films, the title character played by Harrison Ford intersects with living history, first outmaneuvering Nazi occultists in *Raiders*; navigating British imperialism in India in *Temple of Doom*; coming face-to-face with Hitler himself in *The Last Crusade*; and finally, waging a one-man Cold War against Russian mad scientists obsessed with aliens in *Kingdom of the Crystal Skull*. In each film, Jones is the rugged American hero, negotiating his own divided loyalties between the pursuit of "fortune and glory" and the high-minded ideal that the artifacts he uncovers "belong in a museum." In overcoming historically motivated foes, Jones becomes an essential part of the cinematic representation of American history even though he never lived in it himself; his fictional quests to prevent powerful icons from falling into the wrong hands make him a guardian of the American way of life.

The ideological implications of Jones's pursuits (is he a noble historical preservationist or a morally dubious grave-robber?) have been grounds for criticism of the Indiana Jones series, most fully in the first two films' stereotypical representations of its non-white characters. For a number of critics, "[e]ven though Lucas/Spielberg upgraded the production values of the old series, they neglected to upgrade the casual colonial attitudes that were embedded in the old Hollywood films" (96). To Nigel Morris, Jones's "[r]ugged individualism recalls the pioneering spirit enshrined in the principle of the Manifest Destiny to conquer the wilderness" (74). If Jones's plundering of artifacts from South America to the Middle East to South Asia are extensions of Manifest Destiny, the films are even further in dialogue with Ford's Westerns, which engage with the same civilizing impulses (though to varying degrees of complexity). Morris argues that "Jones is foremost, American. His hat, leather jacket, open-necked shirt, canvas trousers, stubble, holstered six-gun and lasso-like whip, together with the desert setting of much of *Raiders of the Lost Ark* and the chase in which he gallops a white stallion to cut his enemies off at the pass: these recall westerns" (74). Ford, the Western genre's most well-regarded practitioner, comes in for the same kind of criticism in his depiction of non-white characters. Even in the more sympathetic readings of his films, critics find "John Ford's depiction of people of color is the most distressing feature of his body of work" (75). McBride observes that *Stagecoach*'s "savage Indian warriors and the comical or duplicitous Mexican servants, are unmodulated caricatures dating back to the earliest days of the genre" (286). J.P. Telotte says that Ford's films are frequently "callous or condescending in their ethnic portrayals, especially of Indians" (114).

While the Indiana Jones films have garnered their share of criticism on racial grounds, critics also accuse them of taking up the "morning in America" mantle of Ronald Reagan's 1980s in their dismissal of the anxieties and darkness that dominated American cinema for much of the previous decade. Molly Haskell saw this effort as part of the films' project from the first installment, *Raiders of the Lost Ark*, which "came to be considered a sort of bellwether of the Reagan era, with its patriotism and good humor, a welcome relief from raucous anti–American anti–Hollywood rhetoric and loose-cannon auteurs" (89). In the aftermath of Vietnam, Watergate, and a number of other national crises, the Indiana Jones movies "melded the blockbuster into the Reagan ideology of resurgent America. A larger metaphor behind the action in *Raiders* was the American emotional desire to never lose again" (Wasser 97). Similar charges might be leveled at Ford's films, especially when viewed in hindsight: "To contemporary audiences, Ford's films, most often characterized by a mixture of comedy and pathos, patriotic Americana and family-centered romanticism, might well seem as old fashioned as anything that D.W. Griffith ever made" (Studlar and Bernstein 10). Throughout his career, "Ford balanced epic themes and intimate dramas in a personalization of the past" and his films "became increasingly self-conscious in their vision of an American past, representing it not as a pure celebration of myth, but exploring it as a constructed discourse" (4). In other words, Ford's perspective on history matured as he got older and began to revisit similar ideals (especially in Westerns), often through his complex, contradictory heroes.

Ford's depiction of *Stagecoach*'s noble outlaw, The Ringo Kid (John Wayne), seems to set the stage for Spielberg's own representation of Jones. Much has been written on the defining moment when Ringo is introduced, alone in the desert and flagging down the coach for a ride. Ford's sudden dolly-in to Ringo, standing against the rear-projected backdrop of Monument Valley, introduces John Wayne anew, who had spent the better part of the 1930s toiling in obscurity after the failure of Raoul Walsh's *The Big Trail* in 1931, Wayne's first Western star vehicle. To McBride, "Wayne's first entrance in *Stagecoach* is one of the great star entrances in film history," a moment that is both "breathless and unexpected" (297). Schatz calls the moment "an archetypal flourish—a true epiphany of star-genre iconography" (38). The moment speaks to Ford's comfort with delaying the introduction of his hero; the entire opening of the film, set in Tonto before the stagecoach has departed, works to establish the central characters who will be its passengers, but withholds the appearance of the protagonist until the journey is already underway. Watching the film with the knowledge of Wayne's subsequent screen persona, the dolly-in to Ringo flagging down the coach, waving his Winchester repeating rifle, seems like an obvious tactic for suddenly revealing the character and star, their images intertwined. At the time, however, because of Wayne's relatively low stock in the industry, such a decision might not have seemed like such a no-brainer.

In each of the Indiana Jones films, Spielberg uses similar delaying tactics in introducing Indy. During the character's inaugural appearance in *Raiders of the Lost Ark*, Spielberg's camera wanders through a noir-esque jungle landscape, with cluttered frames full of trees and hanging vines, sunlight streaking brightly through in brilliant hot spots before coming to rest on the forest floor. Jones is always just slightly unclear—the scene's ostensible point of view belongs to his local guides, Barranca (Vic Taliban) and Satipo (Alfred Molina), who trail behind him with a coterie of other frightened members of the expedition. Jones is thus seen from behind or making his way through the thick jungle with a camera tracking alongside him, the foreground foliage obscuring a clear look at him. His face, when hinted at in images, is obscured by heavy shadows created by the jungle canopy. When Spielberg finally reveals Jones, as the hero wards off Barranca's treachery with a snap of the whip, his camera glosses on Wayne's famous introduction in *Stagecoach*. Though the camera does not rush in as Ford's does, Jones approaches the camera from shadowed darkness and steps into the light for the first time in the film, his rugged, unshaven face and steely gaze marking him as the film's competent, engaging hero. In Buckland's view, "the delay in seeing his face has created an aura of mystery around him" (138). Interestingly, Nigel Morris views the intensity of Jones's introduction in far different terms: "Jones' ominous first shot, in which he looms out of the darkness, sinisterly lit, accompanied by threatening music, introduces him as dangerous—Robert Mitchum in *Night of the Hunter* (1955)" (78). Actor Harrison Ford, with more recent success on screen than Wayne would have had at the time of *Stagecoach*, may have mitigated some of this impression of danger as a result of having garnered audience goodwill from his two appearances as Han Solo in *Star Wars* (1977) and *The Empire Strikes Back* (1980). Solo, like Jones, is a character equally understood by audiences for his contradictions—roguish humor balanced out by ruthless, even murderous pragmatism, both of which conceal hidden, eventually revealed nobility.

In the subsequent Indiana Jones films, Spielberg reinscribes the delaying device he established in *Raiders*, further withholding the reintroduction of the hero's visage, despite the fact that he is clearly known to the audience. In *Temple of Doom* (set in 1935, technically making it a prequel to the 1936-set *Raiders*), Indy is first seen in a starkly different setting, a glitzy nightclub in Shanghai where he is dressed more like the "American James Bond," as George Lucas originally conceived the character, in a white tuxedo jacket and bright red boutonniere, than the dirty-faced, dust-covered, leather-jacketed adventurer of the first film. Like so much of *Temple of Doom*, the film's perspective of Indy is radically different, but Spielberg still finds it important to use framing techniques to withhold the audience's first glimpse of the character. His camera follows Indy from waist-level down a staircase into the club's main floor, his left hand the main focal point. When he is finally shown in close-up, without his iconic hat and whip, the effect (again, like much of *Temple of Doom*) is disorienting. The delayed introduction in *The Last Crusade* is equal parts more conservative (owing to Spielberg's increasing discomfort with the darkness of *Temple of Doom*) and more extreme. The film's opening action sequence doesn't feature Harrison Ford at all; instead, it is a 1912-set prologue that establishes a kind of origin story for young Indy (played by River Phoenix). When Ford-as-Indy is finally revealed, it is in a match cut bridging twenty plus-years of intervening time, as young Indy's bowed head, newly adorned with the trademark fedora, rises to reveal's Harrison Ford's visage underneath before a fist slams into frame and connects with his jaw. Finally, in *Kingdom of the Crystal Skull*, Spielberg first introduces Indy via his hat, lying on the cement outside a secret government warehouse (revealed as Area 51 in production design, but not dialogue). Hauled out of a car trunk by Russian military, Jones is seen in a series of shots from behind that delay the audience's first look at his face, which he finally reveals in a quick turn to the camera that once again recalls Wayne's first appearance in *Stagecoach*. Though Spielberg is self-reflexively quoting his own initial visual introduction of the character in *Raiders*, he also delays Indy's reappearance because of the nearly twenty-year gap between *The Last Crusade* and *The Kingdom of the Crystal Skull*, building audience anticipation of seeing Harrison Ford in his familiar costume, though now looking noticeably older.

Though each of the four films plays with the physical relationship between the heroic subject, Indy, and the camera through delaying the introduction of the hero in the manner of Ford's perspective on Ringo in *Stagecoach*, Spielberg's most overt quotation of the shot comes partway through *Temple of Doom*. In the film's very bleak middle section, Indy is captured by Thuggee cult members after witnessing a human sacrificial ritual and forced to drink blood, which turns him into a possessed, obedient member of the cult. While under the hypnotic influence, he slaps his young friend Short Round and helps prepare singer and female companion Willie Scott for sacrifice.

When he is finally freed from the spell, Spielberg takes the opportunity to reintroduce the hero, newly reborn in his fedora, whip at his side, in a dolly shot directly reminiscent of Wayne's entrance in *Stagecoach*. In the mine where village children are being held captive and forced to work by the cult, Indy stands at the edge of a tunnel entrance, silhouetted, smoke rising around him. As Spielberg pushes the camera in, Indy seems larger than life, renewed in purpose not just to obtain the film's MacGuffin (the Sankara Stones), but to free the enslaved children. Though Indy's methods sometimes verge on the anti-heroic, especially in *Temple of Doom*, the films generally treat him as honorable, quick-thinking, and resourceful, traits he shares with Wayne's Ringo Kid. Throughout *Stagecoach*, "Wayne's physical presence, his bearing and gait, seems perfectly to embody Ringo's charming combination of romantic innocence and unwavering toughness" (Grant 5). The same might be said of Harrison Ford. In a moment played for comedy in *Temple of Doom*, Indy must stop a racing mine cart with failed brakes by using his own boots to slow it down. After he averts the crash, he hops in the dirt to extinguish his smoking feet, repeating "Water!" as a verbalization of his pain. When he sees the tunnel filling with water, the Thuggees' attempt to drown him, he repeats "Water!" with different intonation, now turning the same word into a warning. Actor Ford's performances across all four films are full of such turns, as Indy embodies various heroic and admirable traits, depending on the situation.

According to John Ford biographer Tag Gallagher, *Stagecoach*'s Ringo is "as basic and raw as a hero can be" (149). In his book's conclusion, Gallagher offers a cumulative analysis of what makes up a Fordian hero. According to

In *Temple of Doom* (1984), Spielberg's camera finds Indiana Jones (Harrison Ford) in a pivotal moment—a visual recall of John Wayne's iconic first appearance in John Ford's *Stagecoach*.

Gallagher, this character, "perceiving that myths (even defective) are necessary to sustain us, seeks to mediate between myth (repressive order) and reality (chaos), in order, by purifying myth, to revitalize society" (479). Assume that Ringo fits into Gallagher's paradigm—Indiana Jones does as well. Indy spends each of the four films passing between two seemingly opposing systems of belief: persistent commitment to rationality ("I'm a scientist," he tells Willie) and acquiescence to the power of the unknowable ("It's a leap of faith," he reminds himself before stepping across a chasm in *The Last Crusade*). Jones is a man struggling to reconcile contradictions in his own worldview—he can dismiss the Sankara Stones as "just rocks" and bear witness to their power when they burst into flames and fell *Temple of Doom*'s antagonist, Mola Ram. Jones is pulled down to Earth by his worldly desires for recognition, for an honorarium, or for "fortune and glory," but transcends these foibles when instinct tells him to keep his eyes closed during the opening of the Ark of the Covenant or that water from the Holy Grail is the only thing that can save his gut-shot father. Whether Jones himself believes or not, he routinely adopts a dismissive attitude in discussing the films' MacGuffins with others; he is frequently given to shrugging off their powers, reminding people that these fantastical events are "just a legend," "only stories," or, especially ambivalent, "if you believe that sort of thing." By maintaining an outward sheen of skepticism, Jones can, like the audience, be carried away by the awe and majesty of what he sees when unexplained forces take hold.

A common critique leveled at the narrative structure of *Raiders* is that Indy is rendered passive by the film's finale—he is a bystander, tied to a lamppost with Marion, while the Nazis open the Ark and are melted and burned to death by the forces they unleash, an outcome that would have come to pass if he were there or not. Perhaps, through the lens of the Fordian hero, Jones's (in)actions may seem narratively justified. According to Gallagher, the hero of John Ford's films "may not be passive" (479). Though the Nazis would, according to the film's narrative logic, have likely been incinerated anyway by the opening of the Ark, Indy's primary function is to bear witness to their deaths and, crucially, close his eyes at the critical moment. The Nazis' transgression is to believe that they can harness the power of God—surely that is Jones's rival archaeologist Belloq's sin—and Jones and Marion are spared because they submit to His power. They do not presume to look upon God, as Belloq and the Germans do, and survive to believe in the strength of the myth that the Ark contains, made frighteningly, powerfully real in the film's climax. In Gallagher's formulation, Indy's actions at the climax of *Raiders* embody the duty of the Fordian hero: "He must, perceiving that life can be hell, strive to keep atop the maelstrom; like Tom Joad, he must climb to critical consciousness of life's contradictions. And then, he must be willing to act, to intervene, to assume authority over others" (479). Indy's rational biases give way to his often-dormant sense of faith in the film's climactic moments, and he intervenes to command Marion to keep her eyes shut no matter what happens, so that she too might be spared. Jones oscillates between consciousness's opposing poles and leans on his own instincts in deciding when the right moment to act appears.

As a character driven almost entirely by externalities, Indiana Jones might sometimes be viewed as a two-dimensional, rather than three-dimensional character. Gallagher's perspective on the Fordian hero asserts that "[e]motional vulnerability rather than physical prowess characterizes the Fordian hero, and he acts from the pressure of outer events or inner conscience rather than from free will" (479). While the "outer events" and "inner conscience" seem right in line with Indy's motivations, the character does often exhibit a strong degree of "physical prowess" that, owing to the films' action-adventure genre, seems to take precedence over "emotional vulnerability." Often, the films do elide Indy's emotional needs, allowing his plot-driven concerns (finding the MacGuffin) to dominate the narrative events. And yet, the emotional undercurrents of his relationships with his fellow characters often motivate his actions. His surrogate father-child relationship with Short Round forms the emotional core of *Temple of Doom*; their partnership reaches its low point during Indy's possession and the aforementioned slap, punctuated by Shorty's pained "Indy, I love you!" as he swipes at his mentor's exposed chest with a torch. The torch's flame is enough to jar Indy out of his trance, and his "I'm all right, kid," and subsequent wink reassure Shorty that all is well again before the two take on the Thuggee guards together. Here and in a later moment, John Williams's triumphant "Theme from Indiana Jones" asserts their paired identity; during the following sequence in the mine, the theme returns over a depth-of-field shot from Spielberg, who catches a foregrounded Indy regaining the upper hand in a fight with an enormous Thuggee and Shorty doing the same with the possessed boy Maharaja over his shoulder in the background.

In *The Last Crusade*, Spielberg gives Indy his most developed emotional arc in his relationship with Henry Jones, Sr. Throughout the course of the film, Indy grapples with his complicated feelings about the elder Jones, whose approval he clearly craves and also flouts. Indy's free attitude towards violence often shocks his father. "I can't believe what you did!" the old man shouts after Indy grabs a machine gun from a Nazi guard and sprays bullets at three men, killing them instantly. Indy both desires his father's approval and refuses to become him ("Don't call me Junior!"), a prospect complicated when the two discover that they have both, at intervals, slept with the same woman, Dr. Elsa Schneider, the traitorous Nazi grail-seeker who accompanies them on their journey and intermittently swaps allegiances. The film's most moving moment comes in the aftermath of the film's biggest set piece, a desert chase between a horse-riding Indy and a Nazi tank, when the elder Jones believes Indy has gone over a cliff along with the tank and its Nazi commander. As Indy reappears, standing next to his father staring over the precipice, the suddenly vulnerable Senior grabs his son in a full embrace, choking through tears, "I thought I'd lost you, boy." Indy, still a bit discombobulated from his fight, croaks, "I thought you had too, sir." The formal resuscitation of their familial dynamic, "boy" and "sir," momentarily disregards the narrative and allows the estranged father and son shared understanding, the previous absence of which Senior had lamented aloud while staring over the cliff.

As an action hero, Indiana Jones represents a number of various roles. Across the series, he is a teacher, adventurer, skeptic, believer, friend, romantic partner, surrogate father, surrogate son (to Marcus Brody), actual son, and actual father (to Mutt Williams in *Kingdom of the Crystal Skull*), among numerous others. Like Jones, the Fordian hero "is often a combination of soldier, judge, and priest, symbolizing his intervention, authority, and self-sacrifice. And although he may be a fixture of society, he is yet an outsider, because he is purer than the average man in service of such accepted values as tolerance, justice, medical duty, preservation of family, and love (whereas the false hero serves racism, vengeance, law, 'duty,' intolerance, and glory)" (479–80). By the time of the series' conclusion (again, for now) in *Kingdom of the Crystal Skull*, Jones has fully engaged with each of these values to varying degrees. He bests his greedy rivals, Gallagher's "false heroes" like Belloq, *The Last Crusade*'s Walter Donovan, and Soviet scientist Dr. Spalko and fortune-seeker/double agent Mac in *Kingdom of the Crystal Skull*. In overcoming their treachery and showing circumspection (he "chooses wisely"), he offers a contrastive vision reliant upon preservation of history, undermining the implications of the original film's title, *Raiders of the Lost Ark*. By the time the credits roll on *Kingdom of the Crystal Skull*, Indy is no longer a "tomb raider" seeking "fortune and glory." He is a family man, reunited with Marion in marriage, and ready to play the paternal role to Mutt, whom he has only recently come to know. In John Ford's cinema, "lone males at the edge of society, independent of social norms and free of emotional ties to family, are not heroes in the Fordian universe. Either these men are transformed, or they remain immutably transgressive and inevitably marginalized" (Studlar 61). Jones avoids the fate of *The Searchers*' Ethan Edwards, who famously walks away from the homestead he has worked to preserve, no longer feeling welcome there. The final image of Jones on screen represents the simultaneity of his insider/outsider status: in the church, he wears his wedding best, a gray jacket with a red bow tie. As he walks out of the church with Marion on his arm, he swipes his fedora from Mutt, who picks it up when a sudden, mysterious wind blows the iconic hat towards him. Indy places the fedora on his hat, as if to say, "not yet, Junior," and walks out of cinema history forever—maybe.

And it is in history where the Indiana Jones films cross most readily into Fordian territory. Indy, the films' hero, is a historical figure in the mythic sense. As Spielberg would demonstrate throughout a number of his other films, history is one of his major concerns, as it was for John Ford. Spielberg's vision of history in the Indiana Jones films is not a vision of lived history, but a cinematic one. According to Nigel Morris, "Spielberg protagonists inhabit movies, not merely a diegesis resembling reality" (36). By alluding to John Ford throughout the Indiana Jones films, Spielberg makes an implicit case that all history, if it is to be made cinematic, must rely on cinema itself as a conduit. Buckland, borrowing from Noel Carroll, argues that Spielberg's films perfectly encapsulate "reinscribing the past into the present, allusion becomes an expressive device that reinforces the themes, emotions, and aesthetics of contemporary films" (131). Some critics, like Frederick Wasser, argue that in taking this approach, Spielberg's films "avoid the reality of history and instead treat the past as romantic fantasy" (97). But more likely, Spielberg, known cinephile, sees himself in the continuity of cinematic history rather than world history. Viewed in this context, the Indiana Jones films serve as a vehicle for Spielberg to engage with the cinema of the past to tell stories set in imagined history. In an essay on John Ford's Westerns, Robin Wood argues that Ford's films demonstrate that "[i]ndividuals come and go, but the continuity of tradition is unbroken, the individual gaining a kind of immortality through the loss of his individuality and assimilation into the tradition. The emphasis is on continuity rather than development" (33). Spielberg steps behind the camera to capture these imagined stories of mythic proportions, where Indiana Jones reaches into the ancient past to preserve artifacts of legendary import from the encroachment of villains from the recent past, all in the context of the present moment of their production. In doing so, he has preserved Jones himself as an artifact of cinema history, destined to be discovered by film studies' own archaeologists. As Belloq tells Jones, waving his hand over the Ark of the Covenant, "We are just passing through history. This is history."

Works Cited

Buckland, Warren. *Directed by Steven Spielberg: Poetics of the Contemporary Hollywood Blockbuster*. New York: Continuum, 2006.

Eyman, Scott. *Print the Legend: The Life and Times of John Ford*. New York: Simon & Schuster, 1999.

Gallagher, Tag. *John Ford: The Man and His Films*. Berkeley: University of California Press, 1986.

Grant, Barry Keith. "Introduction: Spokes in the Wheels." *John Ford's* Stagecoach. Edited by Barry Keith Grant. New York: Cambridge University Press, 2003, pp. 1–20.

Haskell, Molly. *Steven Spielberg: A Life in Films*. New Haven: Yale University Press, 2017.

Helpern, David. "At Sea with Steven Spielberg." In *Steven Spielberg: Interviews*. Edited by Lester D. Friedman and Brent Notbohm. Jackson: University Press of Mississippi, 2000.

Matheson, Sue. *The Westerns and War Films of John Ford*. Lanham, MD: Rowman & Littlefield, 2016.
McBride, Joseph. *Searching for John Ford: A Life*. New York: St. Martin's Press, 2003.
_____. *Steven Spielberg: A Biography*, 2nd ed. Jackson: University Press of Mississippi, 2010.
Morris, Nigel. *The Cinema of Steven Spielberg: Empire of Light*. New York: Wallflower Press, 2007.
Ramirez Berg, Charles. "The Margin as Center: The Multicultural Dynamics of John Ford's Westerns." *John Ford Made Westerns: Filming the Legend in the Sound Era*. Edited by Gaylyn Studlar and Matthew Bernstein. Bloomington: Indiana University Press, 2001. pp. 75–101.
Schatz, Thomas. "*Stagecoach* and Hollywood's A-Western Renaissance." *John Ford's Stagecoach*. Edited by Barry Keith Grant. New York: Cambridge University Press, 2003, pp. 21–47.
Studlar, Gaylyn. "Sacred Duties, Poetic Passions: John Ford and the Issue of Femininity in the Western." *John Ford Made Westerns: Filming the Legend in the Sound Era*. Edited by Gaylyn Studlar and Matthew Bernstein. Bloomington: Indiana University Press, 2001. pp. 43–74.
Studlar, Gaylyn, and Matthew Bernstein. "Introduction." *John Ford Made Westerns: Filming the Legend in the Sound Era*. Edited by Gaylyn Studlar and Matthew Bernstein. Bloomington: Indiana University Press, 2001. pp. 1–22.
Telotte, J.P. "'A Little Bit Savage': *Stagecoach* and Racial Representation." *John Ford's Stagecoach*. Edited by Barry Keith Grant. New York: Cambridge University Press, 2003, pp. 113–131.
Wasser, Frederick. *Steven Spielberg's America*. Malden, MA: Polity Press, 2010.
Wood, Robin. "'Shall We Gather at the River?': The Late Films of John Ford." *John Ford Made Westerns: Filming the Legend in the Sound Era*. Edited by Gaylyn Studlar and Matthew Bernstein. Bloomington: Indiana University Press, 2001. pp. 23–41.

"You call this archaeology?"
Indiana Jones and Hollywood's View on the Nature of History

Ryan Staude

In May 1977, two young Hollywood filmmakers built a sandcastle outside the Mauna Kea hotel on the Big Island of Hawaii. One of the directors had gone to Hawaii to escape what he anticipated would be the dreadful news that his latest picture, a science fiction epic called *Star Wars*, bombed during its opening weekend. The other director had just completed principal photography on his own science fiction film and joined his friend as a brief respite before he began post-production. At the start of the trip, a depressed George Lucas told Steven Spielberg that making *Star Wars* had physically broken him, and that he was retiring from directing. However, during a dinner early in the vacation Lucas learned that his film was selling out cinemas across the country, and his mood suddenly livened. As he and Spielberg built their granular fortress, they talked about what movies they wanted to make in the future. Spielberg was on a run of successes with *Sugarland Express* (1974) and *Jaws* (1975), and Lucas could surely command any studio's attention because of *Star Wars'* success. Spielberg mentioned that he wanted to make a James Bond movie, and Lucas replied, "I've got something you might like as much as Bond" (Rinzler 19). Over the course of thirty minutes, as the tide slowly crept upon their sandcastle, Lucas regaled Spielberg with the heroic exploits of his adventurer/archaeologist who traversed the globe in search of precious artifacts. Lucas reiterated that he was not going to direct it, and Spielberg said he would take on the job. The two shook hands and gave birth to one of the most successful and revered film franchises in cinematic history.

The two men envisioned the series as a throwback to the B-movie serial adventures both had enjoyed as children. The film would build toward a series of action climaxes, never allowing the audience to catch its breath. Spielberg formally accepted the role of director in December 1977, and over a period of five days in January 1978, Lucas, Spielberg, and screenwriter Lawrence Kasdan hammered out the story details. They named the lead character Indiana after Lucas's wife's dog. Spielberg had already committed to directing the World War II–set comedy *1941*, which left Kasdan and Lucas to fine-tune the story, and Kasdan to write the script. Filming began in June 1980, and the final movie, titled *Raiders of the Lost Ark*, was released just over a year later in June 1981.

Raiders of the Lost Ark's financial success spawned three sequels over the next 27 years. Collectively, the films have earned almost two billion dollars at the international box office, and been nominated for thirteen Academy Awards. In an American Film Institute survey, Indiana Jones was named the number two cinematic hero of all time ("AFI's 100 Years"). The films have led to television shows, books, video games, amusement park rides, and generations of fans. And while the films have received audience praise, they have also earned the attention of academics and scholars. Scholarly work on the films' religious themes, their notions of masculinity, their portrayal of archaeology and archaeologists, and even their supposed avowal of neoconservative politics have all appeared in print in the last forty years. Yet, almost no work has been done that examines the main character's central occupation: the recovery of the past. For all of the critical discourse on the Indiana Jones franchise, the question remains: what do the films and their main character say about the past and the nature of history?

The films provide viewers with a complicated, nuanced (if at times fantastical) view of the past and of the historical profession. Although Indiana Jones is an archaeologist by training, his discipline is the allied field of history. Doctor Jones may go on field expeditions, and he may spend more time with material objects than traditional historians, but he is engaged in a similar pursuit: to uncover and reveal the truth about the human past. The film depicts Jones as a scholar obsessed with his field (one of his antagonists even says it is his "religion"). He brings the same level of zeal that most scholars bring to their fields, and he uses deductive reasoning to piece together clues to form conclusions. Moreover, he evinces one of the most important traits a scholar must possess: skepticism. Jones takes nothing at face value, and he must prove to himself that evidence is genuine and worth following. His process resembles that of an earnest historian in that he pieces together clues and uses research and deductive reasoning to arrive at answers. He even admonishes students to spend a considerable amount of time in the library because that is where the best archaeology takes place (although he later reverses this advice in the last entry in the series). Lastly, Indiana Jones may risk life and limb in pursuit of historical artifacts, but he never truly possesses them. Just as historians seek to recapture an ever-elusive truth, Indiana seeks to reclaim lost objects. If the objects in questions are taken as symbols for absolute truth, then it is clear what Spielberg and Lucas are saying about historians and the quest to promulgate the truth: scholars may come close, but they can never present an undisputed, truthful view of the past.

David Lowenthal has written that historians "ever stumble on feet of clay." That is, no matter how well they are trained, how thoroughly they investigate and interrogate their sources (written and material), and how rigorous they are in their methods, they will never arrive at an absolute final judgment on why past events occurred in the manner they did. Their interpretations may stand for generations, or they may be turned over by their own students, but historians err when they seek to uncover the absolute truth. Most modern historians would agree with the inestimable E.H. Carr's pronouncement that reaching absolute truth is "not appropriate in the world of history" (qtd. in Phillips 20), with the exception of stating simple historical facts (for example, the battle of Trenton took place on December 26, 1776). Yet, no less a figure than Harvard historian Oscar Handlin contradicted Carr when he wrote, "The historians' vocation depends on the minimal operational article of faith: Truth is absolute; it is as absolute as the world is real. It does not exist because individuals wish it, any more than the world exists for their convenience.... Truth is knowable and will out if earnestly pursued" (qtd. in Phillips 29–30). Here, Handlin was doing his best to channel the German founding fathers of the historical discipline, namely Leopold von Ranke, who argued that with the proper application of the scientific method, historians could relate the absolute truth of the past.

In his 1986 article for the *American Historical Review*, William H. McNeill gave, perhaps, the most eloquent distillation of the role of truth in the historical profession. "Eternal and universal Truth about human behavior is an unattainable goal, however delectable as an ideal. Truths are what historians achieve when they bend their minds as critically and carefully as they can to the task of making their account of public affairs credible" (8). The result of such efforts, according to McNeill, is "mythistory"—a version of the truth that is absolute to some, but myths "for others, who inherit or embrace different assumptions and organizing concepts about the world" (8, 9). Historians locate facts, and then string them together, using what Allan Nevins termed "historical imagination" (260), into a narrative that the public (and other historians) may accept, challenge, or disregard. According to McNeill, as well as most practitioners, it is not the job of a historian to present the absolute truth of history, but rather to use their best judgments in order to offer impressionist views of the past. Contrary to Handlin's edict, then, the past is never completely recoverable, but historians, in the words of Walter

McDougall, must attempt to recover it, even though it is "a quest that can never be fulfilled" (41, 42).

Spielberg and company reflect the discipline's complexity and nuance in their depiction of Indiana Jones and his various quests to reclaim lost objects. Although Jones claims that he is not after the truth (in an opening scene from *Indiana Jones and the Last Crusade*, he tells the students that archaeology is the search for fact, not truth, and that they can take a colleague's philosophy class if they are interested in the latter). Jones may believe that he is not after the truth, but as he assembles facts to determine the locations of the artifacts, he also assembles a larger narrative about their significance. His inability to ever truly possess the relics he seeks mirrors the historian's inability to completely recapture the past, yet both continue on their paths, and along the way they encounter enlightenment and self-awareness.

Indiana Jones, adventurer extraordinaire, is actually Dr. Henry Jones, Jr., a tenured professor of archaeology at the fictional Marshall College. Across the four movies, it is clear that Jones self-identifies, not as a treasure hunter, but as a scholar. Several times he tells people that he is a teacher to dispel any preconceived notions they might hold about the famous "Doctor Jones." Although audiences may relish Indy's more adventurous side, the filmmakers imbue him with realistic characteristics of a scholar in order to further their three-dimensional portrait of this complex character.

To begin, Jones is seen teaching at his university in three of the four films. In all three cases, we first glimpse him in his natural (and definitely safer) element: lecturing to a class about archaeology. And in each instance Jones is seen with the physical trappings, and engaged in the normal business, of a university scholar. Jones has the stereotypical wardrobe of a mid-century professor—tweed sport coat over slacks with glasses. In *Raiders of the Lost Ark*, Jones carries an armful of books and maps to his meeting with federal agents; he is the physical embodiment of the disheveled, unorganized professor. He even carries chalk in his pocket. In *The Last Crusade*, Indy's excursion to reclaim the Cross of Coronado has cost him so much time that he has a stack of term papers to grade upon his return, as well as a large flock of students waiting for a minute of his precious office hours. In the latest installment, *Indiana Jones and the Kingdom of the Crystal Skull*, Jones is involved in that most soul-crushing of experiences, university politics. He also gives the clearest explanation of his job when he tells Mutt Williams in a café that he is a "tenured professor of archaeology." Although the times we see Jones in the university always constitute a prelude to bigger adventures, the filmmakers are accurate in their portrayal of his scholarly existence within the ecosystem of academia.

In addition to looking the part of a scholar, Jones also possesses one of the key traits necessary for success as an intellectual: namely, skepticism of received wisdom. Just as good historians will always seek to divine their own conclusions from the evidence, Indy does not accept the "bedtime stories" or legends that he hears about the objects he pursues. He certainly knows them, and understands their origins, but he does not accept them as fact. The trait of asking "why" is instilled in aspiring scholars from their beginning days as graduate students, and in his pursuit of facts about the past, Jones manifests the skeptical spirit that is so crucial to historians in their work.

Like historians, and indeed many academics, Indy's work consumes his life. When we last see Jones in 1957, he is still searching for priceless artifacts, still teaching (apparently in the same classroom for, at least, the past twenty years), and still a confirmed bachelor. His work is the central organizing principle of his life, and his devotion to it is such that he is repeatedly willing to risk his life, and (one imagines) his professional reputation, in order to obtain the artifacts he seeks. His antagonist in *Raiders of the Lost Ark*, the French archaeologist René Belloq, succinctly captures Indy's obsession when he tells him that archaeology is his "religion." His obsession with the Ark of the Covenant, the Sankara stones, the Holy Grail, and the city of Akator lead to his near death in all four films. Additionally, in *The Last Crusade*, the opening action sequence shows that Indy's relationship with the Cross of Coronado spans his teen years all the way into adulthood. It almost killed him when he was young, and obtaining this artifact nearly drowns him twenty-five years later. Although historians may not be as prone to risking their lives as they pursue their research, Indy's quasi-religious fervor for his field is recognizable in many historians and their work.

One of the reasons that Indy is so zealous in trying to obtain the Cross of Coronado is his belief that "it belongs in a museum." For the most part, Indy sees the artifacts as important totems of human history, and he believes that they need to be in museums where they can be studied and shared with the public. (Interestingly, this is not the case with either the Sankara Stones, which he returns to the villagers because they would "gather dust" in a museum, or the Crystal Skull, which Indy brings back to its home in Akator). Like the Cross, Indy believes that the Ark of the Covenant should be in the hands of experts so it can be studied. Indeed, this was one of the conditions on which he agreed to acquire the Ark for the American government. The past is sacred to Jones, as it is to historians, and, furthermore, it needs to be shared with the wider public. Spielberg and Lucas understand that there is a public side to historians' work, and that presentation (in order to share ideas and inform the public) is a vital aspects of the scholar's work. Although the forces opposing Indy's public exhibition of his findings are more powerful and sinister than the ones facing historians (the American government versus unwilling publishing houses) the comparison is unmistakable.

Historians cannot lay claim to risking life and limb as Indy does numerous times, and it is impossible to draw a connection between the series' fantastical elements and the lived experiences of scholars, but Jones does have a process he follows to reach his conclusions (however heightened, sped up, and dramatized it is), and it resembles the process which historians follow to reach their conclusions.

First, Jones comes to each artifact armed with prior knowledge about it, including the facts and legends surrounding the object. Perhaps because he has spent so much time in the library (as he admonishes his students in *Raiders of the Lost Ark* to do), he is knowledgeable about a variety of ancient artifacts. Jones knows the work of other scholars whom he considers to be more authoritative on certain matters, whether it is his mentor Abner Ravenwood's work on the city of Tanis or his father's research into the Holy Grail. This is the equivalent of historians being able to recite the historiography of a certain field. Understanding a field's literature allows historians to build on the work of their academic forerunners in order to arrive at new conclusions. Likewise, Indy stands on the shoulders of his predecessors so he can find the relics he seeks. In many cases, he takes the clues they have discovered and makes the final connections to determine the artifact's location. He completes the process they began.

Jones analyzes the evidence that he has (or that others have collected for him) to determine the next steps on his quest. Upon his arrival to the library in Venice in *The Last Crusade*, he is able to use his father's diary, the scraps left at his father's work station, and the library's architecture (as well as his knowledge that early Christian burial grounds were located under churches) to find the tomb of Sir Richard, which then leads him to another clue—the starting point in the desert which leads to the Grail's final resting place. Jones's analytical skills serve him well again when the Soviets capture him in *Kingdom of the Crystal Skull*. Once again, Indy's prior knowledge and his ability to decipher his old friend Harold Oxley's drawings and mindless ramblings lead to a conclusion—in this case the location of the city of Akator. Certainly, for the movies' narrative purposes, the speed of his historical process is increased, but, nevertheless, historians must also take clues and find patterns, and then apply their prior knowledge in order to make conclusions and find answers.

Like any good historian, Indy follows the evidence, and does not allow any preconceived notions to sway him during his expeditions. In all four movies, Indy begins as a skeptic. Indeed, he goes beyond skepticism in most cases to outright disbelief. He tells his colleague Marcus Brody that he does not believe in the "hocus pocus" or "mumbo jumbo" legends surrounding the Ark of the Covenant. Likewise, when Walter Donovan relates the story of the three brothers who swore an oath to defend the Holy Grail, Indy stops him with the admonishment that he had already heard the "bedtime story."

Nor can he believe that Oxley has actually found Akator because he does not think it actually exists. However, his skepticism fades as new evidence emerges. Indy warns his students never to believe that "X" will "mark a spot," but he is forced to admit his error in the Venice library. As he uncovers more evidence about the Crystal Skull and Akator, it becomes clear not only that the city is real, but that the skull belongs to a creature not of this earth. The evidence that Indy amasses throughout the movies gradually converts him into a believer. He does not stubbornly cling to his notion that the legends he heard were myths; rather, like a good historian, he follows the evidence to new conclusions and understandings.

Indy pursues his objects of inquiry with zeal, and with a methodology approaching historical research, but like historians searching for an absolute truth they can never find, Jones never fully possesses the artifacts he seeks. He may control them temporarily, but they are never his to share with the world. This pattern is established in the series' opening film, *Raiders of the Lost Ark*. Indy finds the Ark of the Covenant only to have it taken from him (twice) by the Nazis. He has the opportunity to destroy it, but cannot bring himself to obliterate this valuable piece of the past. And although he sees the Ark, he cannot glimpse its contents. A final indignation is when the American government takes it from Indy to have "top men" study it. If the Ark is the truth which Jones seeks to uncover, he gets close to it, but cannot share it with the world. As convinced as he is that the Ark is real, without the physical proof of its existence, the world will disbelieve him. In this case, an impersonal force (the government) removes Indy's "truth" (the Ark) from his grasp. A daunting bureaucracy seals the Ark in a crate to be lost among the items in a vast government warehouse. It is still extant, though, waiting to be discovered, but tantalizingly out of reach. Historians search for the truth, knowing that it is hidden in the occluding fog of the past, but also that it will, inevitably, elude their grasp.

In *Temple of Doom* Indy drops into an Indian village where he undertakes to find the villagers' lost Sankara stone. The villagers attach spiritual significance to the stone, but for Indy it represents "fortune and glory." Ideally, historians hope for similar outcomes in their publications (although, few could claim to actually find such riches). Upon discovering the secret passages of Pankot palace and witnessing a secret Thuggee ritual, Indy risks the lives of his two companions (a woman and a child) in order to obtain the stones. After his inevitable capture and escape, Indy fights the cult's leader, Mola Ram, on a dangling wood bridge over a steep cliff. He holds onto the bridge with one hand while gripping the bag with the Sankara stones in the other. He is so obsessed with the stones that he is willing to risk his life (twice) in order to possess them. Indy does not lose the stones to a governmental authority (as he had lost the Ark in *Raiders*), but rather he willingly returns the one which did not fall into the river to the villagers. His paramour (for this film), Willie Scott, asks him why he did not keep the stone, and he replies that it would just "collect dust" in a museum. This is very unlike the Indiana Jones of *Raiders of the Lost Ark*. Still, as in the previous film, the history that Jones risked his life, and those of his companions, for will not be revealed to the public. There will be no articles published about the stone, nor will it make a grand tour of global museums. Once again, the truth that Indy sought will not be shared with a wider audience.

As in his other adventures, Indy must go to great lengths and travel many miles in order to secure the Holy Grail in *The Last Crusade*. Even more than *Raiders of the Lost Ark*, this movie posits the study of the past as a religious quest that only the truly worthy can fulfill. The Grail's guardian describes Indy as a "strangely dressed" knight, but it is not enough to be clever and worthy enough to find the Grail, one must also have the cunning and integrity to select the correct Grail from a trove of false ones. Of course, Indy knows which one is the rightful Grail, and he uses it to save his father from a mortal wound. His colleague/lover/antagonist, Dr. Elsa Schneider, tries to remove the Grail from its resting place and thereby triggers an earthquake which begins to level the structure in which the Grail is housed. Indy falls into a crevice trying to save Elsa when he sees that the Grail is within his reach. He must make a choice to reach for the Grail and glory, and possibly lose his life, or be rescued by his father. Whereas the Indiana Jones of *Temple of Doom* might have continued to stretch for the Grail, Indy heeds his father's admonition to "let it go." Historians spend years of their lives combing through archives and depositories trying to piece together a narrative of the past. Some are successful, and some, like Indy reaching for the Grail, can never get a firm grip on the truth they seek. The historian may think he sees the truth, and can almost touch it, but can never fully bring it to the public's attention. In the case of the Grail, Indy comes to the realization that his father shares: some truths may be too powerful for the public to know. It is a theme which is continued in Indy's most recent adventure.

In *Kingdom of the Crystal Skull*, Indy finds the titular object, but then he is tasked with returning it to a place that he could *not* find in his youth. The prize here is not the skull, but the city of Akator. The film's antagonist, the Soviet Colonel Irina Spalko, believes that Akator hosts a variety of ancient alien secrets that she can use to help her side defeat the United States in the Cold War. Indy, Spalko, and crew make their way through the jungle, and they locate Akator which, as Spalko hypothesized, is an alien-built city. Indy and his companions discover that the aliens were "collectors" and have amassed a series of artifacts from many ancient civilizations. Upon returning the skull to its skeleton, the aliens merge into one being and grant Spalko her wish to "know everything." However, humans' primitive consciousness cannot comprehend the knowledge which the aliens impart, and Spalko disintegrates from the information's weight. Indy understands that, as with the Ark and the Grail, some forms of knowledge and power are not for human consumption. Nor does Indy stop to collect any of the artifacts which the aliens have collected, preferring to escape with his life rather than pieces of history. Perhaps, since the knowledge is too much for Indy to comprehend and therefore accept, the universal truth might lie beyond the historian's grasp. The truth is too complex and too multifaceted for historians to process and present to an audience, and therefore what they offer, instead, is a version of the truth, McNeill's "mythistory," a truth designed for the public with the intention that people will use it in the manner which best suits them. Like Spalko, historians (and the public) are not ready for the absolute truth, and therefore must be satisfied with the mythistories they formulate in the place of truth.

The Indiana Jones film series is one of the most popular and critically acclaimed adventure film franchises in cinematic history. Although Spielberg and Lucas may have conceived the films as throwbacks to the adventure serials they loved as children, the character of Indiana Jones has taken on a high degree of complexity, and the films have been parsed and analyzed in ways that the filmmakers never contemplated as they discussed the character on that Hawaiian beach in 1977. The movies, which superficially follow a daredevil archaeologist as he races against evil forces to hunt down some of the most sought-after objects in humankind's history, reveal much about the historical profession and what scholars are actually trying to do in studying the past.

Henry Jones, Jr., better known as Indiana Jones, is an archaeology professor. He dresses the part of the bespectacled academic, teaches classes, grades essays, has to deal with student demands, and gets wrapped up in university politics. Like most historians, he is obsessed with the past, and there is a quasi-religious element in his pursuit of relics. He also, for the most part, wants the past shared with the public. Rather than being in private hands, or collected for monetary reasons, Indy wants to put the past on display, where many audiences can experience their collective human heritage. Like historians, Indy has a process he follows which leads him to his conclusions. He is a proponent of spending time in the library to acquire the appropriate background information and context for whatever he seeks. Just as a good historian knows the historiography of his field, Indy knows the stories and legends surrounding the artifacts he seeks. Instead of allowing his skepticism to overwhelm the evidence with which he is presented, he allows new information to persuade him, going where the clues take him. And just as universal truth will always be unattainable for historians, Indy never ends a film in possession of the artifact he chased through the movie. Whether it is taken by the government or by aliens, or whether he willingly gives it back to its rightful owners, Indy has nothing tangible to show for his efforts. Whereas historians publish articles and monographs detailing their findings, Indiana Jones does not come away from his adventures with knowledge or information he can share with the public.

Indy may not win his prize, but his adventures bring him personal fulfillment—a girlfriend in *Raiders of the Lost Ark*, a makeshift family in *Temple of Doom*, a renewed relationship with his father in *Last Crusade*, and a wife and son in *Kingdom of the Crystal Skull*. It can be said, then, that the true importance of these adventures was not the attainment of the ostensible goal, but rather the journeys that helped Indy grow and become a more self-aware person. For historians, while they want to publish and bring their findings to the public, it is the process of research and writing that makes them better scholars. They may not find the truth, but the tools they use in their quest become sharper as a result of the hours in the archive and the constant review of editorial marks on their essays and manuscripts. In the end, historians will not be able to tell people why the past unfolded *exactly* as it did, but they gain more insight into their fields, and they are able to tackle their next projects with new perspectives and outlooks. In a lifelong pursuit of the past, then, what historians may wish for is not the universal truth, but, rather, in the words of Henry Jones, Sr., "illumination" about the human condition.

WORKS CITED

"AFI's 100 Years ... 100 Heroes & Villains," *American Film Institute*, American Film Institute. https://www.afi.com/100years/handv.aspx.

Lowenthal, David. "The Frailty of Historical Truth: Learning Why Historians Inevitably Err." *Perspectives on History*, American Historical Association. https://www.historians.org/publications-and-directories/perspectives-on-history/march-2013/the-frailty-of-historical-truth.

McDougall, Walter A. "'Mais ce n'est pas l'historie!' Some Thoughts on Toynbee, McNeill, and the Rest of Us." *The Journal of Modern History* 58, 1986, 19–42.

McNeill, William H. "Mythistory, or Truth, Myth, History and Historians." *American Historical Review* 91, 1986, 1–10.

Nevins, Allan. "Not Capulets, Not Montagus." *American Historical Review* 65, 1960, 253–270.

Phillips, Paul T. *Truth, Morality, and Meaning in History* (Toronto: University of Toronto Press), 2019.

Cultural Politics

Translocations, Cultural Geography and Anthropological Imperialism in *Raiders of the Lost Ark*

TATIANA PROROKOVA

Introduction

The territorial displacement of cultural objects that has been taking place for centuries is perhaps one of the most complex and problematic issues in cultural history and anthropology. The process of *relocating* or *translocating* cultural artifacts started very early in history and encompasses a vast geography. History knows numerous instances and debates around cultural appropriation, from the Elgin Marbles, which were translocated from Greece to England in the early 19th century, to the Balangiga bells, which the U.S. has recently returned to the Philippines. In one of the most notorious instances of such translocation, Hiram Bingham III, the Yale archaeologist who is often described as "the inspiration of Indiana Jones" (Sloan n. p.), became a household name largely as a result of the Peruvian artifacts he brought from Machu Picchu to New Haven in 1917, and which were eventually returned after a protracted legal battle in 2011. The first film in the Indiana Jones franchise, Steven Spielberg's *Raiders of the Lost Ark*, illustrates the problem of hunting for and relocating cultural artifacts, focusing on the adventures of archaeologist and professor Indiana Jones in Latin America, South Asia, and the Middle East. The plot mainly focuses on the time Dr. Jones spends in Egypt, where he travels in order to save the Ark of the Covenant from the Nazis who want to steal it and ultimately use the artifact for their own purposes. While Indiana Jones evidently portrays a good American in the film, contrasting with the criminal Germans, his invasion of Egypt does not differ substantially from that of the Nazis. Both the U.S. and Nazi Germany are portrayed as colonizers who assume they have the right to fight for one of the local treasures. This problematic colonial treatment of the country is primarily manifested through the desire to possess the artifact and be able to relocate it to the place which this or that party finds best, fully ignoring the legal rights of the local people to the Ark.

This essay investigates the intricate nature of the concept of translocation that is strongly defined by power. In the U.S., translocated objects have turned into a source of cultural and (trans)national knowledge, constructing some of the largest collections in some of the country's most famous museums. Translocation can be considered a tool for introducing a foreign narrative and new knowledge into a local culture. Yet this essay considers translocated objects as malfunctioning cultural artifacts and argues that the process of translocation is, in principle, a process of destruction. The essay also discusses the issue of an anthropological imperialism that justifies and legitimizes colonial dominance in the past in a way that clarifies its influence in the present. The issue of possession is another key concept that informs the notion of translocation. It evidently persists both in colonial and postcolonial times and is reflected in various cultural media, including the films that focus on archeological excavations and translocations. This essay examines *Raiders of the Lost Ark* to identify the visible linkages between translocations and possessions in American culture that continue to complicate the concepts of space/place, identity, and heritage today.

Anthropological Imperialism and the Culture of the Subaltern

The process of colonization was abusing and degrading in relation to the colonized in multiple ways. Transforming or entirely erasing the culture of the locals was part of that process. Cultural violence conducted by the colonizers manifested itself in part through theft. Destroying some cultural objects and forcefully taking others, colonizers not only demonstrated disrespect and neglect toward the religious and social traditions of the locals, but they essentially de-cultured the oppressed. Those objects that, for various reasons, were considered valuable became possessions of colonizers and were translocated to different parts of the globe. Even in postcolonial times, many such artifacts remain outside their countries of origin and inaccessible to the peoples whom they used to belong to.

The process of cultural theft is, significantly, not an act of borrowing. While many archeological objects might have been well cared for, taking them was a criminal act that is better described as stealing, and keeping them in the possession of those to whom the objects did not belong in the first place is, in principle, cultural theft. It is crucial to view these objects not only in terms of material profits but, indeed, as valuable products of a specific culture, people, and place. Their belonging to a specific people is thus not a nominal characteristic but rather a symbolic function that defines the essence of these artifacts. The process of taking away and translocating these objects destroys not only the culture of the locals but also the objects as such. Translocated from the place where they belong and re-appropriated into another context, the objects lose their meanings and functions and turn into devalued items.

Stealing and translocating objects is a way of manifesting imperialism. Understanding the intricate relationship between culture and imperialism, Edward W. Said finds it important "to connect these different realms, to show the involvements of culture with expanding empires, to make observations about art that preserve its unique endowments and at the same time map its affiliations" (5). Said continues: "Territory and possessions are at stake, geography and power" (5). Demonstrating their power through, among other techniques, cultural dominance, colonizers subjugate and suppress the colonized, depriving them of their cultural and ethnic/national identity. The process of oppression is essentially conducted through muting the colonized, thus, in the words of Gayatri Chakravorty Spivak, depriving the subaltern (the colonized) of their own voice. The process goes on as follows: "more powerful people—academics, religious leaders, or people who are otherwise privileged in society—always speak for them [the subaltern]. When they do this, the elite rob subalterns of their own voice. If subalterns could both speak and have a forum in which to be heard…, Spivak hopes these people would achieve an effective political voice" (Riach 11). As Spivak and others have explained, "'the subaltern cannot speak,' means that even when the subaltern makes an effort to the death to speak, she is not able to be heard, and speaking and hearing complete the speech act" (Spivak in Landry, MacLean, and Spivak 292). The process of taking and translocating artifacts is one of the tools colonizers have used to mute the subaltern and impose the only voice that is considered correct—that of the colonizer.

"[T]he influence of colonialism, its ideologies and power relations, on the ways in which objects are understood" (Barringer and Flynn 1) is crucial to consider when examining translocations. The objects like the Ark that appears in *Raiders of the Lost Ark* are not mere souvenirs from colonized lands; they are meaningful artifacts that define the culture of the locals and designate the complex imperial power structure that functions on economic, political, social, and cultural levels. Spielberg's film is a vivid illustration of the unequal relationship between the white man (I use this notion here as a collective term for the invaders from the U.S. and Nazi Germany) and the people of Egypt, who are essentially muted because they function as mere tools to find, hide, steal, or conduct any other manipulations with the Ark that Indiana Jones or the Nazis deem appropriate.

The white man's desire to possess the objects that do not belong to him is at the heart of the film's plot. This is manifested through the masculine dominance that characterizes Indiana Jones's and the Gestapo agent Arnold Toht's intrepid endeavors to get the Ark. While scholars tend to focus on the character of Indiana Jones to discuss the presence of a white male on a colonized territory, I suggest considering both Jones and Toht—a hero and a villain—who both essentially perform a similar function: namely, they portray a white colonizer. In this regard, Claudia Springer's framing of films like *Raiders of the Lost Ark* as "third-world investigation films" (168) is particularly helpful. By accentuating the setting, i.e., the Third World, the scholar shifts attention from the colonizer to the colonized in order to uncover the perversity of the mission that the white man carries out in a foreign territory. Indeed, "action-adventure films [like *Raiders of the Lost Ark*] contribute the convention of placing a Western, usually male, protagonist in the center of third-world settings. The mise-en-scène surrounds him with clichéd signifiers of the third world as mysterious, inscrutable, exotic, sensual, corrupt, and dangerous" (167–68). Juxtaposing the white man and the Arabs, such films attempt to recreate familiar clichés about the brave colonizer and the uncivilized locals—the trope of "us versus them"—only to reinforce the good nature of the white man. Springer contends: "When we understand that constructions of the ethnic Other are linked inextricably to constructions of self-identity, it becomes apparent that in third-world investigation films it is the journalist's ethnic identity at stake. From the moment he arrives in a new location, he is confused by strange, often dangerous, sights and sounds" (169). Indeed, the images of exotic nature, including gigantic spiders, venomous snakes, and sneaky monkeys, contribute to representing the locality as a dangerous, at times even deadly, place for the white man, thus othering it from what the white man would consider home. The mission that the white man has—either to steal the Ark (Toht) or to save it (Jones)—belittles, if not dehumanizes, the locals, portraying the Arabs as incapable of taking care of their own treasures, and, significantly, never being involved in the hunt as active agents. This facilitates the phenomenon of anthropological imperialism portrayed through Jones and Toht, for the two white men are the only people competing for the artifact that, crucially, belongs to none of them.

Importantly, the artifact itself, despite its assumed power, is portrayed as a colonized object, for allegedly a white man can handle it. Nigel Morris laments that "*Raiders of the Lost Ark* [does not] explore the Ark's religious significance beyond it being a force against darkness" (78), which is crucial to the construction of an image of the artifact as a transformed object once it is viewed as entering into the possession of a white man. The Ark turns into a malfunctioning artifact as soon as it becomes an object of pursuit for white men. And even when it is in the Nazis' possession, it does not seem to be powerful enough, for it spares the lives of Jones and his white female companion, who, compared to the Nazis, appear to behave better toward the Ark. The artifact's power is thus not only questioned in the film, but it is, in principle, belittled in such a way that the Ark become nothing more than an exotic object. It draws the interest of the white men who either see it as a source of power (significantly, the locals never use it for this purpose) or as a relic of civilization that should be extracted from the land of the locals, who, in turn, appear in the film as being unable to exist as a nation without the help of the white invaders (especially Indiana Jones). Cultural objectification of the Ark, therefore, not only distorts the meaning of the artifact itself, lessening its cultural and historical importance, it shrewdly illustrates the perverse politics of colonialism whose aim is to enslave not only a certain people but also the environment that this people exists (with)in, cultural products included.

Finally, the idea of white male dominance and the colonizer's aspiration for possessing something that initially does not belong to him is illustrated through the character of Marion—the daughter of Indiana Jones's mentor Abner Ravenwood from the University of Chicago. Marion, in a way, parallels the Ark, for she is constantly kidnapped by one party and freed by the other. The Nazis and Indiana Jones compete in possessing/taking away Marion from each other, just as they compete in finding the Ark. Ella Shohat explicitly calls Marion "the object of competing nationalist male desires" (35). Indeed, "she [Marion] is abducted by the Nazis and their Arab assistants much as the ark is hijacked by them, followed by Dr. Jones's rescue of Marion and the ark from the Nazis. The telos of the voyage into unknown regions—whether mental or geographical—then, is that the Westerner knows the Orient (in the epistemological and biblical senses) and at the same time brings it knowledge, rescuing it from its own obscurantism" (35).

Raiders of the Lost Ark thus addresses the problem of anthropological imperialism via objectification on several levels. First, the film objectifies the locals, displaying them as weak, mute, and essentially incapable of doing anything to protect themselves. Second, it objectifies the culture and cultural artifacts that belong to the locals, portraying them as meaningless treasures that can become powerful only in hands of white people. Finally, it reinforces the gender of the colonizer through subjugation of the white female character, suggesting that the true colonizer who can save the locals is a white *man*. Springer argues: "On one level the films [like *Raiders of the Lost Ark*] are about problems of cross-cultural interpretation, dramatized by the reporter's struggle to understand events taking place in a foreign culture; but more important, they are concerned with constructing white Western male subjectivity" (168). The identity of the white colonizer and his own view on the colonized people and territory are, therefore, the crux of *Raiders of the Lost Ark*'s plot.

Translocations and Possessions: Colonialism in Raiders of the Lost Ark

Set in the 1930s and distinguishing two types of geographies, namely the U.S. and Germany (as a white world), and Peru, Nepal, and Egypt (as a non-white world), *Raiders of the Lost Ark* is essentially a film about colonialism. Scholars pinpoint its resemblance to such traditionally colonial stories as H. Rider Haggard's *King Solomon's Miles* (1886) and *She* (1887)—in case of the latter "[the] beautiful but deadly Arab goddess [She] who presents an obstacle to a white adventurer [is] sometimes considered a prototype of Indiana Jones of the *Raiders of the Lost Ark* films" (*A Study Guide* n.p.). Elspeth Kydd elaborates, arguing that Indiana Jones's "origins are in comic books, earlier serial films and colonial adventure novels (such as H. Rider Haggard's *King Solomon's Mines*). These stories feature similar characteristics and use the same colonial backdrops, with 'exotic' locations and stereotypical 'native' characters. *Raiders of the Lost Ark* becomes part of the process of mythification of these colonial images" (249). The film's colonial nature is, indeed, explicit.

Raiders of the Lost Ark is described as "a popular adventure story that takes the audience on an exotic and wild journey through many different countries in search of archaeological treasures. It is a useful film to study when examining mainstream Hollywood's perception of Third World cultures" (Kydd 249). The film, to be sure, is a useful guide to understanding the portrayals of colonized people and lands, but it also provides a powerful dramatization of how the colonized's cultural possessions change their function and meaning once taken away by colonizers. The film thus directly addresses the nature of colonialism as such. "Set in the mid-1930s when most of the world was still under colonial rule, the film regards the imperial presence in Egypt [...] as completely natural, eliding a history of Arab nationalist revolts against foreign domination" (Shohat 33–35). The film's aim is, hence, not to reveal the true nature regarding the Third World in general and Egypt in particular, but rather, it painfully distorts the image of the colonized, representing them as powerless against the evil white man (Toht) and, thus, being vitally dependent on the good white man (Jones).

Indiana Jones's image is highly problematic in the film. While he seems to embody a hero who comes to the land that is invaded by the Nazis shortly before World War II, risks his life to save the artifact, and also saves the girl—Marion—multiple times, his character is, in principle, a white male colonizer. Morris singles out the elements that help the audience recognize Jones as a hero and a man who does the right thing:

> Jones is, foremost, American. His hat, leather jacket, open-necked shirt, canvas trousers, stubble, holstered six-gun and lasso-like whip, together with the desert setting of much of *Raiders of the Lost Ark* and the chase in which he gallops a white stallion to cut his enemies off at the pass: these recall westerns. There are echoes, too, of jungle explorers—explicit in the opening—such as his archaeologist alter-ego: this connotes class, expertise, "disinterested" pursuit of truth and officially-sanctioned authority, tempering his maverick tendencies and imbuing him with unquestioned right to control. Such qualities relate him to a British tradition, adopted by Hollywood in the 1920s and 1930s: adventure yarns from boys' magazines and Victorian and Edwardian popular novels [74].

The scholar also accentuates the fact that it is through Jones's heroic nature that we perceive the others, including the Arabs, as subjugated: "His [Indiana Jones'] heroism, seemingly innate, despite his apparent autonomy (the credits list him as 'Indy') necessitates defining others as inferior" (74). Moreover, his image as a colonizer is largely intensified through his name: "This dual tradition, manifest in his name (a State named after wars against Native Americans hitched to a quintessentially British patronymic), mythologises colonial conquest by white English speakers" (74). One can conclude, therefore, that the representation of Indiana Jones as a "good" colonizer helps portray the U.S. as the country that has the right to invade another territory to save the colonized. In other words, "*Raiders of the Lost Ark* assumes America's divinely-appointed role as protector of the Ark" (74).

Shohat's analysis of *Raiders* highlights the historical context of World War II: "Often portrayed as a cowboy, the American hero transmutes into an archaeologist in an implicit search for the Eastern roots of Western civilization. Indiana Jones liberates the ancient Hebrew ark from illegal Egyptian possession,[1] while also rescuing it from immoral Nazi control, subliminally reinforcing American and Jewish solidarity vis-à-vis the Nazis and their Arab assistants" (35). And while the references to World War II, U.S. participation in the war, and U.S. liberation of some of the imprisoned Jews during the Holocaust are legitimate in the context of a film that was released after the war but whose plot is set shortly before it, I would argue that the film's chief focus is on the confrontation between the white male colonizer and the colonized, as well as on the overt domination of the former over the latter and the white man's exploitation of the latter. Thus, I do not reduce the film to the exploration of the Holocaust and Jewish persecution but rather see it as a text that, first and foremost, tackles colonialism.

Raiders of the Lost Ark's focus on translocations and possessions is overt from the film's very beginning through its end. Framing the plot in such a way that the United States (personified by Indiana Jones) appears to be the invader in the opening scene and the triumphant winner in the end, the film reimagines Indiana Jones's adventures as colonialism. Thus in the opening sequence of the film, the viewer witnesses Indy's brazen theft of the golden idol from the Hovitos in Peru. The issue of colonialism, projected through the character of Indiana Jones, becomes apparent. The local man who accompanies Indy is ultimately portrayed as cunning and cowardly; in the end he even attempts to betray Indy—an action for which he pays with his own life, having got into one of the traps set in the cave. Through this character, the film seems to justify the actions of Indy who, according to the criminal colonial thinking, being a white man, seems to have the right, or perhaps even an obligation, to rescue the artifact. Importantly, as Indiana Jones leaves the cave with the artifact, he is surrounded by the locals who are very invested in the cultural significance of the object Indy steals. This reinforces the unequal power relations between the colonizer and the colonized, as well as the illegitimate nature of Indy's actions. Curiously enough, the film's final scene comments on the might of the colonizer through an art object, too. The scene takes place in the heart of the U.S., Washington, D.C. The image of the Washington Monument on the National Mall swiftly transfers the viewer to a new geographic location. Significantly, unlike the Ark that is entombed by the U.S. military, the Egyptian-style monument is proudly displayed to the viewers from all over the world, advertising the power and political dominance of the United States.

Part of the film's explorations of colonialism concern cultural transformations that take place both in relation to the colonizer and the colonized. This emphasis on cultural transformation is connoted through the artifact, the Ark. The Ark is the object that determines the dominant nature of the white man—whether of the Nazis who want to use the Ark's magic to make their soldiers invincible or of Indiana Jones who wants both to prevent Nazis from carrying out their scheme *and* to bring the Ark to a museum. While the Ark itself suffers from the intentions of the white colonizers and its translocation is inevitable, it also stands for the colonized in general, being used, abused, practically destroyed, desecrated, etc. Indiana Jones's stance on the artifact is rather ambiguous, too. Before travelling to Egypt, he tells one of his colleagues (who seems to try to scare Jones, mentioning the alleged power of the Ark): "I don't believe in magic, a lot of superstitious hocus-pocus. I'm going after a find of incredible historical significance. You're talking about the bogeyman." While valuing the artifact as a historical treasure, Indiana Jones also refuses to acknowledge its cultural significance to the locals. The archaeologist, therefore, views the object as decent enough to be added to the collections of white people's museums, but, crucially, absolutely devalued as part of someone else's culture. Shohat ponders the meaning of archaeological excavations, the process of translocating various objects, and their role in colonial discourses:

> The origins of archaeology, the search for the "roots of civilization" as a discipline, we know, are inextricably linked to imperial expansionism. In the cinema, the *Indiana Jones* series recycles exactly this colonial vision in which Western "knowledge" of ancient civilizations "rescues" the past from oblivion. It is this masculinist rescue in *Raiders of the Lost Ark* that legitimizes denuding the Egyptians of their heritage and confining it within Western metropolitan museums.... *Raiders of the Lost Ark*, symptomatically, assumes a disjuncture between contemporary and ancient Egypt, since the space between the present and the past can "only" be bridged by the scientist. The full significance of the ancient archaeological objects within the Eurocentric vision of the Spielberg film is presumed to be understood only by the Western scientist, relegating the Egyptian people to the role of ignorant Arabs who happen to be sitting on a land full of historical treasures—much as they happen to "sit" on oil [33].

Shohat shrewdly connects historical excavations that were taking place throughout the colonial times to the continuous postcolonial interest of certain Western countries in the natural resources of the Middle East. In doing so, the scholar outlines a long tradition of hegemonic robbery that has been taking place since the colonial times up until today.

Analyzing the visual aesthetics of archeological excavations that the film recreates is helpful to elucidating the colonial message of *Raiders of the Lost Ark*. One of the scenes included in the film focuses on Indiana Jones dressed in an outfit to pass as a local. He succeeds in doing so, and, walking through the place where the excavations are intensively taking place, the archaeologist identifies the spot where the artifact might be located. Holding a spade, he whistles, and a group of locals come to him; they all start digging. The scene is set during the day and the appearance of the diggers, including the disguised Indiana Jones, seems to legitimize their actions. However, as the scene goes on, the audience observes the group of locals digging feverishly at sunset. The setting changes dramatically. Indiana Jones is now able to shed his local outfit and is shown wearing his American clothes; the camera lingers on him, slowly but steadily putting on his cowboy hat. The locals, in turn, are represented as the archaeologist's tool with the help of which he is able to get the artifact while, pivotally, not working himself any longer. The audience hears the locals singing along while they are working; wind is loudly blowing and the sky that fills most of the image is red as blood—a metaphor for the colonizers' deadly influence on the colonized. As the night comes, the sky changes its color to blue-black and a storm begins, signifying the excavation's "success"—the locals tell Indiana Jones that they have found something. The scene is powerful, for it explicitly speaks about the true nature of colonialism,

Through the body silhouettes, the audience unmistakably identifies the colonizer—Indiana Jones (Harrison Ford)—and the colonized in *Raiders of the Lost Ark* (1981).

which is essentially based on exploitation, abuse, and deprivation. This is probably the only time in the film when Indiana Jones appears not as a heroic cowboy from the West but rather as a white colonizer. In his American clothes, he is no longer one of the locals; the power relations are strictly defined: Indiana Jones observes and ultimately reaps the profits, while the locals toil. The film's skillful use of nature imagery helps the viewer realize the true nature of the white man's actions in foreign territory.

The artifacts insistently displayed in the film as objects of possession and translocation change their meaning upon being transformed from objects that belong to the colonized to objects that belong to the colonizers. This is vividly illustrated in one of the film's final scenes when the Nazis decide to use the Ark. As they open it, ghosts fly out of the artifact and burn alive everyone witnessing the ceremony. The only survivors are Indiana Jones and Marion, who close their eyes and thus do not see what is happening. Tom Brass interprets this scene as follows:

> [T]he supernatural—in the form of ghosts emanating from the recently discovered Ark of the Covenant—is mobilized in defence of nationalism, this time that of the United States. The hero Indiana Jones, the embodiment of American individualism, is impervious to the malign ancient power unleashed by the Ark. Moreover, the film ends with the inference that science—the Manhattan Project that resulted in the nuclear bomb—is itself nothing more than the activation of an ancient force (= the Ark of the Covenant). As such, supernatural power will henceforth be harnessed discursively to the colonial ambitions of the United States, just as previously it was deployed on behalf of either British colonialism (Kipling), the English ruling classes (M. R. James), or the whole British nation resisting colonization (Kneale) [185].

In the scene, evil seems to be triumphantly destroyed. Indeed, the murder of the Nazis is an expected ending in such an adventurous film about American heroism. However, that the Ark is helpless against the white invaders—and, essentially, colonialism—becomes clear when Jones and Marion miraculously survive. With the help of this scene, the viewer finally realizes that *Raiders of the Lost Ark* is not about the Nazis; nor does it attempt to foreshadow World War II. The film is much more complicated in its analysis of such issues as invasion and colonization. Here, the Nazis are used only to intensify the heroism of Indiana Jones: indeed, being aware of the atrocities committed by the Nazis during World War II, the modern viewer can be easily trapped and made to think that the division into good and evil characters is that simple. Yet the film should not be limited to the explorations of Nazism; its larger aim is to discuss the role of the white man in the world. Thus colonization and its consequences are the key issues explored in *Raiders of the Lost Ark*. One can speculate that having spared the life of Indiana Jones, the Ark has taken the side of the "good" colonizer, accepting him as a new owner. Jones's survival complicates the attempt to decolonize the locals through the powerful artifact (which is partially completed, for the Nazis are dead) because it foregrounds the necessity to *translocate* objects that belong to the locals who are incapable of taking good care of these precious things. Possession and translocation are showcased not only as the prerogatives of the white man; they are necessary and inevitable tasks to be performed. The intricate relationship between the local artifact and the white man is thus what makes *Raiders of the Lost Ark* a disturbing colonial text.

Conclusion

Touching upon the problem of archeological excavations and the processes that emerge afterwards, including possession and translocation, *Raiders of the Lost Ark* raises profound questions related to colonialism. While the relationship between the colonizer and the colonized is determined through numerous spheres, including politics, economics, and culture, it can also be vividly studied through archaeological objects that perform the role of mediators between the two agents. Taking the cultural artifacts of the locals into their possession, the colonizers not only deprive the colonized of their culture, essentially destroying it, but they also transform the meaning and the role of the artifacts. Translocation facilitates transcultural exchange, but it also reinforces anthropological imperialism, particularly so in the context of colonialism. The hunt for the Ark displayed in *Raiders of the Lost Ark* is illustrative of the white man's exploration and colonization of the Third World. And while the film attempts to rehabilitate the white American character through the inclusion of German Nazis, overtly foregrounding Indiana Jones's good intentions, compared to those of evil Nazis (which, indeed, helps win the hearts and minds of the audiences), Indiana Jones is, in principle, an embodiment of a white male colonizer who knows better how to take care of the business related to the Third World than the region's own native populations. Jones's intention to "save" the artifact by bringing it to a Western museum rather than helping the locals to preserve it on the territory where it historically belongs disregards the cultural traditions of the locals. Translocation, and the ultimate refusal of repossession, blurs the boundaries of cultural geography, reinforcing the power of the white colonizer, as represented in *Raiders of the Lost Ark*, and continues the long and unjust tradition of the subjugating and muting of the colonized. The film does not see a possibility for the Third World to gain certain political, economic, and cultural powers, and be heard; instead, through the precious historical artifacts, it skillfully erases the framework of colonization as a criminal act and sustains the motif of "the White Man's burden" (Kipling n. p.), suggesting that the act of cultural robbery is performed not for the sake of the white man but for that of the locals and their own culture. In doing so, *Raiders of the Lost Ark* turns into a dangerous Western narrative that attempts to illuminate the advantages of colonialism, instead of showcasing this criminal policy in an authentic and objective way.

NOTE

1. The Ark is an ancient Hebrew artifact that dates back to Moses and the creation of the Ten Commandments. The fact that the Ark was forcefully taken from the Hebrews by the Egyptians in ancient times significantly complicates the issues of possession and translocation as well as the meaning of the Ark itself in *Raiders of the Lost Ark*. Focusing primarily on the relationship between white colonizers and the colonized from the Third World, however, in the context of this essay, I consider the Ark an Egyptian artifact, for during European colonialism, as well as long before that, it was, ostensibly, located in Egypt.

WORKS CITED

Barringer, Tim, and Tom Flynn. Introduction. *Colonialism and the Object: Empire, Material Culture and the Museum*, edited by Tim Barringer and Tom Flynn. Routledge, 1998, pp. 1–8.
Brass, Tom. *Class, Culture and the Agrarian Myth*. Brill, 2014.
Kipling, Rudyard. "The White Man's Burden: The United States and the Philippine Islands." 1899. ux1.eiu.edu/nekey/syllabi/british/kipling1899.pdf. Accessed 7 Dec. 2018.
Kydd, Elspeth. *The Critical Practice of Film: An Introduction*. Palgrave Macmillan, 2011.
Landry, Donna, Gerald MacLean, and Gayatri Chakravorty Spivak. "Subaltern Talk: Interview with the Editors." *The Spivak Reader: Selected Works of Gayatri Chakravorty Spivak*, edited by Donna Landry and Gerald MacLean. Routledge, 1996, pp. 287–308.
Morris, Nigel. *The Cinema of Steven Spielberg: Empire of Light*. Wallflower Press, 2007.
Raiders of the Lost Ark. Directed by Steven Spielberg, performances by Harrison Ford, Karen Allen, Paul Freeman, Ronald Lacey, and John Rhys-Davies, Paramount Pictures, 1981.
Riach, Graham K. *An Analysis of Gayatri Chakravorty Spivak's* Can the Subaltern Speak? Routledge, 2017.

Said, Edward W. *Culture and Imperialism*. Vintage Books, 1994.
Shohat, Ella. *Taboo Memories, Diasporic Voices*. Duke University Press, 2006.
Sloan, Gene. *USA Today*. 23 Sept. 2005. n.p. https://usatoday30.usatoday.com/travel/destinations/2005-09-22-peru_x.htm. Accessed 9 Jan. 2019.
Springer, Claudia. "Comprehension and Crisis: Reporter Films and the Third World." *Unspeakable Images: Ethnicity and the American Cinema*, edited by Lester D. Friedman. University of Illinois Press, 1991, pp. 167–89.
A Study Guide for "Colonialism." Gale, 2016.

"I said no camels!"
Indiana Jones and the Catalogue of Orientalism
MAT HARDY

Of the original trio of Indiana Jones films, two are set largely in the Middle East and center on quests for legendary Judeo-Christian artifacts. In utilizing this central foundation, both *Raiders of the Lost Ark* and *Indiana Jones and the Last Crusade* fall squarely into an established tradition of Hollywood portrayals of the Middle East where no matter how innovative the action and dialogue might be, the prevailing depictions are invariably orthodox. Just as the plot MacGuffins of the Ark and Grail are steeped in ancient beliefs and customary legend, so too is the manner in which the films use the Middle East and its peoples merely as an exotic and clichéd backdrop for Western characters to strut across and demolish. This attitude is an inheritance of generations of European representations of the East, not just in film, but in all forms of media.

This tradition has some of its basis in the Arabian fantasy genre that was established by nineteenth-century writers such as Sir Richard Burton. The release of his translation of *The Book of the Thousand Nights and a Night* (Burton) at a time when mass-literacy and printing technologies were extending the reach of fiction made an indelible contribution to Western conceptions of the East. Characters such as Ali Baba, Aladdin, and Sinbad, as well as tropes like flying carpets, cruel caliphs, genies in lamps, and the perils of three wishes are standard fare in fictional representations of the East. The 2019 release of a live-action version of Disney's *Aladdin* bears testament to the enduring impact of Burton's legacy.

The nineteenth century also saw the height of the Orientalist art movement, where European painters provided exotic visual representations of the

Middle East. The "truths" established in these images provided further basis for European imaging of the East. Depictions of naked slave girls, eunuchs, bath houses, arid landscapes, and chaotic marketplaces were stock fare. These places, and those who lived in them, were represented as different from the civilized orderliness of Europe. There are overtones of cruelty, depravity, and mystery. The purported realism of these paintings made them the photographs of their age and a contributor to mass cultural imagining of the Orient (Nochlin 57).

That very term "Orient" is intrinsic to this perspective. The "othering" of the East as a defined zone inherently different from the West is itself an artificial construction born of centuries of religious rivalry, cultural relativism, and colonial condescension. In *Orientalism* (1978), Edward Said stated that the attitudes that the West espoused were based upon that history of assumed supremacy. With this contempt for the inhabitants and cultures of the East, Westerners stamped them with a limited series of stereotypes and assumptions that became so engrained over the centuries that they were eventually understood as truths. With each subsequent generation of explorers, artists, scholars, authors, leaders, and so on accepting and building upon these mischaracterizations, a self-perpetuating cultural othering was cemented: "the Orient is an idea that has a history and a tradition of thought, imagery and vocabulary that have given it a reality and presence in and for the West" (Said 5). Upon its advent, cinema became part of this Orientalist trend.

The treatment of the Middle East and the Arabs in particular is invariably negative in Western film. In the same way that those repeated tales and images of the nineteenth century formed the platform for the public's understanding of the East, decades of cinematic depiction has further cemented these attitudes. "For more than a century Hollywood, too, has used repetition as a teaching tool, tutoring movie audiences by repeating over and over, in film after film, insidious images of Arab people" (Shaheen 23).

The Indiana Jones franchise is an inheritor of these traditions and arguably perpetuates them in a more potent way because the films are themselves an homage to a past era. Both *Raiders* and *Last Crusade* deliberately borrow from the glory days of the motion picture industry and in particular serial production houses such as Republic.[1] By masquerading as films of the 1930s/40s, *Raiders* and *Last Crusade* can more blatantly adopt the formulaic representation of the Middle East and those who live there.

The visuals and screenplays of the two films illustrate this Hollywood ancestry. Scenes such as the pursuit through the streets of Cairo in *Raiders* reference even earlier formulae for Arabian adventures. *The Thief of Bagdad* (1924), a silent version of a tale from Burton's *Thousand Nights* cycle, was remade in 1940, and the story went on to inform the more familiar tale of Disney's *Aladdin*. The influence of this lineage cannot be underestimated.

Eisele notes that the 1924 version includes a chase through a market, which has become a staple element of films with an Arabian setting, "including a run through the obligatory jars (the first of its kind and alluded to many times after)" (Eisele 80). Indy's pursuit among the baskets of the Cairo marketplace in *Raiders* is derivative of this cliché.

Similarly, the use of maps to show Indy's journeys is not just a convenient short-cut for noting his progress but a direct link to earlier works set in foreign locations. They are a signal to the audience that the hero is no longer "in Kansas" and has entered another world. Showing maps of far-flung corners of the globe has long been a staple of Hollywood cinematic practice, as epitomized in one of the most well-regarded films of all time, *Casablanca* (1942). The Bogart-Bergman masterpiece is another example of the use of an exotic Arab background for a story that has nothing to do with the region itself. However, this alien setting is essential to the glamor of the film and it is a map that helps authenticate this location. "When Michael Curtiz chose a map of Morocco as an establishing shot ... he was unashamedly trading on the associative power such an image holds for a Western audience. The sense of lawlessness, corruption and vice that Curtiz was attempting to distil had been handed down from the Orientalist tradition so that a simple map, or the name of a city, sufficed to conjure a kaleidoscope of exotica" (Smith 75).

This associative power was well-understood by George Lucas. By setting the films in the past, he could convey a whole range of narratives without need for explanation. During a story conference that took place in early 1978, Lucas described what was going to happen to his future hero, Indiana Jones, as he traversed the city of Cairo: "every once in a while somebody throws a knife at him, or he beats somebody up, or somebody beats him up, typical middle-eastern [*sic*] stuff" (Lucas, Spielberg, and Kasdan 28). Indeed, so apparently "typical" was this action, that the exact setting was unimportant to Lucas: "Whatever, it's in Cairo, but it doesn't have to be. I only use that because it's one of those thirties cities. In the research it will probably be an Israeli city.[2] In the middle east [*sic*] somewhere we will be able to find a plausible city" (*ibid*. p. 55).

Such a genesis identifies *Raiders* and *Last Crusade* as a sub-genre of Hollywood film: The Eastern. These are films that are largely set in the Middle East but concern Western narratives. The location of the films is there to offer that Orientalist tradition of "a land of adventure, ancient knowledge, magic, and fantasy ... as well as land of ignorance and corruption, savagery and decadence, just waiting for the hand of Western civilization to 'recivilize' it" (Eisele 70). While the "Eastern" is not as well recognized as the "Western" in movie terminology, there is a strong case that both of the Indiana Jones films discussed in this essay sit within this pantheon.

Indiana Jones and the Eastern Sub-Genre

In describing a specific film genre he had dubbed the "Eastern," Eisele identified ten narrative attributes typically found in those movies set in a Middle Eastern locale. These are (1) transgression, (2) separation, (3) abduction, (4) reduction, (5) induction, (6) seduction, (7) redemption, (8) revelation, (9) reaffirmation, and (10) mutilation (*ibid.* p. 73). Not all Easterns will display all of these attributes, though as explored below, *Raiders* and *Last Crusade* satisfy this full list.

To deal with the simplest attribute first, Eisele mentions mutilation through menaces like "ugly Arabs" wielding "oversized scimitars" (Eisele 76). This is of course vividly displayed in *Raiders* when Indiana is confronted by the black-clad swordsman. However, mutilation also manifests in the stereotypical threat of amputation in the Western imagining of Islamic punishments. This latter is not in evidence in the Indiana Jones films, since there are no real instances of Middle Easterners being sufficiently empowered to inflict such judicial outcomes on the hero. The dangers of mutilation in the films are instead rather more conventional, including the abovementioned scimitars, but also the formulaic fight scenes in the proximity of lethal machinery and the decapitation booby trap in the Grail cavern. It could also be argued that the attempted poisoning from the monkey-owning Arab represents a chemical form of mutilation and a typically cowardly oriental form of assault. The use of poison is historically seen as a "woman's weapon" by Westerners, so this tactic subtly questions the masculinity of the underhanded Arab.

In Eisele's canon, transgression and separation usually involve the hero being accused of something (often without good cause) and then being forced to leave his idyllic home. In the case of *Raiders*, this transgression comes in the form of Indiana's broken relationships with Marion Ravenwood and her father. In *Last Crusade* his estrangement from his father is part of the plot's set-up. Eisele notes that separation is often depicted by contrasting "lush, green estates" with arid North African landscapes (Eisele 74). In the case of the Indiana Jones films, the academic arcadia of New England stands in place of European family seats. Abduction and reduction are even more obvious in the Indiana Jones franchise, with Marion, Henry Jones, Sr., and then Marcus Brody being kidnapped, as well as sundry imprisonments and escapes involving the hero. The abduction of women is a particularly persistent trope in the Eastern and carries overtones of "white slavery" (*ibid.*). The idea of Western women being kidnapped by lascivious Middle Easterners has been a staple plot in all sorts of fiction for decades, from romance, through action, and on to pornography (Hardy 104–5). This trope was even considered in the Lucas-Spielberg story conference about what role Marion might play as a plot point:

LUCAS: How about if we have her kidnapped?
SPIELBERG: Who would kidnap her, and for what reason?
LUCAS: The Arabs. Maybe they're going to rape her. White slavery.
SPIELBERG: I would rather have a plot kidnapping than just a carnal kidnapping [Lucas, Spielberg, and Kasdan 65].

Induction usually involves "a European or American character putting on Arab clothes (a kiffiya or head scarf, a jellaba/galabiyya or loose, robe-like garment, a veil, etc.)" (Eisele 74). Indiana's infiltration of the Tanis dig site dressed as an Arab laborer fits this criterion perfectly. (In an atypical genre example, Marion's donning of the evening gown and girlish "cheap drunk" act in order to catch Belloq off guard also symbolically shift her identity.)

Seduction is closely linked to the narrative attribute of redemption. In a literal sense, the seduction can be sexual. Those romantic encounters involving Marion or Elsa Schneider are the obvious cases, but the rekindling of the father-son bond between Jones Senior and Junior is another example. On a different level, the seductive power of knowledge and discovery is Indiana's greater weakness. He is repeatedly prepared to place himself in the way of danger to retrieve historical treasures steeped in the supernatural history of the east. In the climax of *Last Crusade*, his seduction by the Grail and its power nearly costs him his life, until he is "wooed" back to reality by his rejuvenated father and thus the redemption takes place. By contrast, Elsa is irredeemable and so dies.

The revelation attribute is also displayed in the two films, though not in the standard manner of an individual ultimately recognizing "the true character or identity of another character, enabling either rejection or acceptance to take place" (Eisele 75). Nevertheless, the discovery of Elsa's Nazi persona would fit this criterion. Eisele expands his revelation narrative, however, to include "unveiling the mysteries of the Orient" (Eisele 76). In this case, the entire films become a series of revelations as various clues are solved. Ultimately, the revelation of the power of the Ark or the Grail are capstone unveilings and testaments to the ultimate discovery that supernatural power is treacherous.

Reaffirmation includes an acceptance or reinforcing of the state of a character and/or his environment and often occurs in the dénouement of the Eastern (*ibid.*). This can occur in an overt manner (for example the refreshed romantic bond between Indiana and Marion), or a covert one. In the latter case, the affirmation might be of "prevailing cultural, social, and political values" (*ibid.*). This is easy to identify in the two films: Americans are good and clever; Nazis are bad and stupid. Each team gets what they deserve. In the context of the Middle Eastern environment though, there is another reaffirmation for the audience: Westerners are on the whole superior, and the peoples, the culture, and the landscapes of the East are largely irrelevant; there to be used and then discarded when they no longer have significance.

Indiana Jones and the Middle Eastern Window Dressing

There are innumerable ways in which *Raiders* and *Last Crusade* follow the pattern of using the East merely as an exotic locale for an intrinsically Western "goodies versus baddies" adventure. Firstly, the very use of Judeo-Christian religious artifacts as MacGuffins justifies the Middle East as a location for the intrigue while also underscoring the importance of the quests. These objects do not need to be significantly explained, because they are intrinsically linked to Western culture, if not familiar in their own right.[3] It is merely enough that they are *of God* for their potency to be ascertained. It is notable that while Jewish and Christian traditions are invoked, any reference to Islam is absent in either film.

The careless use of the Middle East as a generic historical-cultural space is exemplified by the factual and geographical muddling of the terms and places depicted. For example, Tanis is explained in *Raiders* as a city of antiquity lost in a year-long sandstorm and only recently uncovered by the Germans. Tanis *is* a real archaeological site, but its ruins were never lost and excavations had in reality been going on there for decades prior to the film's setting. Furthermore, the Well of Souls, said by Indiana to be in Tanis, is actually a cave under the Dome of the Rock on the Temple Mount in Jerusalem. This is approximately where the Temple of Solomon (or First Temple) was built and this is correctly identified in the film as the place where the Ark was stored, though this would not have occurred until hundreds of years after the timing given in the script.[4] Contrary to Indiana's narrative, this temple was definitely not looted in 980 BCE by an Egyptian pharaoh. Indeed, it had likely only just been built at that point. Instead it was destroyed by the Babylonians in 587 BCE and, as of that point, the fate of the Ark is undeniably a mystery to this day.

It is perhaps unfair to criticize action-adventure films for not having documentary-like accuracy. However, when they make free use of real names and locations, it is worth examining the way in which these elements add an imprimatur of authenticity for the audience. By salting the script with enough genuine terminology and spiritual-historical references, the Indiana Jones films are able to draw upon their audience's pre-existing knowledge and beliefs about the Middle East, and this makes it easier for them to accept the screenplay. Balfe describes how this "embedding" of received Orientalist touchstones allows the creators of even the most fantastic oriental tales to make audiences feel at ease with the incredible, simply because there is enough of the (perceived) real in what they are seeing. This "constructs an image positing a claim on the 'truth' of the Orient, precisely because it seems so 'real' and 'historical'" (Balfe 85). It was in this manner that the exquisite details rendered by Orientalist painters of past centuries acted as a form of documentary assurance of the authenticity of the overall scene or subject. Detail, however, does not equal reality.

A further example of this is the depiction of the Sultan of Hatay in *Last Crusade*.[5] Hatay did exist as a short-lived autonomous republic for a few months during 1938–1939. Despite the inclusion of this rather obscure historical detail, Orientalist fantasy starts to inject itself almost immediately. The notion that a republic would have a monarch in the form of a Sultan might seem bizarre to a student of politics. Nevertheless, a Sultan is *expected* by the audience. It is the default terminology for any imaginary Middle Eastern leader. Naturally, the Sultan (played by an Anglo-Lithuanian actor) is dressed in Ruritanian finery, has an opulent palace full of toadies, is greedy for Western industrial marvels such as a Rolls-Royce, and has surplus military equipment to lend out. These are all stereotypical ingredients for fleshing out an oriental autocrat and they are easily digested with little thought on the part of the audience. The obsessive detail the Sultan provides about the Rolls-Royce further serves to drape the imagined on isolated anchors of the real and to invest the screenplay with plausibility.

Finally, the Middle East is further genericized in the shooting locations of the films. In *Raiders* Tunisia stands in for Egypt. *Last Crusade* sees Jordan's Petra used as a stand-in for the mythical location of the Grail, which should roughly lie in modern day Turkey. The tank chase scene was filmed in Spain. As long as there is sand, markets and arid terrain, the audience needs little else to sustain their belief.

The Good Arab(s)

The generally negative depiction of Middle Easterners in the two films is an indication of their Orientalist perspective. Examples of positive Arab characters in either film are limited and really come down to the singularity of Indy's old friend, Sallah. Played by a Welshman, Sallah is the prototypical benign Arab buffoon. He is amiable, naïve, and bumbling, and alternates between bravery and cowardice as the story demands. He has a formidable but hospitable wife who is mother to their nine children. Like many "good" Arabs in Hollywood films, his benevolence is signified by his straddling of the two cultures. His English is very good, though accented. He is often dressed in a pastiche of the tropical dandy, with white linen jackets and absurd

Sallah (John Rhys-Davies) is the archetypal benign Arab buffoon with a penchant for camels and operetta, as seen in *Indiana Jones and the Last Crusade* (1989).

ties. This might be topped with a fez or turban, however, to make it clear that he is not wholly Westernized. His attachment to the music of Gilbert and Sullivan when in a good mood also parades him as a civilized Arab, and thus one to be trusted.

The use of a hybrid Western-Eastern appearance as a signal of trustworthiness for the audience is pervasive in the sorts of fiction that the Indiana Jones franchise is built upon. In another archeological action tale, Captain W.E. Johns' plucky pilot-adventurer, Biggles, also finds himself in Cairo and is importuned by a local historian hot on the trail of a lost Persian treasure. This Egyptian is a "good Arab" and that is obvious to the English chums from his exterior: "a native but obviously one of the better class, and his skin was not much darker than that of a sunburned white man.... His clothes were of good quality and might have been made in London; indeed but for his distinguishing *tarboosh*, he might have passed for a European" (Johns 28).[6] By contrast, the antagonist, also an Egyptian antiquarian, is sensed to be disreputable despite his equally impressive tailoring: "a middle aged man of undoubted eastern extraction, notwithstanding the fact that he was dressed in expensive European clothes.... His skin was dark, as were his eyes, which, like those of many orientals, appeared to be heavy and curiously expressionless.... He was, in fact, of a type common in the Middle East, where east and west are all too often blended with unfortunate results" (*ibid.* 51–52).

Heir to this legacy and part plot enabler and part comic relief, the rotund Sallah is burdened with many of the standard tropes regarding Arabs. Besides his own gaggle of offspring, we are presented with the cliché of extended familial relationships, partially based upon transactional favors. In *Last*

Crusade, Sallah provides a car that belongs to his brother-in-law. This is later destroyed by the tank that the suddenly childlike Sallah later refers to as a "metal beast," despite his own familiarity with motor vehicles. In need of alternative transport, he and Indy decide to go after the animals that other members of the expedition are riding. There ensues a brief argument about the targets:

> INDY: I'm going after those horses.
> SALLAH: I'll take the camels.
> INDY: I don't need camels.
> SALLAH: But, Indy—
> INDY: No camels!

Nevertheless, after some interstitial action scenes, the pair are reunited, with Sallah, contrary to orders, appearing with a team of camels.

> INDY: Sallah, I said no camels! That's five camels. Can't you count?
> SALLAH: Compensation for my brother-in-law's car.

Here Sallah is not just bearing the racial humiliation of being the dumb Arab who can't comprehend simple instructions, but also the ethnic stereotype that camels are a standard form of exchange and an irresistible temptation for any Egyptian.

The Bad and the Ugly

Aside from those Arabs that appear as decoration in the background (such as in the street scenes and Tanis dig), the majority of Easterners who take part in the action are mere obstacles and cannon fodder. They exist as opponents to the heroes, Nazi dupes and one-punch henchmen summarily disposed of in fight and chase scenes. Referring to them as "bad" is not academic exaggeration either. This is exactly how they are described in the *Raiders* screenplay and continuity notes. For example, "Sc. No. 68. Monkey leads German & 2 bad Arabs to Marion's hiding place" (Lost Ark Productions [UK] Ltd). There are also "fearsome" Arabs (Kasdan and Lucas 47) and those that are just plain despicable: "The large square is ringed by the mangy, wretched offal of Cairo society, those Misfits the ordinary people want always to avoid. They huddle against every inch of wall space in their filthy robes" (Kasdan and Lucas 45). Perhaps the only Eastern extra given any semblance of humanity is the soldier of Hatay forced into the booby-trapped tunnel leading to the Grail. That the emotion displayed is sweating fear nevertheless places him in the category of the un-manly oriental.

There are only a handful of individually identified Easterners who appear in more than one scene in the two films. One is "Monkey Man," the grimy, eye-patch-wearing German accomplice and owner of the little primate that spies upon Indy in *Raiders*. It is to be noted that the Ottoman style waistcoat that the monkey wears was a deliberate attempt to make the creature look more Arab, and thus malign (Lucas, Spielberg, and Kasdan 70). In *Last Crusade*, the character of Kazim, a Turk, acts as a neutral obstacle to all who seek the Grail. Linking him to some centuries-old oriental secret society serves to increase the mystique around the treasure and lets the audience know that this object is so real there are those who walk among us charged with its protection. Ultimately, his suicidal ambush of the German column is another cannon fodder performance, demonstrating the inferiority and recklessness of Eastern martial effort against the superior technology and discipline of the Europeans.

This latter point is also exhibited in another of the most iconic scenes from *Raiders*: Indy's confrontation with the swordsman in a Cairo market. The Arab's skill with the scimitar and fearsome appearance are representative of the old, primitive world. He might have once been dangerous, but no longer. He is efficiently gunned down from a distance by the quicker-thinking and better-armed Western hero.[7] This sequence is often noted by people as a favorite scene in the film and was greeted with roars of mirth from audiences

Indiana Jones (Harrison Ford) confronts raw Orientalism in the marketplace in *Raiders of the Lost Ark* (1981).

(Shaheen 546). Tomasulo points out though that "if an Arab had calmly shot Jones while Jones was elaborately brandishing his whip, for instance, the race reversal would mitigate against American laughter" (Tomasulo 335).

Conclusion

Both *Raiders* and *Last Crusade* are films that invoke mystical traditions in their narrative. Overtly, these traditions are concerned with their plot goals: religious relics of Biblical significance. Beyond the obvious though, the films are also ritualized artifacts of their own Orientalist past, both in the form of centuries of Western imagining of the East and stereotypical Hollywood conventions. In expounding on the legend of the Ark to the military intelligence agents, Indiana draws upon an illustration from an enormous antique book.[8] In this scene, Jones has entered the auditorium carrying this heavy tome, apparently coincidentally, and it is quickly opened to the exact page needed. The volume's assumed veracity is signified by its very size and age, and Indy's explanation of the Ark goes unquestioned. It is possible to see this book as unintentionally allegorical for the Orientalist framework Westerners bring to the imagining of the Middle East. That is, without much effort, we are swiftly able draw upon the received wisdom of previous generations that we all carry in order to construct an acceptable interpretation of virtually anything having to do with the East. Blockbuster adventure films are simply another form of this decrepit book.

NOTES

1. The character and appearance of Indiana Jones was based upon various matinee heroes and the leather jacket and fedora costume derived from Charlton Heston's character of Harry Steele in the 1954 adventure *Secret of the Incas* (French and Verschuere).
2. The casual anachronism here is indicative of the muddled approach to the Middle East: Israel did not exist in the 1930s.
3. It could be argued that the lesser popularity of *Temple of Doom* among the original trio of films may be because the setting (and the MacGuffin) were harder for a Western audience to identify with.
4. The existence of the Ark is not proven beyond some sparse scriptural references. In this tradition, it contained not only the tablets of the Ten Commandments, but also a golden jar of manna and the rod of Aaron.
5. That he is a Sultan is indicated in the screenplay, though he is addressed by Donovan merely as "Your Highness."
6. "Tarboosh" is an Arabic term for the fez.
7. In a case of art imitating life, the decision to shoot the swordsman was an expedient shortcut to a logistical problem encountered during filming. The original scene was supposed to have been a lengthy whip versus sword affair that would have taken up to three days of shooting and it was the last sequence to be shot on location in Tunisia before the production packed up and returned to the UK. Harrison Ford was suffering from dysentery at the time and was unable to remain on set for periods of greater than 10 minutes. Ford later recounted the solution: "I was puzzling how to get out of this three days of shooting, so when I got to

set I proposed to Steven that we just shoot the son of bitch and Steve said 'I was thinking that as well.' So he drew his sword, the poor guy was a wonderful British stuntman who had practiced his sword skills for months in order to do this job, and was quite surprised by the idea that we would dispatch him in 5 minutes. But he flourished his sword, I pulled out my gun and shot him, and then we went back to England" (Kovach).

8. In *The Last Crusade*, the diary of Jones Sr. fulfills a similar role.

WORKS CITED

Balfe, Myles. "Incredible Geographies? Orientalism and Genre Fantasy." *Social & Cultural Geography* 5.1 (2004): 75–90. Print.

Burton, R. *The Book of the Thousand Nights and a Night*. A Plain and Literal Translation of the Arabian Nights' Entertainments, Now Entituled [sic] the Book of the Thousand Nights and a Night; with Introduction Explanatory Notes on the Manners and Customs of Moslem Men and a Terminal Essay Upon the History of the Nights by Richard F. Burton. Kamashastra Society, 1885. Print.

Eisele, John C. "The Wild East: Deconstructing the Language of Genre in the Hollywood Eastern." *Cinema Journal* 41.4 (2002): 68–94. Print.

French, Mike, and Gilles Verschuere. "Deborah Nadoolman Interview." TheRaider.net. 14 September 2005. Web. 29 May 2019.

Hardy, Mat. "The Eastern Question." *Game of Thrones Versus History: Written in Blood*. Ed. B. Pavlac. Hoboken: Wiley Blackwell, 2017. 97–109. Print.

Johns, Captain W.E. *Biggles Flies South*. London: Oxford University Press, 1950. Print.

Kasdan, Lawrence, and George Lucas. *Raiders of the Lost Ark: Screenplay*.

Kovach, Steve. "Harrison Ford Explained the Story Behind the Best Scene in 'Indiana Jones.'" *Business Insider Australia* (2014). Web. 29 May 2019.

Lost Ark Productions (UK) Ltd. *"Raiders of the Lost Ark" Continuity Breakdown*. Borehamwood, Harts.

Lucas, George, Steven Spielberg, and Larry Kasdan. *"Raiders of the Lost Ark" Story Conference Transcript, January 23, 1978 Thru January 27, 1978*.

Nochlin, Linda. *The Politics of Vision: Essays on Nineteenth-Century Art and Society*. New York: Thames and Hudson, 1991. Print.

Said, Edward. *Orientalism*. New York: Vintage, 1978. Print.

Shaheen, J.G. *Reel Bad Arabs: How Hollywood Vilifies a People*. Gloucestershire: Arris, 2003. Print.

Smith, Lara Nancy. "'I'll Be Back': Orientalism and 90's Hollywood." *Metro Magazine* 109 (1997): 73–78. Print

Tomasulo, Frank P. "Mr. Jones Goes to Washington: Myth and Religion in *Raiders of the Lost Ark*." *Quarterly Review of Film Studies* 7.4 (1982): 331–40. Print.

The Temple of Orientalism
Debaditya Mukhopadhyay

Much of the pleasure derived from watching films of the Indiana Jones franchise reverts into guilty pleasure when one pays attention to the politics underlying the narratives. A politics of misrepresentation pervades the films in general. Throughout the travels of the eponymous hero of the films, Dr. Indiana Jones, the countries he visits, the people he meets, and the beautiful women who feature in his adventures all appear as stereotypical representations, and this stereotyping appears in its most shocking form in *Indiana Jones the Temple of Doom*. The extremely distorted portrayal of Indian culture in the film is both repulsive and intriguing. While the first film of the series does exoticize Egypt and stereotype the Nazis, it does not offer an abundance of viscerally shocking moments when depicting the geographical space or culture of Egypt. Even while presenting the villainous Nazis, the film did not deviate from history to an absurd extent. When *Indiana Jones and the Raiders of the Lost Ark*, set in 1936, shows the great archaeologist fighting a group of Nazis desperate to acquire powerful occult objects, it does not exaggerate significantly. Heinrich Himmler led a Nazi troop to the exotic land of Tibet in 1939, and, as discussed by Alex McKay, "Nazi leaders such as Heinrich Himmler believed that Tibet might harbor the last of the original Aryan tribes, the legendary forefathers of the German race, whose leaders possessed supernatural powers that the Nazis could use to conquer the world." While the second film reprised the charisma of Dr. Jones with utmost fidelity, it unapologetically fiddled with Indian history and culture. This essay will explore the manifestation of the politics of misrepresentation in this film and trace the manner in which the films reflect the influence of the contemporary sociocultural milieu of America in the 1980s.

Unlike the other three films of the series, *Temple of Doom* opens with a song and dance sequence. The spectacular sequence, taking place in a lavish night club in Shanghai, introduces the female lead of the film, Willie Scott.

Among all the female leads featured in the series, Willie is the most cartoonish and hypersexualized. Both Marion Ravenwood and Elsa Schneider are stronger and more intelligent. Elsa does seduce both Indiana and his father, but she is an Olympic gold medalist as well as an archaeologist with a doctorate. Marion does not have any academic credentials, but both in the first and the fourth films, she is shown as an aggressive tomboy. In *Raiders of the Lost Ark*, for instance, she makes her entry as an intractable owner of a bar in Nepal who can win drinking contests at ease and greet her ex-lover Indiana Jones with a punch. In contrast to both, Willie is just a lush singer and a spoiled brat. Throughout the film, she remains a helpless damsel in distress. In place of the self-reliance of Marion and Elsa, Willie is perpetually helpless and vulnerable. It is constantly hinted that she needs to be supervised and controlled in order to be protected. Before going to enter the ominous temple for the Sankara stones, Indiana instructs the ten-year-old Short Round to "keep an eye on her," which shows how important it is to "govern" her every moment. It is certainly not without significance that the female lead appears to be the weakest in *Temple of Doom*. She is associated with the East right from the beginning, with her Oriental-style dress and her Mandarin rendition of "Anything Goes," and, just like the East, she requires the protection of a superior binary opposite, a Western male.

Every Indiana Jones film opens with the hero facing off against a group of adversaries for some invaluable relic. In *Temple of Doom*, Indiana is shown in a significantly different situation. He meets Lao Che for a deal in which Lao cheats him. Not only does Lao refuse to keep his side of the bargain, but he also attempts to kill Indiana by slyly offering him a poisoned drink. René Belloq, the henchmen working for "Panama Hat," and even the Nazis played fair compared to Lao. All these "white" enemies of Indiana oppose him openly, but Lao, the eastern crime-lord, constantly uses deception. Lao is certainly more civilized than the Thuggees of India, but they are both deceitful. Both take undue advantage of the white men who trust them. The eastern men are essentially frauds and liars in the film. Exceptions to this pattern are Wu Han and Short Round, who are both sidekicks of Indiana. Short Round, as mentioned in the film, was a pickpocket whom Indiana trained. Though nothing specific is mentioned about Wu Han, he too had accompanied Indiana in many of his adventures, and it is clear that both of these Chinese men owed a great deal to the "civilizing missions" of the West.

Upon their arrival in India, Willie, Short Round, and Indiana meet an old man who guides them to their village. Though the ravaged condition of the village is explained as an outcome of the misrule of the Maharajah of the nearby Pankot Palace, the village scenes are problematic enough for their focus on the wretchedness of the Indians. At the end of the opening song sequence, a title informs us that the film is set in 1935. At this time, the Indian

Freedom Movement was at a very advanced stage, and, for leaders like M.K. Gandhi, the villages were to play a vital role in the initiation of mass-struggle. The unnamed Indian village in the film, however, shows no trace of any such political activity. Bipan Chandra explains that, around 1934–35,

> Gandhiji emphasized constructive work in the villages, especially the revival of village crafts. Constructive work, said Gandhiji, would lead to the consolidation of people's power, and open the way to the mobilization of millions in the next phase of mass struggle.

But the village in the film consists of submissive, uneducated, and helpless people who prostrate themselves for help when they see Indiana and his friends. The physical appearance, attire, and food of the villagers together create an image of absolute bleakness. The old man does insist that the stealing of the sacred *Shiva Linga* from the village has drastically changed their circumstances, but the way the film continues showcasing the squalor of the setting—both before and after the rescue of the sacred stone—betrays a deliberate highlighting of the poverty and abhorrent condition of the Indian village.

While depicting the forests during the characters' journey to Pankot palace, *Temple of Doom* portrays India as a lethal place infested with sinister-looking animals and insects. Apart from one panoramic view of the surroundings, no attempt is made to capture the scenic beauty of the setting. Instead, disgusting and at times dangerous animals make their appearances one after another. Even outlandish animals are recruited for the purpose of associating the Indian forests with an atmosphere of intimidation. While crossing a runnel, the group sees giant shapes flying above, and when Willie gets excited, Indiana, to her and the audience's shock, informs her that they are actually "giant vampire bats." The species he refers to is a native to South and Central America, and though the shooting location of the film, Sri Lanka, along with select regions of South India, do reportedly have a species of bat that sucks blood, they are notably distinct and less sinister than the South America variant. According to Ishwar Prakash, the South Asian species is called the "Indian false vampire bat" or "Megaderma lyra lyra." The data of a surveyor mentioned in his article reports that "false vampires feed on smaller bats, grasshoppers and crickets, but that frogs appear to constitute their chief diet" (545). These basically harmless creatures are used to offer a jump scare moment while the group is camping at night. A monkey, a scary looking lizard, an owl, and a snake pop up back-to-back within minutes. Even the apparently friendly baby elephant given to Willie is shown as a nuisance. The horde of insects shown during the dungeon scenes inside the palace also adds to the shock, and, though dungeons may be expected to have insects, the bugs' absurdly large size attests to their artificiality and the scare tactics lying behind their presentation. All these horrific creatures contribute to the depiction of India as scary and uninhabitable.

Stereotyping continues when depicting the Royal Palace of Pankot as well. The website dedicated to the film franchise, in the section "Scouting for Locations and New Faces" of the entry on *Temple of Doom*, reads:

> for interior shots Watts hoped to film many scenes in the Rose Palace of Jaipur in the Indian state of Rajasthan, but the local government, scandalized by the script's horror-comic character, demanded so many changes that he and Lucas decided Elstree's soundstages would be just fine [TheRaider.net].

Apart from presenting the reaction of the administration of Rajasthan to the film as a knee-jerkish one, the passage also discloses the filmmakers' particular interest in the Indian state of Rajasthan as a filming location. Their desire to shoot the film in a Rajasthani palace, and to equip the palace with hidden underground dungeons that lead to the epicenter of black magic, suggests the film's connection with "imperial medievalism" and "Oriental Gothic." As Ananya Jahanara Kabir explains, "Spanning the long eighteenth century, imperial medievalism signals those processes of European self-formation that constructed its 'other' along temporal and spatial axes of alterity" (66). In her essay, Kabir focuses on the impact of the imperial medievalist discourse disseminated by James Tod's *Annals and Antiquities of Rajasthan*. To quote Kabir, "The self of European Enlightenment located its pre-modern other in the Middle Ages—an other that was both foil to the Enlightened self and its own point of origin" (66). When Tod depicted Rajasthan in his nineteenth-century book, "construction of a temporally distant other met the construction of spatially distant other" (66), resulting in a process whereby "identities were 'exported' from different moments in Europe's past to delineate and describe India's present" (67). Kabir sums up the overall effect of such discourses, commenting, "What resulted was an enormously popular portrait of Rajasthan and, by extension, of India, which was turned to repeatedly by colonial administrators seeking to buttress their views of 'Rajput feudalism,' 'Maratha banditry,' and 'Mughal despotism'" (67). In short, Rajasthan became less a geographical space and more a metonymy used for representing a regressive image of India. While speaking about the other manifestations of the discourse, she adds that the Gothicizing of "Indian architecture" began "around the same time" (73) as a result of the continuous linking of Rajasthan with medieval Europe. The portrayal of the hidden dungeons that harbor monsters like Mola Ram in *Temple of Doom* certainly echoes the discourses outlined in Kabir's essay. After showing the dark forces of Kali taking over Indiana Jones's mind, a low-angle shot is used to show the huge structure of Pankot Palace, and the image, by evoking the outlines of a typical haunted castle, Gothicizes the palace vividly.

Indiana and his companions are invited inside Pankot Palace by Chattar Lal, the Prime Minister of Pankot. Though he appears to be a perfect gentleman, he is soon revealed to be a cunning villain. Just like everything else inside the palace, he too has a shocking secret. The film attempts to present the exoticism of Indian culture in the dinner scene and, while at it, uses its politics of misrepresentation in a shocking manner. After a very brief and unclear portrayal of the Indian Fine Arts, using a few singers and dancers doing generic acts, the filmmakers choose to demean Indian cuisines in a reckless manner. The guests are all offered stomach-turning dishes such as live snakes, insects, chilled monkey brains, and eyeball soup. While Willie and Short Round get the shock of their lives from this outlandish bill of fare, the Indians look overjoyed and eat with great relish. Shashi Tharoor, trying to express the effect of these horrid moments, writes, "Many NRIs recounted tales of foreigners cancelling prior commitments to dinner for fear of being served stewed snakes and monkey brains by their Indian hosts." The grotesque food items hint at the underlying savagery of Indians and thereby justify the "Western civilizing mission" in India. Along with Indians, the dinner includes Captain Blumburtt, of 11th Poona Rifles, as a guest. Blumburtt is represented as an ideal gentleman who trusts and respects the Royal authority of the Maharajah to the fullest, but the Indians, including Prime Minister Lal, take undue advantage of his trust and carry on their nefarious activities secretly. The scenes justify colonization through their portrayal of the ridiculously incapable Maharajah as well. The Maharajah of Pankot is a child named Zalim Singh. He yawns during the dinner, which shows how little he cares for his subjects. Eventually he is shown to be hypnotized by Mola Ram. He can help Indiana and his friends at the end only by seeking help from Captain Blumburtt, which thoroughly justifies the presence of the British in India.

The dinner scenes reveal important details about the secrets of Pankot Palace. The old man of the ravaged village said earlier that the palace again "has the power of the Dark Light" and adds that "the evil start at Pankot and then like monsoon it moves darkness over all country." When Indiana tells Chattar Lal that Captain Blumburtt has informed him about the role played by the palace "in the mutiny," it is hinted that the film equates the evil forces represented by the worshippers of Kali, such as Mola Ram, with the anti-British risings. These hints are confirmed and fully explained when Mola Ram proudly asserts his agenda to Indiana before contaminating his mind and body with the blood of Kali. He claims that the Sankara stones originally belonged to the temple presided over by him. To him, every white man is a thief and the British are interlopers. He has a grudge with the British particularly for the massacre they committed a century ago at their holy temple. The history of the presence of colonizing forces from Europe in India does include notable instances of the desecration of Hindu temples. An article by

Mallicia Kumbera Landrus describes how both Hindu and Muslim forms of worship were banned during the colonization of Goa by the Portuguese. The regent Queen Catarina passed a decree in March 1559 which described the festivals of the Hindus and Muslims as "diabolic rituals" (308). Landrus also mentions violation of Hindu temples in particular, saying:

> It is difficult to gain an accurate picture of the number of temples that were demolished by the Portuguese colonists. It is claimed that some 160 were razed within the island of Goa and a further three hundred destroyed by the Franciscans in the province of Bardez. Between 1566 and 1567, approximately 300 temples were razed to the ground in Salcete. Despite conflicting evidence, these figures nonetheless give a sense of the scale of the destruction of Hindu temples [309].

Discursive strategies make their presence strongly felt even in the supposedly hilarious comic moments showing Willie and Indiana seducing each other in the royal palace. Indiana uses Willie as a bet during his confrontation with Lao, and eventually she gets swept up in Indiana's adventure, but she never becomes a fit companion of Indiana. Instead, she is continually ridiculed for throwing tantrums and being impractical. Indiana never develops a genuine amorous feeling for her as he does for Marion and Elsa. Even when Willie sleeps next to Indy in the forest with her body barely covered, he hardly notices her charms. Inside the bedroom of Pankot Palace, however, he behaves in a significantly different manner. All of a sudden, he expresses interest for observing Willie's "nocturnal activities." They both start trading phrases like "mating customs," "love rituals," and "primitive sexual practices." Indiana claims to be an expert on all of these areas, and Willie responds accordingly. None of the other films has Indiana expressing such carnal desires. He does get intimate with Elsa, but the plot of *Last Crusade* suggests that Indiana genuinely cares about Elsa, whereas, in the case of Willie, a sudden rush of lust seems to take him over, causing him to capriciously overcome the aversion to her he had evinced previously in the film. He gets drawn into the conversation instantly when Willie says she wants to sleep like a princess, wearing only her ornaments. The image Willie tries to evoke immediately triggers Indiana's fantasy, and, considering the similarity between said image and the traditional images of Indian princesses, it seems justified to argue that the film draws on the stereotypical presentation of the East and Eastern women as a stimulant of sexual fantasy of the forbidden kind. In the words of Gina Marchetti:

> Mysterious and exotic, Hollywood's Asia promises adventure and forbidden pleasures. Whether in a Chinatown opium den, a geisha house in Japan, or a cafe in Saigon, romantic involvements and sexual liaisons unacceptable in mainstream Anglo-American society become possible. Erotic fantasies can be indulged, sexual taboos broken [1].

The royal palace of Pankot becomes a setting for the Western male to indulge fantasies of conquest and mastery that are both political and erotic.

Scenes featuring Mola Ram give vital insights into the problematic treatment of history in *Temple of Doom*. As suggested by Justin Jacobs in his thesis, while George Lucas claimed that the films were premised on detailed research conducted by his co-writer Philip Kaufman (228), in reality the franchise was a "classic example of cultural recycling" (226). In Jacobs's words:

> Collectively, what we are seeing here is a significant debt to pre-existing Hollywood productions; fantasy, science fiction, and detective novels; and mainstream popular culture. Missing from this list is anything resembling history [227].

The scenes in the underground temple and Mola Ram's Thuggee origin directly echo George Stevens's film *Gunga Din* (1939), where "thugs appeared as monstrous religious fanatics and rebels against the Raj" (Carter). Additionally, the film also has its underpinnings in the "Imperial Gothic" genre. Patrick Brantlinger observes that "the three principal themes of imperial Gothic are individual regression or going native; an invasion of civilization by the forces of barbarism or demonism; and the diminution of opportunities for adventure and heroism in the modern world" (230). Mola Ram converts Indiana into a supporter of Kali by forcefully making him drink a gruesome dark liquid described as "the blood of Kali." Under the influence of the intoxicant, Indiana behaves exactly like the brutish assistants of Mola Ram. He participates in their ritualistic killing ceremony and slaps Short Round savagely. The scenes of Indiana's transformation that portray a Western civilized man getting corrupted strongly resemble scenes from colonialist narratives like Rudyard Kipling's horror story "The Mark of the Beast." In a similar vein, the cult of Kali becomes the demonic force that intends to invade at first the "civilized" British empire of India and then the whole world. The film has Mola Ram telling Indiana, "The British in India will be slaughtered. Then we will overrun the Muslims. Then the Hebrew God will fall. And then the Christian God will be cast down and forgotten. Soon, Kali Ma will rule the world." Indiana Jones, however, the true-blue White adventurist from the West, vanquishes Mola Ram and his team, proving the superiority of the enlightened Westerners. The momentary torching used for bringing people out of the "black sleep of Kali Ma" also appears to symbolize an antithesis between the dark forces of the subcontinent and the light of Western consciousness.

The Thuggees led by Mola Ram are depicted as a serious threat to the helpless Indians. As the literal meaning of their name suggests, the cultists are "thugs" or cheats of a dangerous kind. They attack from behind and are absolutely unethical and immoral. It is not the British but these nameless menacing men who torture Indians in the film. They loot the village, steal the children, and use them as child laborers. While Indiana protects children and apparently loves Short Round deeply, the Thuggees whip the poor children mercilessly. Despite the extermination of these murderous men by the capable British administration, the Thuggees were secretly gathering strength, preparing for their return. It is Indiana, the fearless American adventurist, who literally unearths their scheming and saves the innocent. Although this denouement itself has an interesting politics lurking behind it, as the latter part of this essay will show, the politics involved in the use of Thuggees is no less significant. As suggested by Kim A. Wagner, Thuggees

> were a fraternity of ritual stranglers who preyed on travellers along the highways of nineteenth century India. Their unsuspecting victims were first deceived into joining the thugs and later at some secluded spot strangled, plundered and buried, supposedly assuming the status of human sacrifices to the goddess Kali. Thuggee was said to be an ancient practice sanctioned by Hinduism and the thugs supposedly observed a plethora of religious rules; they relied on omens, performed rituals and spoke a secret language [1].

Wagner succinctly points out the cultural politics at work involving the Thuggee:

> While thuggee proved to be an important element in the founding of the early colonial state in India, it also became one of the most potent images of colonial lore and fiction, and one that has survived almost unaltered till this day. As 1839 saw the demise of thuggee in India, nominally at least, it also saw its birth as a literary subject [1].

Alexander Lyon Macfie comments that the Thuggees "inspired one of the strongest and most long-lasting orientalist discourses ever invented" (383) and identifies *Temple of Doom* as a part of this tradition. After a thorough survey and analysis of relevant primary and secondary sources, Macfie reaches the conclusion that Major General William Henry Sleeman, a British soldier who became an administrator in nineteenth-century British India, "did to some extent at least invent thuggee as a widespread religious conspiracy, illustrative of the backwardness and irrationality of the Indian people" (395). As argued by Wagner, the British writers demonized the Thuggees while "inventing" them. The Thuggees were set apart from "economically motivated banditry" by these discourses through their association with the Kali cult, but Wagner argues that "there is no mention whatsoever of thuggee as a religious practice in the material predating Sleeman's involvement in the campaign to eradicate thuggee" (953). The goddess Kali too is demonized in the process. As explained by Devdutt Pattanaik, Kali is Devi Durga transformed into "the dark goddess," and she is traditionally shown licking blood because she had to defeat the demon Raktabija who had the magical power of being reborn in a new full-grown body the moment a drop of his blood touched the ground (143). "The later Orientalist fascination of Kali as a bloodthirsty and barbarous deity to whom human sacrifice" was due (Devdutt 953), however, led her to becoming frequently represented as "the 'cannibal goddess' of the thugs" (954).

Each of the Indiana Jones films centers around the quest for objects with miraculous power. The way these sacred objects are treated at the end of each film conforms to a clear pattern, but *Temple of Doom* makes a distinct departure from this formula. The Ark of Covenant is brought to the American government; the Holy Grail could not be acquired only because the rules of the sanctum would not permit its removal. Indiana consciously searches for these holy objects of Western origin, and it is repeatedly mentioned that these quests constitute a noble task, but when it comes to the Sankara stones, Indiana adopts a notably different approach. Firstly, he does not deliberately search for the stones; his circumstances cause him to stumble into this quest. Secondly, although Indiana is insistent throughout the first and third films that archeological objects belong in a museum, he willingly restores the sole remaining Sankara Stone to the villagers. When Willie says that she could have kept the Sankara Stone he remarks, "What for? They'd just put it in a museum. It'd be another rock collecting dust." The stone was a mythical object just like the Ark or the Grail, but Indiana is uncharacteristically uninterested in this magical relic of Eastern origin. As suggested by Jacobs:

> The Sankara Stones are also the only wondrous curiosity of the film franchise to be used solely for sinister purposes, with no apparent redemptive qualities. To put it another way (again borrowing the lexicon of Egyptomania), the Western and alien artifacts turn out to be "wondrous curiosities," while the lone non–Western artifact is portrayed as a "monstrous curiosity" [244].

As frequently mentioned in the above discussion of the film, *Temple of Doom* is a film thoroughly tinged with Orientalism in the Saidian sense. Orientalism is "the processes by which the 'Orient' was, and continues to be, constructed in European thinking" (Ashcroft 167). Orientalism should not be conceptualized as "a Western plot to hold down the 'Oriental' world" (Ashcroft 168). Instead, in the words of Said himself, "It *is*, rather than expresses, a certain *will* or *intention* to understand, in some cases to control, manipulate, even incorporate, what is a manifestly different world" (12). Though Said had confidently asserted that, unlike the Orientalists of European origin, "Americans will not feel quite the same about the Orient" (1), *Temple of Doom* shows that Americans too had the will or intention that he described.

The representation of India in *Temple of Doom* reflects the political climate of its contemporary American milieu. To quote Katherine Biber, "Indiana Jones embodied American heroism in the 1980s" (67), and 1980s heroism is inextricably bound up with the cinematic charisma of Ronald Reagan. Though Biber does not make an attempt to see *Temple of Doom* in the light of Reagan's political relation with India at the time, the film echoes the tension between Reagan's America and India during the first few years of the 1980s. Chidanand Rajghatta points out that "Washington and New Delhi went through hard times in the early Reagan years," adding, "The Soviet Union had just invaded Afghanistan, and Reagan, sworn opponent of the 'evil empire,' felt that New Delhi had not opposed it." Moreover, as suggested by Malone and Mukherjee, America was not at all feeling comfortable with India's emergence as a nation empowered with nuclear arms since the 1970s.

> The US received a major jolt in 1974 when India conducted its first nuclear weapon test at Pokhran. It came to light that India had diverted nuclear materials imported for civilian purposes, much of it from the US, in order to initiate a weapons program. Although India assured the world that its test was a "peaceful" one, the event was a blow not just to American influence in south Asia but also to the emerging global nonproliferation regime in general [1059].

In this context, it is highly significant that Spielberg's film shows India as a poverty-ridden and primitive nation. Shashi Tharoor points out that due to "the colossal global ignorance about India in those days, the Indiana Jones view of India was swallowed without challenge by cinegoers around the world." The film aspired to replace the anxiety of Reaganist America with a pleasure derived from the film's Orientalist vilification of wild-eyed Indians intent on world domination.

Works Cited

Ashcroft, Bill, Gareth Griffiths, and Helen Tiffin. *Post-Colonial Studies: The Key Concepts.* London: Routledge, 2009.
Biber, Katherine. "The Emperor's New Clones: Indiana Jones and Masculinity in Reagan's America." *Australasian Journal of American Studies* 14.2 (1995): 67–86.
Brantlinger, Patrick. *Rule of Darkness British Literature and Imperialism, 1830–1914.* Ithaca: Cornell University Press, 1988.
Carter, Miranda. "Confessions of India's Real-life Thugs." *The Telegraph*, 17 January 2014.
Chandra, Bipan, et al. *India's Struggle for Independence: 1857–1947.* Gurgaon: Penguin Books India, 1989.
Jacobs, Justin. "Hollywood vs. History: Separating Fact from Fiction in the Indiana Jones Film Franchise." *Indiana Jones in History: From Pompeii to the Moon.* 2017. 225–250.
Kabir, Ananya Jahanara. "'Oriental Gothic' : The Medieval Past in the Colonial Encounter." *Reorienting Orientalism.* Ed. Chandreyee Niyogi. Sage Publications, 2006. 65–88.
Landrus, Mallica Kumbera. "Parish Churches, Colonization and Conversion in Portugese Goa." *Parish Churches in the Early Modern World.* Ed. Andrew Spicer. London: Routledge, 2016. 297–320.
Macfie, Alexander Lyon. "Thuggee: An Orientalist Construction?" *Rethinking History* XII.3 (2008): 383–397.
Malone, David M., and Rohan Mukherjee. "India-US Relations: The Shock of the New." *International Journal* 64.4 (2009): 1057–1074.
Marchetti, Gina. *Romance and the "Yellow Peril": Race, Sex, and Discursive Strategies in Hollywood Fiction.* University of California Press, 1994.

McKay, Alex. *Hitler and the Himalayas: The SS Mission to Tibet 1938–39*. Spring 2001. https://tricycle.org/magazine/hitler-and-himalayas-ss-mission-tibet-1938-39/.
Pattanaik, Devdutt. *Indian Mythology Tales,Symbols,and Rituals from the Heart of the Subcontinent*. New Delhi: Inner Traditions India, 2003.
Prakash, Ishwar. "Foods of the Indian False Vampire." *Journal of Mammalogy* 40.4 (1959): 545–557.
Rajghatta, Chidanand. "Reagan and India: Great Expectations." *Times of India*, 6 June 2004.
Said, Edward W. *Orientalism: Western Conceptions of the Orient*. New York: Vintage Books, 1978.
Tharoor, Shashi. "Indiana Jones and the Template of Dhoom." *The Times of India*, 10 March 2007.
TheRaider.net. 7 June 2019. http://www.theraider.net/films/todoom/making_2_newfaces.php.
Wagner, Kim A. "The Deconstructed Stranglers: A Reassessment of Thuggee." *Modern Asian Studies* 38.4 (2004): 931-963.
_____. *Thuggee Banditry and the British in Early Nineteenth Century India*. Basingstoke: Palgrave Macmillan, 2007.

The Quest for "Alien" Indigenous Knowledge in *Indiana Jones and the Kingdom of the Crystal Skull*

KASEY JONES-MATRONA

Introduction

The fourth film in the Indiana Jones franchise, *Indiana Jones and the Kingdom of the Crystal Skull*, presents the mysticism surrounding Indigenous knowledge along with the desire to obtain and weaponize this ancient knowledge. The film, directed by Steven Spielberg, portrays typical harmful stereotypes of Indigenous peoples as language-less dart-shooting warriors and half-naked chanting musclemen. Another pressing issue is the representation of Indigenous societies through the study of artifacts. Scholars in Indigenous museum and curatorial studies have long been concerned with the representation of peoples through corpses and artifacts. These portrayals often help assert that Indigenous cultures and knowledge are "dead" or only knowable through objects, and they allow non–Indigenous people to create narratives for Indigenous societies. In the film, the Crystal Skull and legendary city of Akator become the encapsulating representations of Indigenous knowledge, which is inherently alienated from Western knowledge. The main characters also discredit Indigenous knowledge throughout the entirety of the film.

In *Indiana Jones and the Kingdom of the Crystal Skull*, Indiana Jones voyages to South America with young Mutt Williams (later discovered to be his biological son) to find his old colleague and friend Harold Oxley. Oxley is said to have discovered the mythical Crystal Skull, assumed to be a pre–Columbian artifact, and gone mad. Dr. Spalko, a Russian KGB agent, also seeks Oxley and the Crystal Skull for her own purposes. Early in the film, Jones first comments on the interesting craftsmanship of the Crystal Skull but argues that there is no deeper importance. By the end of the movie, Jones defines the Mayan translation of gold as treasure. The treasure found in Akator, he asserts, is knowledge. This knowledge never quite leads to a confrontation of the painful history of archaeology for Indigenous peoples, nor of Jones's own positionality and cultural looting. Dr. Spalko, meanwhile, transparently seeks to weaponize knowledge gained from the Crystal Skull for military purposes. When Spalko's wish is fulfilled at the end of the film, she is overwhelmed by the knowledge and consumed by an ominous portal. This conclusion conveys the repercussions of desiring sacred knowledge solely for malicious intents. These shifting and varying attitudes toward the skull and its knowledge still provide little promise for the representation of Indigeneity, though.

The Crystal Skull never moves beyond serving as the driving force and legend behind Jones's adventure plot. The Mayan-speaking alien who awakes toward the end of the film is linked to the Indigenous civilization and embodies the ultimate "Other" who appears fascinating and/or fear-inducing to dominant culture. The film constructs a blurred and careless representation of ancient Indigenous civilizations that blends together Inca, Maya, and Aztec, and invents the fictional Ugha tribe. The predominantly white cast of protagonists seeks and searches for Indigenous artifacts and knowledge, all the while demonizing and disrespecting Indigenous peoples and cultures.

Anthropological, Archaeological and Museological Impact on Indigenous Populations

In order to analyze the film, it is important to first discuss the fraught history of archaeology, anthropology, and museology in regard to global Indigenous populations. Ethnological research and museum exhibitions have long contributed to commodification of the Indigenous body. From classification systems to artifact collection, Indigenous bodies have quite literally been bought, sold, and displayed. Henry Lewis Morgan, nineteenth century ethnographer, created a classification system of savagery and barbarism in his book *Ancient Society*, which laid the groundwork for patronizing and destroying Indigenous cultures in the Americas. In his book, Morgan concludes that "the Indian family of America ... illustrated each of these conditions, and especially those of Lower and Middle status of barbarism, more elaborately and completely than any other portion of mankind" (16). Morgan's speculation became much-needed "proof" that the Indigenous cultures of the Americas were uncivilized in order for white settlers to justify delivering colonization through the guise of civilization. Much pseudo-intellectual work came to follow and the Academy itself began to organize and praise ethnographic research from largely outsider perspectives.

In his article "The Representations of Indian Bodies in Nineteenth-Century American Anthropology," Robert E. Bieder writes, "The bodies of Indians became important for the investigations of ethnologists and anthropologists throughout the nineteenth century. Here they found the imprint of the environment, searched for Indian origins, observed effects of disease and customs, and defined the body's limitations and deficiencies" (166). Samuel Morton, a Philadelphia physician, studied "Indian crania from North and South America. To collect these crania, Morton enlisted the aid of Indian agents, along with civilian and military physicians, in various parts of the country.... Angry and horrified Indians tried to prevent the desecration of their graves but such activity often was carried out by military personnel against defeated tribal groups" (Bieder 170). Indigenous peoples were often doubly traumatized by being enlisted to help archaeologists with false promises of preserving and helping their peoples when their true goals were to dig up bodies and artifacts for their own fame and personal advancement.

Indiana Jones's role as archaeologist is crucial for viewers to consider. At the start of *Indiana Jones and the Kingdom of the Crystal Skull*, we learn that Jones has been found in Mexico digging. He is captured and brought to a compound in Nevada with a warehouse of artifacts and mummified remains. In his *NPR* review of *Kingdom of the Crystal Skull*, Christopher Joyce writes, "As a teenager in *Indiana Jones and the Last Crusade*, he chases after tomb raiders and manages—albeit briefly—to recover what *they* were stealing: the Cross of Coronado. Indy insists it should be in a museum. So the young Indy believes artifacts should be studied by scientists, not stolen by treasure hunters." Joyce recognizes the sense of entitlement that scientists display in their appropriation of cultural artifacts, and he points out that Jones's denunciation of looting in *Indiana Jones and the Last Crusade* is hypocritical. He writes, "The history of archaeology is replete with real characters who would now be considered looters." Archaeologists were, and some continue to be, looters, and this looting was justified for the sake of Western knowledge.

Another example of Jones's intent to loot occurs upon his arrival to South America. When Jones and Mutt reach Peru in the film and find the grave of Spanish conquistador Francisco Orrellana, Mutt points out a sign that states "no grave robbers," to which Jones replies, "Good thing we're not grave robbers." Once inside the tombs, though, Jones removes and pulls skulls from dead bodies, handles skeletons disrespectfully, and disturbs unmarked graves, eventually finding the Crystal Skull. He also takes a sword off of

Orellana's mummified body in order to keep it before putting it back after receiving a questioning glare from Mutt.

Indigenous scholars have written about the impact of this cultural looting along with the effects of anthropology and archaeology on Indigenous communities. In his chapter "Anthropologists and Other Friends," Standing Rock Sioux scholar Vine Deloria describes the "infestation" of tribal lands every summer by anthropologists (78). These anthropologists write reports from which slogans are mined and "slogans become conference themes" (80). Poor and hasty observations of tribal peoples then spread throughout academic communities and create false narratives, such as the narrative of the "lack of progress" (90). These false narratives are created by sharing "research" within trusted institutions like academia. However, this research is often collected without proper consent and without making tribal nations aware of the intentions and purposes of the observations. Deloria writes, "The fundamental thesis of the anthropologist is that people are objects for observation" (81). For many anthropologists, Indigenous peoples were (and are still) seen as objects for study, not agential human beings to collaborate with.

Museums were complicit in this system of cultural looting and dehumanization of Indigenous peoples for centuries. In her book *Grave Injustice*, Kathleen Fine-Dare writes how "millions of American Indian and Native Hawaiian human remains and cultural objects were obtained by museums and private collection" in order "to convince the public that the possession of territories, resources, bodies and property of natives-turned-enemies is justified" (14). If prestigious museums collected Indigenous bodies and artifacts, then this practice could too easily become normalized. Indigenous "specimens were ... subjected to ... scrutiny necessary to make good decisions regarding the antiquity, purity, creativity, or savagery of humans" (17). The Indigenous body could be read, like the rings on a tree trunk demonstrating the age of a tree, in order to learn about human "progress" from savage peoples to civilization. Museums in the United States began to put the "products of ... looting activities" on display (19). By the 1860s, "hundreds of thousands of Native American skeletons and skeletal parts" were on display or in storage in museums (Fine-Dare 20).

Some countries like the United States and Australia began to create legislation to protect Indigenous communities from further exploitation. The Native American Graves Protection and Repatriation Act (NAGRA) was instituted in the United States in 1990 and sought to discover and return cultural objects and Native American remains to tribal communities and descendants from whom they had been taken (Fine-Dare 44). This is one example of a practice that still yields acts of repatriation today. In South America, though, looting and lack of consent from Indigenous populations was even worse than in the United States and other countries that slowly began to enact safeguards for Indigenous communities. In *Relics of the Past*, Stefanie Ganger describes how "many cities in Peru and Chile became home to lively communities of antiquities collectors" (1). Collectors were fascinated with precontact artifacts and "members of the elite owned a collection or at least some scattered 'antiquities'; things they associated with the time before the Spanish conquest" (1). There are significantly fewer safeguards in South America in regard to repatriation and exhuming and collecting remains and objects in comparison with other continents. Gustavo Politis writes, "In South America the situation is different and relatively backward in comparison with the USA and Australia. First, it is important to recognize that dialogue between archaeologists and indigenous peoples in the region has always been difficult, erratic, distant and basically absent. Tombs, monuments and sacred places were excavated in the name of science without any consideration for the people culturally and historically related to them" (97). Although countries like the United States and Australia began to foster more constructive communication between Indigenous communities and archaeologists, in South America, this communication was never exactly established.

Since South America specifically was (and is) at greater risk for mistreatment and unfair practices from archaeologists and anthropologists, ideas of alienation and other-ness are more easily perpetuated. Robert McGhee problematizes archaeological practices regarding Indigenous cultures, pointing to "a significant element of the intellectual climate that allows marginalized groups to exist as permanent aliens in the societies of settler nations" (579). For McGhee, archaeology is "a set of techniques developed for the recovery of information related to human history, and as a project that is equally applicable to the history of all human communities" (580). But, "Scholars in the Western intellectual tradition have long compared their own societies with that of a mythological Golden Age, or with the societies of barbarian or savage peoples that retained the characteristics of that age" (McGhee 585). This supposed intellectual superiority impacts archaeological practices. McGhee's definition of archaeology argues that all human societies should be treated equally, but white Western families would certainly not want or allow their ancestors and grandparents to be dug up from graveyards, studied, and displayed in museums.

Defining Indigenous peoples as inferior justifies the continued disrespect they receive in terms of archaeology. Scholar Daniel McGuire also discusses the alienation of non–Western cultures. McGuire writes, "Defining Indian people as alien placed them outside the usual rights and privileges of White society; lumping Indian people in a single group denied them an identity except in relation to whites" (817). Archaeology, along with other academic fields and disciplines, creates the fallacy of one entity of Indigeneity where all tribally specific protocols and knowledge systems are blurred and lost. In turn, all Indigenous peoples are alienated and treated as societies and nations of the past rather than the present and future.

Indiana Jones and the Kingdom of the Crystal Skull further creates alienation of Indigenous peoples by both equating Indigenous peoples with actual aliens and inferring that even extraterrestrial beings (along with all "civilized" humans) are more intelligent than Indigenous peoples. At the end of the film, Jones makes an interesting comment about archaeology in relation to the alien figures in the film. When Jones and the crew enter the room in the temple of Akator with the twelve alien figures and crystal skulls, they find artifacts from every era of early history. Jones identifies the aliens as archaeologists themselves. This is an interesting departure from the film's pattern of alienating Indigenous peoples, and it seems to completely differentiate the movie's Indigenous peoples from the aliens. Jones views the aliens as earlier iterations of archaeologists like himself and this explains the history of archaeologists serving as "superior" figures of culture. Dr. Spalko specifically deems the aliens as more intelligent beings than Indigenous peoples and discredits Indigenous knowledge systems.

Although this history of archaeologists and Indigenous peoples is a difficult one, I do want to acknowledge that many efforts are being made to decolonize archaeology. Scholars like Alejandro Haber propose methods for decolonization in South America specifically: "Decolonizing archaeological thought in South America is being fostered through three simultaneous paths: (a) a critical approach to the ways archaeology contributes to coloniality, (b) a criticism of the mechanisms by which coloniality informs archaeology, and (c) a varied exposure of archaeology to subaltern (that is, non-hegemonic and counter-hegemonic) knowledge" (471). Critiquing art forms like film that project colonialism as an ideal and further colonize Indigenous peoples and audiences is another step in decolonization as well.

The Legend of the Crystal Skull and Indigenous Knowledge

The entire plot of *Indiana Jones and the Kingdom of the Crystal Skull* is driven by the protagonists' quest to obtain the ancient artifact of the Crystal Skull. The Crystal Skull is the ultimate representation of the acquisition of ancient Indigenous and/or alien knowledge in the film. This artifact of the Crystal Skull is based on a widely debated artifact that was found in the nineteenth century. The Crystal Skull has long been speculated to be a pre-Columbian artifact, but many researchers and scientists have proven that it was produced much more recently and sold as a phony artifact. Various crystal skulls were privately owned and displayed in museums in the twentieth century. In his case study of these crystal skulls, Joseph Laycock traces their origins and passage through various museums and owners. In 1878, The Musee d'Ethnographie du Trocadero in Paris "displayed a carving of a human skull made from rock crystal. It was the first time such an object was presented to the public. The previous year, the British Museum in London had also acquired a crystal skull—this one life-sized—from Tiffany's in New York" (Laycock 166). Laycock writes, "these skulls were presented as pre–Columbian Aztec artifacts and scholars pondered how ancient peoples had constructed them. In the 1930s, a third, even more skillfully crafted, crystal skull surfaced in a private collection" (166). Different tests were used to determine the age of the Crystal Skull: "In 1992, a skull was donated to the Smithsonian Museum of American History, prompting curators to reexamine the origin of these objects. Carbon dating is not effective on rock crystal and there is no way to conclusively determine the age of the skulls. However, experts agree that the skulls are almost certainly not genuine pre–Columbian" (Laycock 166). Geologist George Kunz noted "that the style of the carving resembles Mexican art" but "crystals of this size are not found in Mexico" (Laycock 171). Scientists estimated that the crystal skulls "were likely created in nineteenth century Germany using crystal imported from Brazil" (Laycock 180). Therefore, the skulls were not actually Mayan pre–Columbian artifacts, but German productions from Brazilian crystal.

Although the skulls most likely did not originate from a South American tribe, many still believed in their spiritual powers. Many people believed that when they channeled a skull, "their experiences [were] understood to be transmitted from an outside source rather than an introspective insight or epiphany" (Laycock 170). People believed that there was an outside force that could be accessed through interaction with the skull. The tales of the skull were that originally "a Mayan priest would have manipulated the detached jaw, causing the skull to 'speak' and give prophecies" (Laycock 175). Moreover, the "skull was actually a kind of ancient 'memory bank' that functioned similarly to a computer" (Laycock 176). This legend explains why Spalko believes she can harness powerful knowledge from the skull in the film. It supposedly encapsulates generations of knowledge along with prophecies of the future.

The legend of the skulls inspired many writers. Laguna Pueblo theorist and author Paula Gunn Allen was one writer who published stories and poems about the skulls. Whether she completely believed that the skulls were authentic or not, she was interested in their symbolism in regard to spirituality and power. Paula Gunn Allen's 1991 collection *Grandmothers of Light* includes poems and stories where she uses the "crystal skull as a metaphor for the return of women-centered spiritual power" (Toohey 36). As a self-labeled tribal feminist and theorist whose work largely inspired Indigenous feminism today, Gunn Allen utilized the symbol of the Crystal Skull to represent and

94 Cultural Politics

empower Indigenous women. Gunn Allen claimed to "directly [channel] the words of this Crystal Woman, a personification of sacred anotherness" (Toohey 46). This sense of "anotherness" or otherworldliness/other-ness is associated with the skull and represented differently by certain writers and scholars.

The film hastily re-traces the supposed legendary history of the skull, but it is not given the Indigenous spiritual power that theorists like Paula Gunn Allen attribute to it. It is merely mystical and apparently created by aliens, not created and utilized by Mayan people. Jones says that the crystal skull was stolen in the fifteenth or sixteenth century and the legend is that whoever returns it will gain its power. It was stolen from and should be returned to Akator, the mythical city of gold, also known as El Dorado, which Jones and the other characters place somewhere in South America. A Spanish conquistador named Francisco de Orrellana sought the skull (in the film's history) and Jones later finds out that Orellana actually made it out of Akator and buried the skull with his men. Oxley does speak to the skull in Mayan in the film, so there is a tie to the Mayan language at least.

The film identifies the Crystal Skull as belonging to aliens who appeared to ancient civilizations. Jones tells Mutt that the Nazca Indians used to bind their heads to elongate the skull in order to resemble the interdimensional begins. Mutt speculates that the aliens must have been their gods. Jones describes the skull as a piece of "seamless quartz" and "even with today's technology it would shatter" if anyone tried to create it. The film leaves out the discourse about the lack of authenticity of the crystal skulls and the history of their multiple exhibitions.

Although Jones completes a quest to locate the skull, Spalko is the ulti-

In *Indiana Jones and the Kingdom of the Crystal Skull* (2008), Jones (Harrison Ford) finds the crystal skull during his Peruvian tomb raiding and describes how it is too intricate to have been created by (indigenous) people.

mate representation of wanting to locate and consume knowledge in order to use it for personal achievement and harmful intent. Spalko is obsessed with the desire for some kind of total knowledge that she can abuse and use against others. In the beginning of the film, Spalko states that she "knows things before anyone else" and will learn anything that she doesn't know. She engages in psychic research science and looks for artifacts with potential "paranormal military application." She wants to weaponize knowledge and history in any way she can for warfare. Her aggressive intentions reflect archaeology's history of harming Indigenous and vulnerable populations.

Spalko believes that the crystal "opens the psychic channel" of the human brain. When she reaches the room with the twelve alien skulls at the end of the film, she places the thirteenth Crystal Skull back onto the alien body and says, "Tell me everything you know." The skulls fuse together and gleam knowledge, represented by bright light, into Spalko's mind and she is transported to another dimension. She achieves what she wanted the entire time, but the viewer can infer that Spalko is unhappy with the results, since she cannot possess the knowledge and remain on earth to use it against others. The temple quickly begins to collapse and is overtaken by water. Once Jones and his fellow adventurers are safely outside of the temple, Mutt questions where the gold was in Akator, the "city of gold." Jones then tells him that the Ugha word for gold translates as treasure. He states, "The treasure wasn't gold, it was knowledge." Therefore, although both Jones's and Spalko's camps sought the crystal skull and its place in revealing treasure, this artifact represented and/or possessed knowledge. Ultimately, both Jones and Spalko hunt Indigenous knowledge, whether Mayan, Incan, or Ugha. The protagonists both conflate and separate Indigeneity and alien-ness.

Representations of Indigeneity

The Indiana Jones franchise has received wide criticism for its Orientalism, exoticism, and plainly racist representations of non–Western characters and cultures. There are few Indigenous or South American characters represented in *Indiana Jones and the Kingdom of the Crystal Skull*. The few who do appear are tertiary characters at best, with minimal-to-no speaking roles. They are antagonists to Jones or merely aid him in finding certain locations or information. When Jones and Mutt arrive in Peru, they encounter a couple of men speaking Quechua in the marketplace. They are shot from the side and angled in the background. They tell Jones where he can find the sanitarium where Oxley was being held. Jones tells Mutt that Quechua is an Incan dialect. This encounter serves mainly to demonstrate Jones's linguistic knowledge and to carry Jones and Mutt to their next Peruvian location in the film, not to educate audiences about Inca people, their history, or their place in Peruvian/South American history.

In her article "Hollywood's Transnational Imaginaries: Colonial Agency and Vision from *Indiana Jones* to *World War Z*," Lena Jayyusi critiques the Indiana Jones film *Raiders of the Lost Ark*. Jayyusi writes, "We first meet Indiana Jones, an archaeologist-adventurer in the jungles of South America where he is trying to bring back a golden idol for a local museum back home, fighting off treacherous Latinos, primitive yet deadly natives and the dangers of the cave in which the sacred idol is placed" (359). Both the South American space and the natives are threatening to Jones. Further, Jayyusi argues, "The narrative structure and organization of *Raiders* involves a classic projection of a neo-colonial optic. Indeed, it is marked by visibly racist tropes and by an ethic of Western entitlement" (359). In the Indiana Jones films, protagonists "are constantly threatened by, and yet manage to overcome, various non–Western others, represented in typical manner as backward, incompetent, and evil, not to say also ugly" (Jayyusi 359). Non-Westerners are painted in the most unflattering and discriminatory of strokes.

We can see extremely similar representations of South Americans in *Indiana Jones and the Kingdom of the Crystal Skull*. At the sanitarium, a nun leads Jones to the room where Oxley stayed. The nun again serves as a vehicle for Jones to make his own discoveries. As she guides Jones and Mutt, a crazed dark-skinned man howls and reaches out from his cell. This is another quick and minor scene to demonstrate the irrational "primitive-ness" of Jones's surroundings. When Jones is later reunited with Oxley, he is met with a crazed version of his old friend who is unable to speak in complete sentences and dances around a campfire as entertainment for Spalko's team. Oxley draws pictures in his cell in the sanitarium and the images he leaves behind make him appear unstable to Jones. Oxley also later draws images to form a map for Jones and Spalko to follow to get to Akator. These moments allude to the notion that pictographs are inferior to alphabetic text and language. Indigenous peoples across the world did not document written language but privileged oral traditions and also shared stories and histories through images in pottery, weaving, cave paintings, and other mediums. Jones does not value these methods of language and communication, though (at least not to the same level as Western alphabetic text), and believes Oxley has regressed into savage behavior that was induced by communicating with the skull (an alien/Indigenous entity).

Perhaps the most offensive representations of Indigenous peoples are the "warriors" throughout the film. When Jones and Mutt find Orellana's gravesite, South American warriors climb and scale the trees in an animal-like fashion until they attack. They yelp indistinguishably as they try to blow poison darts. One wears a skull over his own face and Jones is able to blow the dart back into the warrior's own mouth when he aims for Mutt. The other scurries off when Jones pulls out his gun, the ultimate symbol of Western superior technology. In the film credits, these characters are called the "cave warriors" (IMDb). They have no specific nationality or identity; they are empty stereotypical dark-skinned barriers for the heroic Indiana Jones.

Similar to the cave warriors, when Jones and his crew make it to Akator, there are Ugha warriors. Like the swarming ants in the previous jungle scene, the Ugha men swarm out of nowhere in a large group to attack. Some wear black or white paint and they yell and try to attack until Oxley points the skull at them and they become afraid and back off. The "warriors" in the film are animalized and dehumanized as shown through their crawling, climbing, swarming, nakedness, and lack of language.

The film blurs and blends aspects of Mayan, Incan, and Aztec history, culture, and identity, and it creates the fictional Ugha tribe without providing them with any tribally specific history. Jones acknowledges that modern day Peru was part of the Incan empire, the skull is described as having some relation to Mayan culture (but is also entirely alien and interdimensional), and the Ugha tribe is the fictional tribe that resides in Akator and supposedly interacted with the aliens. Jones treats all of these ancient Indigenous empires as one, along with indicating that these cultures are dead and all that is left is their artifacts for archaeologists to now find and study. No distinction is established among these tribes and groups, although they are all rooted in specific locations across Latin/Central/South America.

Multiple characters ignore and discredit Indigenous knowledge throughout the film. Jones reads cave paintings when he reaches Akator that seem to indicate that another group (the aliens) taught the Ugha agricultural skills. The film is written so that Jones can discredit tribal Indigenous knowledge and argue that the Ugha must have been taught these skills, although many Indigenous peoples of the Americas had sophisticated agricultural systems. Spalko also insults Indigenous knowledge throughout the film. She refuses to believe that the skull was created by humans. She states that "early men could not have conceived [Akator], much less built it." Spalko recapitulates the myths that aliens must have built ancient wonders like the Egyptian pyramids, Nazca lines, and other architectural anomalies like temples and tombs around the world. For Spalko, Indigenous peoples just did not have the knowledge or ability to plan and construct these phenomena.

Although the film works to enforce stereotypes about lack of Indigenous ingenuity, it is important to acknowledge the complex and advanced knowledge systems of ancient Indigenous peoples that still live on today. Advanced education and higher education is just one way Indigenous knowledge manifested in pre–Colombian spaces. In his article "Colleges Before Columbus: Mayans, Aztecs and Incas Offered Advanced Education Long Before the

Arrival of Europeans," Steven Crum notes that "the Mayans of Central America were perhaps the first to establish advanced education" (1). In fact, "the Mayans developed an elaborate hieroglyphic written language which is still being studied and analyzed by scholars today. They were also scientists and mathematicians" (Crum 1). Colonists worked to destroy these knowledge systems, though. Crum writes, "When the Spanish leadership militarily defeated the Aztec empire in 1521, they destroyed the visible Aztec institutions, including the calmécacs, and replaced them with Spanish ones" (1). Although lasting harm was inflicted upon Indigenous peoples and their knowledge systems, there is still survival and revitalization today.

Overall, the Indigenous characters in *Indiana Jones and the Kingdom of the Crystal Skull* have no purpose other than to protect Akator from invaders. They have no stories of their own and there is no fictionalized history to the Ugha tribe. The warriors exist in the film solely to create conflict and challenge for Jones and to remind the audience of the superiority of Western civilization. There is little representation of South American or Indigenous presence in the cast and crew. David Knopp, George Lucas, Jeff Nathanson, and Philip Kaufman (all white men) wrote the film (IMDb). There is one Brazilian producer, Flavio Tambelini, and some cast members are Latinx who fulfill the minor roles of offensive warrior stereotypes (IMDb). Some of the filming locations include Argentina, Brazil, Hawaii, New Mexico, and California (IMDb). Indigenous participation and contribution in directing, production, writing, and acting will always lead to more complex, accurate, and respectful representations. This franchise is largely missing this crucial input.

Conclusion

Although Indigenous peoples and knowledge are not fairly or accurately represented in the Indiana Jones franchise, I can agree with one quote from Dr. Jones: knowledge is the ultimate treasure. Knowledge is powerful. Traditional knowledge can decolonize and destabilize colonial and imperial institutions. There are rumors of a fifth Indiana Jones film. One can hope Steven Spielberg and the cast and crew will work to address the complex and complicated histories of the cultures they have thus far represented in one-dimensional ways. It is imperative as viewers, though, to be critical of Western control of historical narratives through institutions like archaeology, to realize how they are circulated and perpetuated in mediums like film, and to demand better.

Works Cited

Bieder, Robert. "The Representations of Indian Bodies in Nineteenth-Century American Anthropology." *American Indian Quarterly*, vol. 20, no. 2, 1996, pp. 165–179.

Crum, Steven. "Colleges Before Columbus: Mayans, Aztecs and Incas Offered Advanced Education Long Before the Arrival of Europeans." *Journal of American Indian Higher Education*, vol. 3, no. 2, 1991, pp. 1–7.

Deloria, Vine. *Custer Died for Your Sins: An Indian Manifesto*. University of Oklahoma Press, 1988.

Fine-Dare, Kathleen. *Grave Injustice: The American Indian Repatriation Movement and NAGPRA*. University of Nebraska Press, 2002.

Ganger, Stefanie. *Relics of the Past: The Collecting and Study of Pre-Columbian Antiquities in Peru and Child, 1837-1911*. Oxford University Press, 2014.

Haber, Alejandro. "Decolonizing Archaeological Thought in South America." *Annual Review of Archaeology*, vol. 45, no. 1, 2016, pp. 469–485.

IMDb. "Indiana Jones and the Kingdom of the Crystal Skull." *IMDb*, https://www.imdb.com/title/tt0367882/.

Indiana Jones and the Kingdom of the Crystal Skull. Directed by Steven Spielberg, Lucas Film, 2008.

Jayyusi, Lena. "Hollywood's Transnational Imaginaries: Colonial Agency and Vision from *Indiana Jones* to *World War Z*." *Continuum: Journal of Media and Cultural Studies*, vol. 32, no. 3, 2018, pp. 355–369.

Joyce, Christopher. "Indiana Jones: Saving History or Stealing It?" *NPR*, April 21, 2008, https://www.npr.org/templates/story/story.php?storyId=89724552.

Laycock, Joseph. "The Controversial History of the Crystal Skulls: A Case Study in Interpretive Drift." *Material Religion*, vol. 11, no. 2, 2015, pp. 164–188.

McGhee, Robert. "Aboriginalism and the Problems of Indigenous Archaeology." *American Antiquity*, vol. 73, no. 4, 2008, pp. 579–597.

McGuire, Randall. "Archaeology and the First Americans." *American Anthropologist*, vol. 94, no. 4, 1992, 816–836.

Morgan, Henry Lewis. *Ancient Society*. Charles H. Kerr and Company, 1877.

Politis, Gustavo. "On Archaeological Praxis, Gender Bias and Indigenous Peoples in South America." *Journal of Social Archaeology*, vol. 1, no. 1, 2001, pp. 90–107.

Toohey, Michelle Campbell. "Paula Gunn Allen's Grandmothers of the Light: Falling through the Void." *Studies in American Indian Literatures*, vol. 12, no. 3, 2000, pp. 35–51.

Identity

Indiana Jones and the Crusade for Authenticity

SIOBHAN LYONS

"Archaeology is the search for fact ... not truth."
—Indiana Jones, *Raiders of the Lost Ark*

The Indiana Jones franchise evokes themes of nostalgia on two fronts: on the one hand Indiana himself, as a devoted researcher and archaeologist, spends much of his time searching for priceless historical artifacts from historical eras. Indiana's connection to these ancient relics is one that he himself describes as being motivated by "fortune and glory," and yet the films ultimately portray an ethereal appreciation for these artifacts that transcends monetary reward. On the other hand, Indiana Jones is primarily set in the 1930s and '40s, a crucial era of socio-political change that has since been lionized in popular film. The first three Indiana Jones films, released in the 1980s, deliberately tap into these feelings of nostalgia for an era defined by nomadism, adventure, political upheaval, and international intrigue. The script, the cinematography, and the characters all radiate a glow of nostalgia.

Adam Gopnik of *The New Yorker* declared that there should be a "40-year rule" for nostalgia. The '80s, he explains, "somehow managed to give the Second World War a golden glow," a tendency epitomized by *Raiders of the Lost Ark*. As with many of Spielberg's films, from *The Goonies* to *Jurassic Park*, the Indiana Jones films place a precarious emphasis on retrieving a moment in time or on staging a fantasy of reanimating the past, whether in the form of biblical figures or those of pirates and dinosaurs, all of whom have left behind certain relics or fossils.

But Indiana Jones projects a highly romanticized version of the past, wherein even the Nazis are, as theorists note, "cartoonish." What we see in the films is a *cinematic*, somewhat counterfeit nostalgia. In this sense, Indy's search for "authentic" artifacts parallels the audience's search for authenticity. An examination of the films' historical setting alongside their years of release reveals notable contrasts: rugged masculinity alongside emerging metrosexualism, the intrepid traveler in a time of an increasingly technological travel industry, and the priceless artifact against the American yuppie generation. This essay will explore how Indiana Jones speaks more to the 1980s than it does to the 1930s, while investigating the ways in which the Indiana Jones films attempt to frame notions of authenticity.

The story behind the development of the film franchise is almost as well-known as the plot of the films themselves. After Tom Selleck was initially cast in the role of the titular character, Harrison Ford was eventually selected despite resistance from co-creator George Lucas, who had just worked with Ford in *The Empire Strikes Back*, which was released in 1980, the year that filming for *Raiders of the Lost Ark* began. Focusing on a search for the Ark of the Covenant, the film would go on to become an enormous box office success, cementing Ford as a rugged, sarcastic, yet well-meaning action hero. Like Han Solo, Indiana Jones pursues personal rewards at the same time that he tries to do right by history, even if such ideals waver in the face of reality.

As with *Star Wars*, Indiana Jones was a modernized version of film serials from the 1930s and '40s. Its use of ancient relics, exotic locations, and an assortment of colorful characters including brave adventurers and "cookie-cutter Nazi villains" (Umland & Umland, 167) adds up to a story that has an ambiguous relationship with notions of authenticity. The character of Indiana Jones was reputed to have been based on several different historical figures, notably paleontologist Roy Chapman Andrews, though both Spielberg and Lucas have stated that this is not the case. The Nazis in both *Raiders* and *The Last Crusade* have been described as cartoonish and even comedic, lacking the severity of other filmic Nazis, such as those portrayed in Spielberg's *Schindler's List* (1993). The two most important relics in the franchise—the Ark of the Covenant and the Holy Grail—are not merely important in their own right, but possess supernatural qualities to give them added attraction for viewers following the journey. For every feature or plot device that is based in fact, there is a highly fanciful element added that puts Indiana Jones movies in a bizarre category between historical adventure and supernatural drama.

The 1980s and the Quest for Authenticity

The 1980s were a pivotal era in American culture. Defined by Ronald Reagan's celebrity presidency from 1981 to 1989, the decade was one in which corporate America thrived, motivated by an ethos memorably summed up by the character of Gordon Gekko in Oliver Stone's film *Wall Street* (1987): "Greed is good." Yuppie culture saw younger Americans aspiring to surpass the wealth and success of their parents' generation. While fights for social and cultural freedoms defined the 1960s, and Watergate and the Vietnam War were emblematic of the 1970s, the 1980s was the era of MTV, Ted Turner's 24-hour cable news network CNN, and PC (personal computer) culture. The 1980s' emphasis on emerging media technologies, which would only accelerate as the decade progressed, operated in stark contrast to the modest, rugged terrain of the Indiana Jones films. When Marion Ravenwood looks out admiringly over the rooftops in Cairo (filmed in Kairouan, Tunisia, known as "Little Cairo"), there is not a power line in sight, as the crew removed the 350-plus television antennas to portray an authentic 1930s Egyptian skyline. This epochal separation is crucial to the success of the franchise, removing audiences from the cultural landscape of the 1980s—from AIDS to the Wall Street Crash, and from MTV to Who Shot JR?—and placing them in an era idealistically characterized by authentic places and authentic people. In contrast to the globalization emerging in the 1980s, which contributed to a smaller world of more seamless interconnectivity, Indiana Jones augments the texture of the physical world by identifying authenticity with arduous world travels, face-to-face communication, and priceless relics. Such contrasts provoked a desire for the more "authentic" worlds of the Indiana Jones films which were, nevertheless, far removed from the true nature of the 1930s. As Cornelius Holtorf writes:

> The contemporary mass media, the Internet, expanding tourism, and trends towards a global economy have no doubt been instrumental not only to the spread of themed environments and "Disneyization" but also to the global popularization of archaeological themes such as those contained in the Indiana Jones–type hero [157].

A nostalgic fondness for a less hedonistic, less mercantile world sits at the center of the Indiana Jones film franchise and drives the plots of the films. While films of each generation differ in themes, one of the more enduring elements that is an inevitable part of every decade's cinematic output over the last fifty years is the theme of authenticity—whether it takes the forms of a celebration of authentic people or things, or of a direct criticism of the notion of authenticity and its idealistic expectations. 1980s cinema, for example, challenged notions of authenticity, with divergent approaches to ghosts—*The Shining* (1980), *Poltergeist* (1982) and *Ghostbusters* (1984)—time-travel—*The Terminator* (1984), *Back to the Future* (1985)—and extraterrestrial life—*E.T. The Extra-Terrestrial* (1982), *Aliens* (1986) and *Predator* (1987). The implications of artificial intelligence were also examined, with Ford starring as Rick Deckard in *Blade Runner* in 1982. But the Indiana Jones franchise has a specific kind of stance on notions of historical authenticity: the notion that authentic lives and pursuits were not to be found in the future, but in the past. Nathaniel Lewis writes, for instance, that the notion of authenticity: "is often freighted with the burden of the golden past, a nostalgia for an earlier age that seems, in retrospect, more real" (5).

Michael Albrecht similarly observes that "authenticity is one of the key lenses through which we view contemporary mediatized society and the anxiety around the consumption of the inauthentic is central to modern life" (5). In the 1980s, yuppie culture and consumerism were booming. The notion of a successful life was tied to one's financial status, however precarious that status might be. Indiana Jones, in contrast, offered the notion that a worthier pursuit was to dedicate oneself to the quest for ancient relics. In contrast to the materialistic consumption of capitalistic products, Indiana Jones shows the same kind of frenzied adoration for "authentic" artifacts that the yuppie culture lavished on expensive cars. We see the fatal consequences of the fake or counterfeit object and this "anxiety around the consumption of the inauthentic" in *The Last Crusade*, when the antagonist Walter Donovan drinks from an opulent gold and emerald chalice, which he mistakes for the Grail. The table in the Knight's chamber is literally covered with a number of Grail duplicates, with only one ensuring eternal life. The comparatively modest appearance of the true Grail conveys the film's message about 1980s capitalism and the error of consumer choice in fetishizing visually appealing but false or misleading products.

Yet while the films do attempt to remove the viewer from the era in which the films were produced, the 1980s do not completely disappear from

Walter Donovan (Julian Grover, left) "chooses poorly" in *The Last Crusade* (1989) as (from left) Elsa (Alison Doody), the Grail Knight (Robert Eddison) and Indiana Jones (Harrison Ford) watch.

Indiana Jones's radar at all. Characters such as Dr. René Belloq, Major Arnold Toht, Walter Donovan, and even Indy's very first guide, Satipo, express the same greed that became a hallmark trait of the 1980s. Indiana's own search for relics, while depicted as far more noble in motivation, nevertheless veers close to obsession, even when Indy chastises his father for the same blind determination in *The Last Crusade*: "This is an *obsession*, Dad. I never understood it." And yet his actions throughout the franchise illustrate just how far Indy is willing to go to recover these authentic artifacts.

Moreover, Indiana Jones's deliberate focus on priceless artifacts works as a counter-narrative for the world of the 1980s, where mass-production and planned obsolescence had become normalized. In this sense, the films reflect a desire for the authentic artifact. As Holtorf argues, the authenticity of monuments "lies in the process of natural decay and gradual vanishing" (113), in contrast to the abundance of mass-produced products in the late twentieth century, which never properly decay. Holtorf also notes that "authenticity is what distinguishes an original and unique work of art from a mechanical reproduction" (112), an allusion to Walter Benjamin's theories on mechanical reproduction and its negative impact on the "aura" of a work of art.

Importantly, Lewis sees authenticity as the "true condition of the western cultural imagination" (1), while Holtorf similarly argues, "The notion of authenticity is a product of western cultural history with roots in antiquity" (112). This is certainly evidenced in *Raiders* when both Sallah and the Imam caution Indy against searching for the Ark. While the Imam offers Indy a sign warning him against disturbing the Ark, Sallah is much more insistent, explaining, "If [the Ark] is there, at Tanis, then it is something that man was not meant to disturb. Death has always surrounded it. It is not of this earth." Yet in his desire for fortune, glory, and authenticity, Indy ignores these warnings and pursues the Ark regardless, epitomizing the West's covetous nature and the notion that one must obtain the item of desire at all costs, whether those costs are monetary or mortal. As Kazim—one of the knights in *The Last Crusade*—asks Indy, "Ask yourself: why do you seek the cup of Christ? Is it for his glory, or for yours?"

In *The Authenticity Hoax*, Andrew Potter argues that "the quest for authenticity is a quest to restore that lost unity. Where once we did it through actual religious rituals, prayer, and communion with God, now we make do with things such as Oprah's Book Club" (12), which, he says, is a "fluid mix of pop-psychoanalysis, self-help, sentimentality, nostalgia, and yuppie consumerism" (12–13). Indiana Jones bridges these two seemingly contradictory elements of nostalgia and yuppie culture by making its hero an archaeologist who verges on the brink of tomb-raiding, hence the title of the very first film, *Raiders of the Lost Ark*. Indiana Jones furthermore imbues religious artifacts with an additional element of occultism to appeal to an era whose ambiguous attachment to spirituality required an element of spectacle to maintain interest in an otherwise antiquated, "stuffy" phenomenon. Indy can't simply go after these relics for their religious value, nor can he be seen to go after them for their monetary value either. The spiritual transforms into the supernatural, and the artifacts' source of power becomes the thing that verifies their authenticity and confirms their value for an audience whose sense of value is almost entirely defined by the era in which the films were made.

Indeed, Potter argues that "there really is no such thing as authenticity." Authenticity, he says, "is a way of talking about things in the world, a way of making judgements, staking claims, and expressing preferences about our relationships to one another, to the world, and to things" (13). Indy's relationship with the world deliberately eschews authenticity; not only are the locations carefully curated to embody the rugged look of the 1930s as depicted in popular culture, but the people, from the Nazis to the natives, are conveniently stereotypical, notably in *The Temple of Doom*, which depicts Indy as the "white savior" to rescue the "helpless" Indians.

Indy's relationship to his father, moreover, is an important motif in the final film, informing Indiana's relationships with others, including Dr. Elsa Schneider, with whom both he *and* his father become intimate. With father and son both having a sexual relationship with Schneider, Indy's own relationship with his father takes an odd turn. Indy observes, "you're old enough to be her grandfather." Henry's rendezvous with a much younger woman who is closer to Indiana's age shifts the dynamic of their father-son relationship, with the two becoming more like rivals or associates rather than father and son. The film was also released two years after the "womanizer" scandal involving American politician Gary Hart in 1987, when Hart, then 52, was purported to have had an affair with model and author Donna Rice, a woman 22 years his junior. But while Indy admonishes Henry for his actions, his own relationship with Marion Ravenwood is vulnerable to the same critique: Marion was 15 when she and Indy—ten years her senior—were together. As Marion says in *Raiders*: "I was a child! It was wrong and you knew it!" (A transcript between George Lucas and Steven Spielberg also reveals that they originally intended Marion to be eleven when she and Indiana began their affair.)

Throughout *The Last Crusade*, we see repeated attempts on Indy's behalf to become closer to his father and to cement an authentic father-son relationship. This theme is introduced in the flashback that opens the film, in which a young Indiana Jones attempts, to no avail, to get his father's attention after his acquisition of the stolen Cross of Coronado. Henry is too busy working on his Grail notebook to pay attention to his son. Later, while on a zeppelin, Indy once again tries to connect with his father, claiming they "never talked," only for his father to dismiss his concerns once more, insisting that he at least gave his son plenty of "space." Even after he believes Indy has fallen over a cliff to his death, when Henry discovers that his son has survived, he embraces Indy only briefly before pulling away and resuming his composure.

The parallels between the Jesus-God relationship (with God giving His only son so that humanity shall be saved, one of the Bible's more ambiguous doctrines) and the relationship between Indy and Henry are not only evident, but deliberately foregrounded amidst the backdrop of Grail mythology. Indiana plays the Jesus figure who is sent to recover the Grail and appease his wounded father, while Henry stands in constant judgment of his son, ridiculing his methods. It isn't until the end when Henry, ever the obsessed seeker of the Grail, convinces his son to "let it go" that we see their relationship mended. Henry at last chooses his son's life over the Grail, and both father and son come to realize that their lives are more important than the artifact they have been pursuing.

Indeed, it is Indy's relationship with "things," as Potter puts it, or artifacts, that drives the franchise as a whole. The artifacts, in a way, act more like red herrings, whose importance to the plot is simply a means to an end for arriving at the deeper meanings that these objects represent.

Truth/Fact, Real/Fake

Fact and legend converge in the Indiana Jones film franchise, with the mythology of Jesus and the various artifacts attached to Christian mythology—the Ark of the Covenant, the Holy Grail—used as metaphors for a variety of tropes, including good vs. evil and the father/son relationship. Lucas employed a number of different sources for the films' narratives, including Trevor Ravenscroft's 1972 book, *Spear of Destiny*, a book that focuses on the occult power of the spear which pierced Christ. And although, as previously mentioned, both Lucas and Spielberg deny the link, many archaeologists see similarities between Jones and real-life archaeologist Roy Chapman Andrews.

While the Ark's powers and its utility for the Nazis remain slightly more ambiguous, the Grail, in contrast, has a very specific use and value, as it is said to imbue the one who drinks from the chalice with eternal life, a promise that motivates Walter Donovan's heedless pursuit of it. Even Elsa Schneider, whose pursuit of the Grail for the first half of the film appears motivated purely by scholarly appreciation, succumbs to the Grail's occult appeal at the cost of her life, prompting Henry to remark, "Elsa never really believed in the Grail. She thought she'd found a prize." For Henry, then, as it is for Indy, the Grail is not merely a prize to be coveted, but is much more than what it represents to unscrupulous treasure hunters. As Umland argues, "Donovan's myopia prevents him from understanding that the cup grants only spiritual immortality, and then only to the worthy. It cannot be bought, nor can it be wrestled away from its keeper" (171). Filmed during a thoroughly capitalistic era during which value was often considered only in monetary terms, *The Last Crusade* depicts Donovan's materialism as the basis for the mistake that costs him his life. Donovan fails to distinguish between the "simulacra grail and the genuine item" (171), as Umland puts it, a fact that conveniently taps into the yuppie preference for "authentic" products over cheap, counterfeit objects. But while the "real" item represents wealth for the yuppie culture in contrast to poverty, the Grail's authenticity engenders spiritual wealth and spiritual poverty. The notion that an item's value can only be measured in capital undermines the true significance of the Grail's existence and further identifies the world of Indiana Jones as a contrast to the values of the world in the 1980s. Even though materialistic values certainly existed in the time in which Indiana Jones is set, the audience is meant to see the 1930s as a time that is contrastingly more virtuous than the 1980s, even as greed accompanies the pursuit of sacred relics in the films.

In contrast to the physical bravado of Indy himself, Umland further notes that the real heroes of the franchise are the academics, "the true guardians of what the grail represents" (171). The Grail's significance for the film's academics, chiefly Marcus Brody, emphasizes fact over superstition, even when they acknowledge the artifact's powers. As Brody says to Donovan, "You're meddling with powers you cannot possibly comprehend." He offers the same cautionary advice to Indy during *Raiders*: "For nearly 3,000 years, man has been searching for the Lost Ark. Not something to be taken lightly. No one knows its secrets. It's like nothing you've ever gone after before."

While the film is driven by the exaggerated properties of these otherwise immobile artifacts, academics are there to remind Indy and the audience that underestimating the true value of such artifacts and the immaterial value they represent will likely lead to one's downfall, for that is the price paid when one fetishizes items of a sanctified nature that cannot be quantified by any capitalistic system. These items, as Sallah and Brody rightly posit, are not of this world; that is, they do not belong to a world dominated by capital exchange.

The relationship between what is real and what is fake both in regard to artifacts and the field of archaeology itself largely defines the franchise. Indy himself acknowledges that archaeology is the search for fact, not truth, and this distinction is key to the franchise's paradoxical approach to artifacts. Imbued with magical properties, the artifacts, from the Ark to the Grail, symbolize Indiana's pursuit of his own truths regarding his relationship with his father and his relationship with the world at large, a pursuit that ironically abandons any sense of fact in the process. As Henry puts it, "The quest for the Grail is not archaeology; it's a race against evil." The concept of evil, a prominently biblical term, transforms Indy's practice of archaeology from the pursuit of fact, as Indy sees it, to one of truth and of good vs. evil, a crude binary that defines many of Lucas' films, most notably *Star Wars*, with its emphasis on the dark side vs. the light. In *The Last Crusade*, the Grail becomes the impetus for thwarting the Nazis and restoring goodness.

The character of Belloq in *Raiders* constitutes an interesting element in the films' "good vs. evil" motif. The determined, unscrupulous archaeologist and rival to Jones describes Indy as a "shadowy reflection" of himself. Indy holds himself up as the archaeological poster boy, demonizing Belloq's methods, and, to a significant extent, Indy is right; Belloq allies himself with the Nazis in his pursuit of the Ark in the same way that Donovan does for his pursuit of the Grail. Yet Belloq's description of Jones is nevertheless apt. There is a fine line between the two in regard to their equally dubious practices, and while Jones sees his pursuit as virtuous, his own coveting of the artifacts and the destruction left behind add credence to Belloq's assertion. As Belloq later reminds Jones: "All your life has been spent in pursuit of archaeological relics. Inside the Ark are treasures beyond your wildest aspirations. You want to see it open as well as I." This is also what makes Belloq a much more interesting villain than Donovan: he is as charming as he is devious.

In the same scene in which Indy distinguishes between philosophy's pursuit of truth and archaeology's pursuit of fact, he also claims that "seventy percent of all archaeology is done in the library," a claim he undermines in *The Kingdom of the Crystal Skull* when, astride a motorbike in a library, he informs his students: "If you want to be a good archaeologist, you gotta get out of the library!" before driving off with the engine revving. While this is a playful self-reference on the one hand, as Indy has always undermined such an edict by spending most of his time in the field, it also shows the extent to which the fourth installment over-compensated by essentially turning Indy into a caricature of himself.

The actual role of an archaeologist becomes an important element in the film's approach to authenticity. As Indy tells his students about the profession: "forget any ideas you've got about lost cities, exotic travel, and digging up the world. We do not follow maps to buried treasure, and X never, ever, marks the spot." Yet all of these points directly characterize Indiana's career.

As in *Jurassic Park*, which also focuses on archaeological history and paleontology, the Indiana Jones films skirt the realities of archaeology in favor of cinematic exaggeration, something which is unsurprising in filmmaking of this nature. Yet while *Jurassic Park* at least shows the more patient, delicate aspects of dealing with fossils at the beginning of the film, with characters who continually caution against corrupting science and history, Indiana Jones takes a more impulsive approach to artifacts, even as he claims to respect them.

Indy's actual handling of artifacts is clumsy and haphazard, rather than delicate and patient. Unwittingly destroying much of the tombs and temples he raids, from the very first temple in *Raiders* to the lost city in *Crusade*, Indy is not the model archaeologist. In fact, David Germain compares Indy's approach to that of a bull in a China shop: "Though he preaches research and good science in the classroom, the world's most famous archaeologist often is an acquisitive tomb raider in the field with a scorched-earth policy about what he leaves behind."

Indeed, at the beginning of *Raiders* and the end of *Last Crusade*, the temples that Indy explores collapse. In fact, it is only in *Temple of Doom*, the film that was received the most poorly of the three, that sacred temples remain relatively intact. Although the film was rightly criticized for its depiction of Indy as a colonialist patriarch, he manages to return one of the magic stones to its rightful owner (rather than a museum), a practice which he renounces in *Last Crusade*, believing that all objects "belong in a museum."

Archaeologists' opinions of Jones are at once favorable and critical. While archaeologists enjoy Indy's over-the-top antics, they note that his portrayal of archaeologists does not accord with the genuine practice of archaeology: "Real experts in antiquities acknowledge that the movies are pure fiction that present archaeology as blockbuster adventure, yet they cannot help but cringe at the way Indy manhandles the ancient world," Germain says. Archaeologists note the painstaking realities of archaeology. As archaeologist Bryant Wood argues, "You're working at one site tediously, probably for many, many years and spending more time processing the finds and writing reports than you do actually digging at the site. But that wouldn't make for a very good story" (qtd. in Germain).

It becomes integral, then, to point out the playful and ironic tenor that undergirds the franchise. Any analysis of the films must take into account the artistic liberties the filmmakers take in enhancing the audience's enjoyment. As a series about archaeology and fact, Indiana Jones is contrastingly fanciful and deliberately over the top. And whatever flaws Indy possesses in his acquisition of artifacts, he maintains his view that ancient relics are shared property and should be placed in museums.

Conclusion: The Illusion of Authenticity

The Indiana Jones films exemplify the hyperreal impulse in late twentieth-century culture as theorized by Jean Baudrillard. For Baudrillard, the hyperreal is a sense of the real "without origin or reality" (1). In an era increasingly defined by planned obsolescence and plastic-dominated objects with the "made in China" tag, the Indiana Jones trilogy performed history for an audience keen on experiencing a curated nostalgia that was both "authentic" and theatrical. With its elaborate sets and locations and its emphasis on the priceless artifact (in contrast to the mass-produced products of the late twentieth century), audiences are asked to reconcile their conflicting desires between the real and the fake when it comes to Indiana's outlandish escapades. What the fans of Indiana Jones want, then, is not authenticity, but the *illusion* of authenticity, what Dean MacCannell called "staged authenticity" (98). Indeed, philosopher Slavoj Žižek argued that "the problem of the twentieth century's 'passion for the real' was not that it was a passion for the Real, but that it was a fake passion whose ruthless pursuit of the Real behind appearances was the ultimate stratagem to avoid confronting the real" (24).

The Indiana Jones films constituted less of a model of authenticity in a pre-capitalistic world and more of a vehicle of escapism into an *alternative capitalism*, where the rare artifact acts as a substitute for the mass-produced products with built-in obsolescence common in the late twentieth century. The films' emphasis on authenticity is at once timely in the context in which the films were released, calling for more authentic endeavors, and utterly contradictory considering the financial return the films have accumulated at the box office.

Since their release, the films have become a hallmark example of "nostalgia cinema." Despite the prestidigitation through which they replace one brand of capitalism with another, the films nevertheless criticize the 1980s consumerist obsession with fetishizing objects, even as they partake in the illusion of authenticity in an era increasingly bereft of unique curiosities.

WORKS CITED

Albrecht, Michael. *Fake Plastic Trees: Authenticity in Contemporary Popular Media Culture.* Ph.D. Dissertation, University of Iowa. 2008.
Baudrillard, Jean. *Simulacra and Simulation.* Sheila Faria Glaser (trans.). Ann Arbor: University of Michigan Press. 1994.
Germain, David. "Action Hero but No Archaeologist." *Los Angeles Times*, May 23, 2008. https://www.latimes.com/archives/la-xpm-2008-may-23-et-indiana23-story.html.
Holtorf, Cornelius. *From Stonehenge to Las Vegas: Archaeology as Popular Culture.* Walnut Creek: AltaMira Press, 2005.
Lewis, Nathaniel. *Unsettling the Literary West: Authenticity and Authorship.* Lincoln: University of Nebraska Press, 2003.
MacCannell, Dean. *The Tourist: A New Theory of the Leisure Class.* Berkeley: University of California Press, 1999.
Potter, Andrew. *The Authenticity Hoax: How We Get Lost Finding Ourselves*, Melbourne: Scribe, 2010.
Umland, Rebecca A., and Samuel J. Umland. *The Use of Arthurian Legend in Hollywood Film: From Connecticut Yankees to Fisher Kings.* Westport: Greenwood Press. 1996.
Žižek, Slavoj. *Welcome to the Desert of the Real: Five Essays on September 11 and Related Dates.* London: Verso, 2002.

"I came to find my father"
Indiana Jones and the Quest for the Lost Father
LINDA WIGHT

Numerous commentators have observed the pervasive concern with father-son relationships in the films of Steven Spielberg. Lester D. Friedman writes, "No matter the genre, father figures—good and bad, dependable and unreliable, genetic and assumed—pervade Spielberg's movies" (95). Spielberg has been particularly noted for his repeated depiction of "psychologically and emotionally lost boys" and "missing, consumed, distant, or malevolent father figures" (34), a pattern often attributed to Spielberg's own well-publicized troubled relationship with his emotionally distant father (34). Father-son relationships are a feature of each of the Indiana Jones films, though it is in the third and fourth installments that the quest for father-son reconciliation takes thematic primacy. In *Raiders of the Lost Ark*, Indy's seduction of the teenage Marion is framed as a betrayal of her father, Abner, who loved Indy "like a son," while *Indiana Jones and the Temple of Doom* positions Indy as surrogate father to eleven-year-old Short Round and the Indian children whom he frees from a Thuggee cult. The later films expand on these concerns. *Indiana Jones and the Last Crusade* explores the adolescent rebellion implied by Indy's betrayal of Abner in *Raiders*, attributing Indy's immaturity and search for surrogate father figures to the emotional neglect of his biological father, Henry Jones. *Last Crusade* emphasizes that a positive father-son relationship is crucial to both father and son's achievement of a mature, well-rounded masculine identity. Thus, the quest for the Holy Grail becomes inextricably bound up with, and indeed secondary to, the quest for father-son reconciliation. *Indiana Jones and the Kingdom of the Crystal Skull* again positions father-son reconciliation as crucial in the quest for a secure and respected masculine identity. Building upon his role as surrogate father in *Temple of Doom*, Indy discovers he has a biological son, "Mutt," with Marion, and his assumption of the paternal role, in which he inducts Mutt into manhood, reaffirms Indy's value and relevance to stave off fears of the obsolescence of the aging action hero.

The emphasis on father-son conflict and reconciliation reflects not only Spielberg's interests, but also a broader Hollywood concern with absent fathers and troubled sons. Stella Bruzzi observes that the "'fragile' father-son relationship ... has been how Hollywood ... has so frequently 'worked through' its anxieties about masculinity and masculine genealogy in general" (158). From the 1980s, a masculinity crisis narrative has circulated in popular culture, emphasizing the son's need for his father to induct him into a manhood. In *Iron John* (1990), Robert Bly attributed the perceived feminization of society largely to the absence of the father; his ideas were popularized within the men's movement and the ongoing resonance of these ideas at the end of the twentieth century was evident in films like David Fincher's *Fight Club* (1999). The belief that masculinity is "something which needs to be passed from man to man, from father to son" (Coward 155), has fueled what Robin Wood labels the "Restoration of the Father" (172). Wood argued in 1986 that this had become the "dominant project ... of contemporary Hollywood cinema" (172), and it has remained a thematic concern in subsequent decades. Despite the nineteen-year gap in the distribution dates of *Last Crusade* and *Crystal Skull*, both films explore the impact of the father's absence on the son's ability to achieve adult masculinity, and they emphasize father-son reconciliation as crucial to working through the masculine anxieties and inadequacies of both father and son.

In *Last Crusade*, Indy must reconcile with his father in order to achieve a mature masculine identity. The film's opening scene provides an insight into the fractured father-son relationship that has left Indy trapped in a perpetual adolescence. After escaping a gang of grave robbers, thirteen-year-old Indy bursts into Henry's study, eager to show his father the Cross of Coronado that he has recovered from the robbers. Henry, however, fixated on his own work, remains seated with his back to Indy, and treats his son like an impatient child by insisting he count to twenty in Greek. Andrew M. Gordon notes that Henry's face is hidden in this scene, "suggesting his emotional absence from his son" (140). The adolescent Indy thus seeks an alternative paternal role model in the leader of the grave robbers. "Fedora" provides Indy with the praise and encouragement he desperately needs at this formative period of transition from boyhood to adulthood. Although Indy is forced to hand the Cross back, Fedora tells him, "You lost today kid. But it doesn't mean you have to like it," placing his hat on Indy's head in a gesture suggesting the anointing of a protégé. A cut to a scene twenty-six years later reveals an adult Indy still wearing Fedora's hat and a leather jacket almost identical to the one worn by the grave robber. Indy is engaged in taking back from Fedora's employer the Cross he was forced to relinquish so many years ago, suggesting his lasting determination to prove himself worthy of the confidence Fedora expressed in him.

The significance he has placed on this childhood encounter with Fedora, and his own father's emotional absence from his life, means that Indy's adult identity is insecure and incomplete, shifting between two ideals: the leather jacket-clad adventurer, modeled on Fedora, and the bow-tie wearing professor, resembling Henry. Indy resents his father; his adoption of the name "Indiana" (the name of the family dog who showed the young Indy more affection than his own father) constitutes a rejection of the name and role of Henry Jones II—"Junior"—to which his father sought to consign him and in which role, Henry's use of the infantilizing nomenclature implied, Indy would always be lacking. Nonetheless, Indy-as-professor still seeks to emulate his father, perhaps hoping that a successful performance in this role will earn him the paternal approval he craves (Gordon 142; Bruzzi 135–36). Split between these "dual persona[e]," however, "both sides of his personality remain in a type of arrested development" (Catron 67). Indy often resembles a rebellious adolescent, on the one hand disparaging his father and embracing an adventurer identity seemingly opposed to Henry's intellectual persona, while on the other hand remaining fixated on proving himself a better man—braver, smarter, and more physically capable.

Indy's determination to prove his superiority to the father who refuses to acknowledge his worth is emphasized as he begins his quest to find Henry, who has vanished while searching for the Holy Grail. Indy dismisses his father's lifelong intellectual and spiritual pursuit as a "hobby" and the Grail legend as a "bedtime story," contrasting his father's credulity with his own scientific objectivity and exposing his resentment for the legend which displaced him from his father's circle of priorities. Labeling Henry "a book worm" and "old fool," Indy insists Henry is "in over his head." Just as Henry's use of "Junior" suggests Indy is yet to attain a competent adult identity, Indy's references to Henry's age imply his father's inability to cope with the kind of dangerous situations around which Indy has constructed his own adventurer persona. Indy thus reacts defensively to observations of similarities between him and his father (Gordon 142). When Henry's Austrian colleague, Elsa Schneider, observes, "You're a great deal like your father," Indy demurs, "Except he's lost and I'm not." Later, when he and Elsa discover the map to the location of the Grail on a knight's shield hidden beneath a Venice library, he gloats that his father "would never have made it past the rats. He hates rats. He's scared to death of 'em." Ignoring his own fear of snakes, Indy belittles his father in an effort to lessen the pain of his neglect.

Indy's conflicting impulses between rebellion and a desire for paternal approval are evident when the two are reunited in the castle where Henry is

Father-son conflict between Professor Henry Jones (Sean Connery, left) and Indy (Harrison Ford) in *Last Crusade* (1989).

being held captive. Despite his earlier disparagement of his father, Indy responds to Henry's astonished "Junior?" by snapping to attention: "Yes, sir!" However, when Henry berates Indy for bringing his Grail diary back within the Nazis' grasp, Indy reacts with murderous rage. Prohibited from taking his anger out on his father, Indy cries, "I told you! ... Don't call me Junior!" as he turns his machine gun on the Nazis. Indy and Henry escape, but their conflict escalates again when they stop at a crossroads—literal and metaphorical. Indy insists they head straight for Hatay to save Marcus Brody, Henry's friend and another of Indy's surrogate father figures, from the Nazis who have captured him. Henry, however, argues they must go to Berlin to retrieve his Grail diary: "The only thing that matters is the Grail." Frustrated by his father's willingness to sacrifice the people he is supposed to love for the sake of his spiritual quest, Indy swears, "Jesus Christ!" and is shocked when Henry slaps him for blaspheming. This scene emphasizes the disparity of their core values: Henry does not appreciate Indy's emotional needs, while Indy lacks Henry's spiritual faith.

Nonetheless, the quest for the Grail provides the opportunity for Indy and Henry to each come to an appreciation of the qualities and values of the other man which he himself lacks. Henry, perhaps unwittingly, initiates their reconciliation when he sends his Grail diary to Indy, entrusting his son with his life's work. Indy recognizes the significance of the gesture—"This is his whole life," Indy remarks—though he is confused as to how Henry's trust correlates with his apparent lifelong disappointment in his son. Friedman notes that in following the clues in his father's diary, Indy "literally follows in his father's footsteps" (78), eventually coming to an appreciation of his father's spiritual faith and developing this quality in himself. Thus, the quest for the Grail, which Marcus describes as "the search for the divine in all of us," is inextricably linked with Indy's quest to reconnect with his father and, through him, with his own spiritual faith, which his resentment of his father's Grail obsession has prevented from developing.

Yet their reconciliation also requires Henry to come to an appreciation of Indy's qualities as a man and to embrace the emotional connection with his son from which his intellectual and spiritual pursuits have distracted him. When Indy throws a pursuing Nazi from the zeppelin on which father and son seek to flee Germany, Henry reacts with surprised admiration. Immersed in his newspaper, Henry was oblivious to the Nazis' approach. Henry has spent his life immersed in the close study of written texts, which has left him blind to what is occurring in the physical world around him, including his son's repeated entreaties for love and attention. In this scene, the obsessive intellectual starts to realize the limitations of his own perceptions and appreciate his son's ability not only to recognize danger, but also react with quick-thinking ingenuity. Significantly, after they are forced to flee the zeppelin and from pursuing Luftwaffe fighters in a biplane, Indy comes to realize that despite his father's immersion in the life of the intellect, he possesses similar qualities. At first, Henry seems to confirm Indy's habitual treatment of his father as an inept old man by inadvertently shooting the tail off their plane. Once stranded on the beach, however, Henry's quick-thinking invention saves them as, drawing on his knowledge of Charlemagne, "Let my armies be the rocks, and the trees, and the birds in the sky,"[1] he uses his umbrella to frighten the seabirds into the path of the oncoming fighter. Indy's gun is empty in this scene and Catron argues that Henry's ability to defeat the Nazi plane emasculates his son (90). The look Indy casts his father, however, is one of dawning appreciation as he begins to recognize the qualities in Henry—innovation in dangerous situations, and the ability to apply intellectual knowledge of the past to overcome the challenges of the present—in which he himself takes pride.

However, father and son must move beyond an appreciation of the other's qualities and also demonstrate those qualities themselves in order to complete their quest for reconciliation and for each to achieve a more rounded masculine identity. As Friedman observes, "As the film progresses, each becomes more like the other" (98). For Henry, this means embracing the physical and emotional aspects of the masculine self which he has neglected in himself and undervalued in his son. As Henry, Sallah (Indy's longtime friend from *Raiders*), and Indy attempt to rescue Marcus from a Nazi convoy, Indy drops his gun into the tank where his father and Marcus are being held, his yell of "Dad!" an imperative to his father to demonstrate his capacity for physical heroism. Henry rises to the challenge and seizes the gun. Although he incapacitates the Nazi soldier by squirting ink in his eye, he doesn't react to Marcus's quip, "The pen is mightier than the sword!" and instead grasps the tank's gun and shoots. Marcus's exclamation, "Look what you did!" echoes Henry's earlier stunned reaction to Indy's violent dispatch of the Nazi soldiers, but Henry now declares, "This is war!" emphasizing a significant shift in his perceptions and abilities that bring him closer to Indy's adventurer persona.

Even more significant is Henry's emotional epiphany when a tank plunges over the edge of a cliff, apparently carrying Indy to his death. Henry finally articulates how much Indy means to him: "Oh God, I've lost him. And I never told him anything. I just wasn't ready Marcus. Five minutes would have been enough." His regret and sorrow stand in stark contrast to the incomprehension he earlier expressed in response to Indy's attempt to establish an emotional connection. On the zeppelin, Indy had tried to convey the void his father's emotional absence had left in his life: "What you taught me was that I was less important to you than people who had been dead for five hundred years in another country. And I learned it so well that we've hardly spoken for twenty years." Disconnected from his own emotions, Henry asks Indy what he now wants to talk about as if indulging a child's immature request. And, when Indy admits ruefully that he cannot think of anything, Henry cheerfully shifts his attention back to his diary, oblivious to the fact that Indy is not just pleading for an exchange of words, but for an emotional connection. Indy's apparent death, however, shocks Henry into a realization of the depth of his love for his son. Thus, when he realizes Indy is standing beside him, Henry seizes him in a joyful hug, "I thought I'd lost you, boy!" Friedman notes that this is "the first genuine sign of affection between the two men in the movie" (98), and the significance of this moment is confirmed as Indy relaxes into the paternal embrace he has craved his entire life.

Just as a threat to Indy's life was needed to shock Henry into acknowledging his paternal emotions, Indy only achieves spiritual illumination after Donovan (the Nazi collaborator who seeks the Grail for himself) shoots Henry to force Indy to retrieve the Grail. Guided by Henry's Grail diary, Indy must negotiate three tests; only by following his father's intellectual and spiritual example is he able to succeed, not only in attaining the Grail, but also in developing the spiritual qualities that he previously lacked, thus completing his quest for reconciliation with the father for whom spiritual faith is the cornerstone of his identity. To pass the first test, Indy learns that a man must be humble before God; not only must he acknowledge the limitations of his own scientific method, but he must also relinquish the pride that has engaged him in a game of one-upmanship with his father his entire adult life. To pass the second test, Indy must follow in the footsteps of God (choosing the stepping stones that spell the name of Jehovah); the crosscuts between Indy and Henry emphasize that Indy must also follow in the footsteps of his earthly father if he is to fulfill his quest. The final test demands that Indy completely relinquish his spiritual skepticism by taking a leap of faith, stepping into a seemingly empty chasm. With this step, he accepts the spiritual into his life, demonstrating his faith both in God, as well as in his own father, whose diary and own spiritual faith he trusted to guide him safely to the Grail.

Thus, Indy achieves spiritual illumination and is rewarded with the Grail, which he uses to save his father's life. Moments later, Henry returns the favor in a scene that emphasizes his own emotional illumination. As the cavern collapses around them, Indy hangs from the edge of a crevice, desperately reaching for the Grail. Henry, however, has realized that his son is more important to him than the Grail and pleads, "Indiana, Indiana, let it go." This is the first time he has used Indy's preferred name, emphasizing his newfound respect for his son. Father and son grasp hands in a symbolic gesture of reconciliation as the Grail slips away beneath them, bound together by a relationship now marked by respect, spiritual connection, and love. For Indy, this marks a significant movement towards a mature masculine identity. No longer tormented by insecurity and anger, Indy has completed his quest to earn his father's love and respect. Moreover, just as Indy has achieved a more rounded masculine identity by following his father's spiritual and intellectual example, Henry has also proven his own masculine worth by emulating his son. Through his newfound emotional connection with Indy, Henry rehabilitates his paternal credentials and, by demonstrating his capacity for physical heroism, wards off the emasculating threat of advancing age.

The thematic concern with age becomes even more pronounced in *Crystal Skull*. Nineteen years older, Indy's adventurer identity is now under pressure. In the film's opening scene, he acknowledges that the physical heroics that have been a central component of his identity are becoming more difficult. Moreover, the deaths of both Henry and Marcus have heightened Indy's awareness of his own aging and mortality. As his friend Charlie observes, "We seem to have reached the age when life stops giving us things and starts taking them away." However, Indy is soon "given" a son by Marion, his love interest from *Raiders*, who reveals she was pregnant when Indy left her. Now nineteen, "Mutt" Williams provides Indy with the opportunity to secure a paternal masculine identity by inducting his son into manhood. As in the previous film, *Crystal Skull* suggests that a boy needs his father's example and guidance in order to achieve a mature masculine identity. Thus, the film follows Mutt's development from an immature adolescent to a competent young man who has proven himself worthy of his father's respect. Significantly, however, although Mutt demonstrates that he is capable of the physical heroics that have defined his father, his knowledge and abilities remain secondary to Indy's; thus, *Crystal Skull* disavows anxieties that age will result in a loss of capability or status for men.

The return of the older Indiana Jones in *Crystal Skull* reflects a broader Hollywood interest in the aging action hero. Philippa Gates observes that, since the 1990s, prominent 1980s action stars including Sylvester Stallone, Bruce Willis, and Harrison Ford returned in late installments of the franchises which made them famous, reviving their most famous characters—Rocky and Rambo, John McClane and Indiana Jones (277). These films "explore the problems that arise when the will is strong but the flesh not so" (277), in particular the concern that men who previously epitomized a physical ideal of masculinity will now be "undervalued because of their age" (278). In the opening scene of *Crystal Skull*, Indy's escape from his Russian captors reveals that physical heroics are becoming more difficult. Gates notes that as he attempts "a difficult maneuver, he misses, crashing through the windshield of the jeep behind" (285) muttering, "Damn! I thought that was closer." In the eyes of young men like Mutt, Indy's age becomes his defining characteristic, as emphasized by Mutt's repeated use of "old man" as his term of address.[2]

Indy's discovery that Mutt is his son, however, allows him to forge a paternal masculine identity, taking another step in his quest for mature manhood by himself taking on the role of the responsible father, as prefigured by his performance as surrogate father in *Temple of Doom*. *Crystal Skull* reflects a broader Hollywood interest in exploring the mature paternal incarnations of 1980s action stars: "Stallone, Willis, and Ford's heroes focus their emotional efforts ... on shoring up damaged relationships with their own children ... and/or forming bonds with new young people as substitute children" (Gates 278). Hannah Hamad argues that "for many male stars, the discursive addendum of fatherhood to their masculinities serves to positively inflect an otherwise abject aging process" (70). In her discussion of films including *Rocky Balboa* (2006), *Live Free or Die Hard* (2007), and *Crystal Skull*, she contends that these films rejuvenate the stars' masculine identities by recasting their age "as a boon to their masculine selfhood" (75). In *Crystal Skull*, for instance, the focus shifts from concern about the physical limitations that may negatively impact the aging Indy, to his potential to forge a respected paternal identity by positively contributing to his son's development as a man.

Catron argues that despite his maturation in *Last Crusade*, Indy has largely been portrayed as an immature figure. His abandonment of Marion prior to their wedding suggests "a fear of domestication" (117) and the responsibilities of family that might have undermined his freedom. Almost immediately upon discovering Mutt's identity, however, Indy embraces responsibility for guiding his son towards manhood. Where previously he was sympathetic to Mutt's aversion to school, Indy now demands of Marion, "Why the hell didn't you make him finish school?" Predictably, Mutt is resistant to Indy's judgment and expectations: "Don't call me son!" Like Indy in *Last Crusade*, Mutt resents the father who unwittingly abandoned him. His sense of self is also shaken by the realization that his father is "some schoolteacher" rather than "an RAF pilot, a war hero," as he previously believed. Like Indy, he has sought to define his own identity, signified by his adopted name and anti-establishment "greaser" costume of leather jacket and slicked-back hair. Thus, he resists the role of "Henry Jones III" by dismissing Indy as an old man and schoolteacher, just as Indy sought to dismiss his own father nineteen years earlier.

In order to effect a reconciliation, then, Indy must prove himself a worthy role model. In particular, Indy must demonstrate that despite his age he can still embody the physical hero. Gates observes that, once again, this "fantasy of heroic masculinity" (288) is a common pattern in Hollywood films featuring aging 1980s action stars. Citing the tagline of *Red* (2010)—"Still Armed. Still Dangerous.... Still Got It," she writes: "Although our returning action heroes and stars struggle with their age, significantly they all prove their ability to perform physical heroism to defeat the enemy" (288). Indy's ongoing capacity for physical heroism is asserted from the first scene of the film, in which Indy is introduced via a shot of his fedora, the iconic marker of his adventurer identity. In this case, Indy has apparently had his hat (and by implication his masculinity) stripped away, as a Russian soldier tosses it carelessly to the ground beside the car in which Indy and his friend Mac are being held. Over a dozen Russian soldiers, however, immediately raise their guns towards the fedora and Indy as he stumbles from the trunk, emphasizing their recognition of his dangerous potential. Older he may be, but despite the occasional mishap, Indy still manages to escape single-handed from an entire armed Russian military troop, using only his whip and fists, performing physical feats that include leaping from beam to beam and swinging from lights and metal chains. Later, Indy again flees the Russians, this time on the back of a motorcycle ridden by Mutt. Catron observes that Indy is relegated to the "backseat, now occupying the sidekick position of his father in *Last Crusade*" (105). Where Henry sat passively gripping his satchel and umbrella, however, when Indy is pulled from the motorcycle, he escapes by hitting his captors before climbing through the window of their car and back onto the bike. Mutt is mildly impressed, but his reaction shifts to stunned amazement at the cemetery where Indy blows a poison dart back up a blowpipe into the mouth of their attacker, saving Mutt's life.

Indy's heroic competence is contrasted in this scene with Mutt's inexperience and fear, which expose his tough-guy act as a façade. Mutt's hands shake as he follows Indy into the underground tomb, and he panics when scorpions crawl over him, recalling Willie's reaction to the bugs in *Temple of Doom*. Throughout this scene, Mutt follows passively behind Indy, his only contribution an observation that two sets of footprints could have been made by the same person returning. Mutt smiles in response to Indy's praise—"Not bad, kid"—signaling his desire to earn the respect of the older man, although, at this point, he remains unaware of their familial relationship. In order to earn Indy's respect, and to progress from adolescent posturing to a competent adult masculine identity, Mutt must prove that his tough-guy persona is more than a superficial façade by successfully performing the physical heroics modeled by his father. Later, in the Amazonian jungle, as Indy, Marion, and Mutt attempt once again to escape the Russians, this time with Mutt's surrogate father, Ox, and the alien Crystal Skull, which the Russians hope to use as a weapon of mind control, Indy responds to Mutt's adolescent complaints by telling him, "Don't be a child. Find something to fight with!" Mutt rises to the challenge, using a sword to seize the skull from the Russian leader, Colonel Irina Spalko and engaging her in a swordfight from the top of the moving vehicles. The significance of this scene as a test of Mutt's masculinity is emphasized both by Spalko's taunt, "You fight like a young man. Eager to begin, quick to finish," and the plants that hit Mutt in the crotch as he straddles the two vehicles. Spalko comes close to defeating Mutt, but when he is flung onto the hood of the jeep driven by Indy, he responds to his father's evaluative gaze with a retort—"What are you looking at Daddy-o?"—before flinging himself back into the action. The struggle continues until Mutt is caught by a vine and hoisted into the treetops where he comes face-to-face with a colony of monkeys. The implication that Spalko has made a monkey of him is quickly effaced when Mutt demonstrates the same quick-thinking innovation, agility, and physical skill that epitomize his father, swinging from vine to vine through the trees and leading the monkeys in a renewed assault on Spalko's vehicle, which, significantly, was about to push Indy's car over the edge of the cliff.

Mutt's physical heroics earn his father's respect and position him as Indy's successor. Hamad argues that in such scenes Mutt is "heavy-handedly primed to assume his father's mantle" (82). However, the film's "labored refusal to cast Jones's aging masculinity in terms of obsolescence" (82) demands that Indy retain his superiority. The film closes with Indy's marriage to Marion, affirming his ascension to a responsible, mature, paternal masculine identity. Mutt, as best man, smiles his approval, indicating that Indy has overcome Mutt's resentment to earn the respect of his son. However, Hollywood's fantasy of a heroic masculinity undaunted by time, as well as Spielberg's own well-documented investment in Peter Pan heroes (Catron 124), means that Indy cannot relinquish his adventurer mantle to his son. Thus, as Mutt stoops to pick up his father's fedora from the floor of the chapel, Indy swipes it from his hand and places it on his own head as the familiar Indiana Jones theme plays, reinforcing Indy's continued status as action hero.

In both *Last Crusade* and *Crystal Skull*, father-son reconciliation is crucial in enabling both men to achieve a mature, secure masculine identity. For the sons, reconciliation with the father allows them to move beyond immature resentment, rebellion, and posturing, following the paternal example to complete their quest for a competent adult masculine identity. For the fathers, reconciliation with the son affirms their achievement of a responsible, caring paternal identity. In both films, the father earns the respect of his son and plays a crucial role in inducting the younger man into manhood. Thus, Henry and Indy respond to cultural concerns about the perceived obsolescence of older men, not only by demonstrating their paternal capability, but also by performing physical heroics that maintain a fantasy of heroic masculinity untroubled by the passage of time. Increasingly, however, the masculine fantasy promoted by the series is coming under pressure from speculation surrounding the promised fifth installment, which has largely focused on Ford's age (he will be seventy-eight in 2021 when the film is due for release) and the possibility that he will be replaced by a younger actor in future films (Miller; Jones). Ford himself is now a grandfather, and whether the fifth film will be forced by the passage of time to explore a masculine succession (perhaps by a biological or surrogate grandson) that would relegate Indy to the margins remains to be seen.

Notes

1. This quote has been misattributed to Charlemagne and was most likely invented by the scriptwriters of *Last Crusade* to emphasize Henry's historical knowledge.
2. This term attains a new significance when Mutt discovers that Indy is his father.

Works Cited

Bly, Robert. *Iron John: A Book about Men*. Shaftesbury: Element Books, 1990. Print.
Bruzzi, Stella. *Bringing Up Daddy: Fatherhood and Masculinity in Post-War Hollywood*. London: British Film Institute, 2005. Print.
Catron, Evan. "Indiana Jones and the Displaced Daddy: Spielberg's Quest for the Good Father, Adulthood, and God." Master's thesis. University of Central Oklahoma, 2010. *ProQuest Dissertations Publishing*. Web. 24 Apr. 2019.
Coward, Rosalind. *Sacred Cows: Is Feminism Relevant to the New Millennium?* London: HarperCollins, 1999. Print.
Friedman, Lester D. *Citizen Spielberg*. Urbana: University of Illinois Press, 2006. Print.
Gates, Philippa. "Acting His Age? The Resurrection of the 80s Action Heroes and Their Aging Stars." *Quarterly Review of Film and Video* 27.4 (2010): 276–89. Taylor and Francis. Web. 15 Mar. 2019.
Gordon, Andrew M. *Empire of Dreams: The Science Fiction and Fantasy Films of Steven Spielberg*. Lanham, MD: Rowman & Littlefield, 2008. Print.
Hamad, Hannah. *Postfeminism and Paternity in Contemporary U.S. Film*. London: Routledge, 2014. Print.

Jones, Damien. "Harrison Ford: 'No-One Will Replace Me as Indiana Jones When I Give Up.'" *NME*, 27 May 2019. Web. 31 May 2019.
Miller, Matt. "Harrison Ford Doesn't Want Chris Pine, or Pratt, or Anyone to Play Indiana Jones." *Esquire*, 28 May 2019. Web. 31 May 2019.
Wood, Robin. *Hollywood from Vietnam to Reagan*. New York: Columbia University Press, 1986. Print.

Indiana Jones as Educated Swashbuckler

JENNIFER CRUMLEY

On the day Donald Trump was inaugurated as president of the United States, white supremacist and alleged neo–Nazi Richard Spencer was punched in the face by a man in a mask while being interviewed by the Australian Broadcasting Company, whose cameras captured the entire event. In the film, Spencer is responding to questions from both interviewers and protestors when an African American woman asks him if he's a neo–Nazi, which Spencer denies. The interviewer takes up the charge and asks, "Why do you think neo–Nazis love you?" Spencer replies that they actually hate him, and as he begins to explain the meaning of his lapel pin ("Pepe" the frog), a man in a mask jolts in from the side and punches Spencer in the face. The video instantly went viral, with some people cheering for the man in the mask, while others began to be concerned with what appeared to be but one more example of an apparent increase in open violence. Memes sprang up comparing the punch to a scene from one of the original *Captain America* comics, eventually morphing into memes featuring Indiana Jones on top of a tank, arm cocked back ready to strike the enemy—a Nazi—with captions such as "I came here to study the humanities and punch Nazis, and they just cut funding for the humanities." The debate about whether or not it is appropriate to punch Nazis (even though Spencer denies any association with the neo–Nazis of today) led interdisciplinary researcher Samuel Merrill to pen an article about the punching of Richard Spencer, asking the question, "What Would Indiana Jones do?"

Merrill writes that "[t]he choice of Indiana Jones was not coincidental. In fact, it tapped into the growing symbolic value of the film franchise to many of those who resist the world's political slide to the extreme right" (Merrill). Merrill believes that though the Indiana Jones franchise has up to this point been largely ignored in terms of its association with American patriotism, the memes featuring Indy following closely on the heels of those featuring the overwhelmingly patriotic figure of Captain America have sparked a new topic of discussion around the Spielberg films. Merrill writes that the dichotomization of Indiana Jones too easily overlooks some of the more troubling aspects of the franchise, specifically "neo-colonialism and sexism" as two of the main issues (Merrill). And while Merrill lands on the same side of the violence argument as the series' own museum curator Marcus Brody ("the pen is mightier than the sword"), implying that, by allowing for the violence against Nazis, we may also be contributing to a resurgence in anti-intellectualism, I argue that part of the reason Indiana Jones became so quickly associated with the latest wave of Nazi-punching and leftist resistance to fascism is because he represents the Platonic American Hero for the World War II/Cold War era: the educated swashbuckler. It is difficult to argue that a professor of archaeology, whose character has possibly brought more people to the field than a love of ancient artifacts, could contribute to anti-intellectualism. There is a level of depth in the characterization of Indiana Jones that needs to be studied as passionately as Henry Jones, Sr., researched the Holy Grail. Spielberg was able to tap into the ideas and symbols of American patriotism and American ideas of the heroic across several decades, while also drawing from the foundation of the heroic narrative, creating a character who bridges all variations of the very concept of the heroic, thus ensuring the character would continue to be relatable across generations. Indiana's future is largely safeguarded by the simple fact that none of the artifacts he seeks ever ends up in a museum as he desires. These objects are not just plot devices, but they serve to actually further his character development as he has to face his fears, fight for the survival of himself and others, and ultimately watch the physical manifestation of his motivation be locked away in a vault, returned to its rightful owner, or fall into a chasm never to be seen again. The lost artifacts of the Indiana Jones universe are actually a fundamental element of the Indiana Jones mythos: as iconic as his fedora, bullwhip, and gasmask bag. French scholar René Girard wrote that "the ultimate meaning of desire is death," and for Indiana, the same holds true, for if he were ever to actually obtain his wish of seeing one of his artifacts laid to rest behind glass in a museum, it would mean his undoing (Girard 290).

 Professor of literature and author of *The Hero with a Thousand Faces*, Joseph Campbell, laid the foundation for the heroic journey. The journey of the hero from the known world to the unknown and back again is broken into three phases: the departure, the initiation, and the return. During the departure phase, the hero answers a call to adventure, is given supernatural aid to assist on his quest, and upon crossing the threshold into the unknown, meets with threshold guardians and discovers mentors or helpers before having to face an opening trial. In the initiation phase, the hero enters into the unknown world and faces additional challenges and temptations before reaching the ultimate boon (achievement of quest). As the hero attempts to return to the known world, he passes through transformation, on to atonement, and then finally crosses the threshold with the gift of mastering two worlds. The hero's journey is easily overlaid onto the plots of each film in the Indiana Jones franchise, but the important difference is that the ultimate boon, while always obtained by Indiana, never fulfills his personal desire of seeing it come to rest in a museum. In *Raiders of the Lost Ark*, Indiana seeks the Ark of the Covenant only to have it locked in a vault in an army base. *Temple of Doom* sees Indiana fighting Thuggees in order to obtain the "fortune and glory" rewarded by the Sankara Stones, but ultimately he returns them to the village from which they were stolen. *The Last Crusade* follows Indiana and his father on a classic quest for the Holy Grail, and he learns almost too late that the Grail can never cross the threshold of the grail cave without causing certain destruction. In the last installation, *Kingdom of the Crystal Skull*, Indiana is forced by Soviets to locate the Crystal Skull of Akator, inadvertently activating an ancient interdimensional craft. Why is it that Indiana is always denied his desire for the object of his quests? Let us first understand better the purpose of desire as a motivator for heroes in literature and apply those motivations to the character of Indiana Jones.

In his 1961 work *Deceit, Desire and the Novel*, René Girard discusses the meaning of desire in the novel and marries classic works of literature to contemporary themes of psychology, propaganda, and advertising. Even though Girard is discussing such works as *Don Quixote* and *Madame Bovary*, the principles of his arguments are applicable to the Indiana Jones franchise. Girard describes one model of desire as the mediator model—meaning that the object of desire is chosen for the hero, and not something the hero decides upon for himself (Girard 2). Girard goes on to say that "[o]nly someone who prevents us from satisfying a desire which he himself has inspired in us is truly an object of hatred.... Now the mediator is a shrewd and diabolical enemy; he tries to rob the subject of his most prized possessions" (10–11). Adding another layer to the mediator of desire model and pairing it with Campbell's heroic departure phase, we begin to see how Indiana's quests blend Girard's model with Campbell's heroic arc. The hero is called to an adventure and the object of desire is chosen for him by a mediator, who later becomes a clear enemy of the hero by interfering with the hero's attempts to obtain the object of desire that the mediator has named on the hero's behalf. The mediator therefore becomes a part of the trials the hero must work through in order to reach the ultimate prize. This formula is the backbone of three of the four films in the Indiana Jones franchise, with *Temple of Doom* being the only exception, though *Temple* fits in more succinctly with the classical heroic story arc than the other three films. The major contrast between the plots in the Indiana Jones franchise and the epic tales and myths which relay the heroic stories of old is that Spielberg decided to end each film without the closure of the arc typical of epics and mythology—namely, the hero bringing back new knowledge or an important artifact to the culture from whence he hails. For Indiana Jones, this closure would take place in the form of the object he seeks coming to rest in the museums which are curated by Dr. Marcus Brody, thereby bestowing knowledge upon future visitors of the museum. Literature professor and poet Frederick Turner writes in his 2012 monograph *Epic: Form, Content, and History* that the epic journey always has "satisfying dénouements.... Either the hero dies, or he returns alive, bearing the fitting gift for his culture and homeland. In either case, there is closure" (Turner 119). By denying Indiana Jones closure in the form of the artifacts coming to rest in a museum, Spielberg not only allows for the possibility of another film in the franchise, but he also actively creates a character who is continuous and evolving, and this evolution can be seen in small self-referential moments throughout the films.

One of the most poignant examples of the self-referential evolution of Indiana Jones serves not only to remind the audience that he is a professor of archaeology, but also to build a bridge between *The Last Crusade* and *Kingdom of the Crystal Skull*. In *Crusade*, Dr. Jones gives a lecture to his class in which he emphasizes that "we do not follow maps to buried treasure, and X never, ever marks the spot." He goes on to say that "seventy percent of all archaeology is done in the library—research, reading; we cannot afford to take mythology at face value." It is important to note that Indiana is making these proclamations after finally capturing the Cross of Coronado from a lifelong rival, Panama Hat. As a young man, we see Indiana steal the Cross of Coronado from Fedora who was hired by Panama Hat to retrieve the cross. After having to relinquish it to his rival, we are brought to the film's present day, where we see Indiana attempting to take the cross back. After one of Panama Hat's goons restrains Indiana, Panama Hat says, "This is the second time I've had to reclaim my property from you," to which Indiana replies, "That belongs in a museum!" Panama Hat, foreshadowing a world wherein Indiana has been granted the closure of seeing one of the objects of his desire encased in glass, replies, "So do you." After no small amount of effort, Indiana does indeed get the Cross of Coronado back from Panama Hat, and we next see Indiana Jones as professor in the classroom delivering the lecture previously noted. It would seem as though Indiana has finally fulfilled his destiny, and Spielberg shows us, and Indiana, a glimpse of what fulfilled destiny might hold for the future: namely, a demanding student body and a cramped office for grading papers. As Indiana climbs out of the window to escape the student-body mob in his outer office, he is, as Turner describes, blazing a trail, which will move him once again from the world of the known to the unknown. Turner describes the blazing of a trail as it pertains to epic as a space "neither on one side of the line nor the other.... It is within the region of the previously unsayable, the unknown, the future, but within eyeshot of the blaze" (Turner 78). It is here, in this space between, only a few steps from the open window through which he crawled and made a blaze, that Dr. Jones, having completed his own lifelong quest and seen into his future of professorial captivity, is picked up by a car of strange men and called to his next adventure, which marries the past and future by tasking Indiana with finding his father, thereby completing his father's lifelong quest. Moving forward to *Kingdom of the Crystal Skull*, an older Dr. Jones is on the run with his son Mutt and ends up skidding through the library on the back of Mutt's motorcycle. As the motorcycle slides to a stop and Mutt and Indiana try and right themselves, a student asks Dr. Jones a question about a particular scholar, to which Indiana tells the student to read the work of a different archaeologist who spent more time in the field, closing with "[i]f you want to be a good archaeologist, you gotta get out of the library!" It is clear that the earlier blazing of a trail had an impact on Indiana, and he is bringing this lesson to his students. The attention paid to his lectures throughout the series (two of the films even reference the same homework assignment) serves to remind the viewer that Indiana is first and foremost a scholar. He may be an action hero, but he also holds the highest educational degree achievable, and this combination makes him not only unique, but also serves to align him with the societal ideals put forth by intellectuals of the Cold War period, further contributing to Indiana's cross-generational appeal.

 The Cold War era is only truly represented in *Kingdom of the Crystal Skull*, but the values which America was trying to instill in its citizens during those years were a carryover from World War II. Having seen the horrors of fascism, patriotism became second nature to most Americans. But the intellectuals of the Cold War period wanted to make sure the American public was more than just patriotic; they wanted individuals with open minds, who were able to think for themselves and make informed decisions. Intellectual historian Jamie Cohen-Cole writes about the efforts of Cold War–era intellectuals to craft the open-minded citizen in his 2014 monograph entitled *The Open Mind: Cold War Politics and the Sciences of Human Nature*. Cohen-Cole states that "Cold War intellectuals and policy makers saw in open-mindedness solutions to the most pressing problems faced by the nation.... Traditional or authoritarian societies could not be sustained in the presence of a citizen body that thought autonomously" (Cohen-Cole 2). The group of people responsible for crafting the open-minded citizen comprised intellectuals in the fields of cognitive and social science and were counted on the rosters of organizations such as the Ford Foundation, along with universities like Harvard and MIT. The open-minded citizen, in the eyes of these intellectuals, had three characteristics:

> First, this self had a political role in which it served as an exemplary model of citizenship, engaging with others to make America a free and democratic society. Second, this self participated in academic society, partaking of the intellectual and social life of the university community and displaying characteristics of a model researcher, scientist, or thinker. And third, the open mind served as a universal model of human nature ... it was a role model *for* the proper modes of democratic or academic thinking [Cohen-Cole 4].

The new open-minded citizen was crafted through curriculum changes from the primary and secondary educational levels to the interdisciplinary approach, which began to be applied in collegiate environments. The use of cognitive science was an undercurrent throughout the effort, and scientific curricula began to be more present in early education. Though the ultimate result of this attempt to create a more open-minded citizen backfired from a conservative standpoint, as it paved the way for marginalized groups to begin seeking out equal rights, the three basic principles were absorbed into Cold War society, and these features are clearly present in the character of Indiana Jones.

As a scholar of archaeology, Indiana Jones straddles an academic fence between the social sciences and the humanities, embodying the interdisciplinary approach which crafted the model citizen as a researcher and scientist. The evidence of Indiana's political role as it pertains to making America a free society is evident in *Kingdom of the Crystal Skull*. After being left to his death at a nuclear test site by Soviets, Indiana is being debriefed and having his patriotism questioned, like so many in the McCarthy era were. During the interrogation, General Ross enters the room and chastises the men questioning Indiana: "Not everyone in the army's a commie, and certainly not Indy.... Do you have any idea how many medals this son of a bitch has won?" By portraying Indiana as a decorated war hero, Spielberg taps into the American patriotism that resurfaced and was sustained after 9/11, seven years before *Crystal Skull* was released, but he also rekindles the Cold War–era patriotism for the generation that lived through the nuclear duck-and-cover drills of the film's time period. The last element in creating an open-minded citizenry, the "universal role model for human nature," is a theme that is carried through every film in the franchise and ties directly back to the objects which Indiana is always called upon to find: the Ark of the Covenant, the Sankara Stones, the Holy Grail, and the lost skull of Akator (Cohen-Cole 4). All of these objects are entangled with the symbology of a higher power. These symbols, according to Jungian psychologist Joseph L. Henderson, are actually "symbolic representations of the whole psyche.... Their special role suggests that the essential function of the heroic myth is the development of the individual's ego-consciousness—his awareness of his own strengths and weaknesses—in a manner that will equip him for the arduous tasks with which life confronts him" (Jung 101). Self-awareness is essential for the open-minded citizen and was in fact the goal of the cognitive scientists who set forth the criteria to craft the same such people who were capable of thinking critically. Taking a look at the films in the order of their release shows us how Indiana becomes more self-aware and adapts to his adventures as time presses on.

Raiders of the Lost Ark sets the stage for the tropes that become so prevalent throughout the series: the fedora, the bullwhip, the noir-style shadow shots of Indiana's profile, the reliably comical fear of snakes, and the quests for objects at the direction of others (the aforementioned mediator model of desire). Though the main plot of each film centers around an object sought for and lost, each film actually begins with action involving an object that Indiana also fails to hold onto. In each case, the introductory object ends up being lesser than the object of the main quest; said another way, one represents the profane, and one the sacred. For *Raiders*, the film opens with Indiana attempting to steal an idol from a temple in Peru. Though he is successful in obtaining the idol, it is stolen by a rival French archaeologist named Belloq. As Belloq takes the golden idol from Indiana, he says, "Dr. Jones, again we see there is nothing you can possess which I cannot take away," thus indicating this is not the first time Indiana and Belloq have crossed paths. Though Indiana is visibly upset as he relates this story of how the idol was stolen to museum curator Marcus Brody, the loss of the idol is quickly overshadowed by the arrival of Army intelligence officers who ask Indiana to find the Ark of the Covenant before the Nazis do. The Ark of the Covenant, a symbol of Christianity and the founding of the Ten Commandments, is a clearly sacred object, thus moving the golden idol of the film's opening quest to the role of the profane. The pairing of the Ark with the golden idol also invokes the stories of the idol-worshipping Israelites of the Old Testament, upon whose behalf Moses intervened. The Ten Commandments, which the Ark is said to house, were written in response to this idol worship. The Nazis are now set up as the competition to the object of the quest, and their desire for the object leads Indiana to be tasked with this call to adventure by the U.S. Army. The journey to obtain the ultimate reward begins, complete with virtual map for the viewer, as Indiana seeks out his supernatural aid (the Staff of Ra) to help get him through the first trial and across the threshold to the unknown. Indiana faces numerous obstacles on his quest, but is eventually successful, only to have Belloq once again appear to take the Ark. The underworld journey which is so prevalent in the classical heroic quest is represented by the power of the ark reaching its full potential. As Indiana and his "goddamn partner" Marion Ravenwood stand tied to a post, the Nazis, with Belloq at their helm, selfishly open the Ark to view the contents inside. Indiana advises Marion to shut her eyes so as not to be killed by the Ark's power. When the Ark finally calms, only Indiana and Marion remain, having passed through, back to the known world. Here we have the first instance of Indiana being denied his request that the object he seeks be laid to rest in Brody's museum. *Raiders* ends with Indiana and Brody angrily asking about the location of the Ark. The Army intelligence officers assure them it is "somewhere very safe," and the viewer learns it is being anonymously stored in a giant government warehouse. Having been denied the possession of both the profane artifact and the sacred, Indiana persists, and there is no closure, as there would be at the end of a typical heroic journey.

Though the action in *Temple of Doom* takes place prior to that of *Raiders*, the formula remains consistent, with only minor differences. Spielberg actively chose to avoid Nazi villains going forward, so instead the call to adventure happens in India. The film opens with Indiana at a night club in Shanghai as he attempts to trade the ashes of Nurhachi (a seventeenth-century emperor of the Manchu dynasty) for the Peacock's Eye—a one-hundred-forty-carat diamond that was once owned by Alexander the Great. After fighting with Lao and his gang, Indiana barely escapes with his life, but has the addition of a new companion, nightclub singer Willie Scott, and the new character of Short Round as his young sidekick. The three escape Shanghai on a plane flown by Lao's men, who force the plane to crash in India. Here, they are taken in by a village which has been plagued by a newly fortified Thuggee cult, who has stolen the Sankara Stones and the children of the village. The village leaders plead with Indiana to take on their plight, and Indiana, knowing the legend of the Sankara Stones, says that they bring "fortune and glory," and he takes up the call to adventure. Again, we have the set-up of the first object (Peacock's Eye) being a profane version of the primary object. Both are stones, and the Sankara Stones do contain diamonds within their rough outer exterior, but diamonds have only monetary value. The Sankara Stones are sacred and serve as the lifeblood of the village due solely to their existence in the space—the diamonds inside are not what make them sacred to the village. Indiana fights through Thuggees and once again journeys through the underworld to come back to the land of the known, returning both the Sankara Stones and the missing children to the village. When they arrive back from whence they began, Willie says to Indiana, "You could've kept it." To which Indiana replies, "What for? They'd just put it in a museum, and it'd be another rock collecting dust." Here is an interesting turn of events for Indiana. Realizing the value of the sacred stones, and having completed the quest, he returns to the known world with a greater understanding of the value of the stones for the villagers, as opposed to fortune and glory or monetary value they had the potential to bring to Indiana himself. Indiana's sacrifice is a perfect embodiment of the role model for the open-minded citizen mentioned above. Instead of returning to his own people with a sacred object from his quest for external recognition, he has grown internally as an individual, having evolved through the loss of personal financial gain. This theme of personal growth is carried forth through the next installment of the series.

The Last Crusade opens in the same manner as the first two films: Indiana attempts to hold on to an object and loses it, with the difference that this scene takes place in the past with a young Indiana Jones. Here we get some backstory about Indiana's origins: the fedora being passed down, the brief glimpse of the dog whom he named himself after, and the beginning of his fear of snakes. After the opening sequence in which Indiana loses the Cross of Coronado, the next scene, set in the contemporary timeline, shows an older Indiana finally fulfilling his lifelong quest. As previously discussed, however, this will never do. Indiana is tasked with finding his father, and thereby the Holy Grail. Once again, we have a sacred object overshadowing the initial quest of the profane. The Cross of Coronado being but an adornment and symbol of the crucifixion, it pales in comparison to the actual cup which Jesus drank from at the Last Supper and which is believed to bring eternal life. Indiana receives his father's Grail diary in the mail, and this serves as his supernatural guide to begin his adventure. One of the trials Indiana has to face is a fight with the Brotherhood of the Cruciform Sword, who are sworn to keep the Grail safe. Kazim asks Indiana why he seeks the Grail, and Indiana responds, "I came to find my father." In some ways, then, *The Last Crusade* differs in that the object is a person, but Indiana does get caught up in the hunt for the Grail itself as well, and once he obtains it, he learns that it can never pass the seal of the temple in which it is housed. Though Indiana is momentarily seized with blind desire for the Grail, the relationship and respect of his father, which is what he has truly been seeking his entire life, pulls him away from the power of the object. When Henry Jones, Sr., says calmly, "Indiana.... Indiana, let it go," he is not only acknowledging his son, but he is also letting go of his own obsession with the Grail—once again showing a character evolution that fits in line with the role of the symbology being used in the film by showing both Sr. and Jr. their own strengths and weaknesses. This character evolution is necessary to pass to the fourth film, wherein Indiana is faced with his own estranged son, Mutt.

The variation in *Kingdom of the Crystal Skull* on the pattern of the initial object being the profane is that both the profane and sacred object are one in the same, just in different stages of the quest. Indiana is kidnapped by Soviets and taken to a military base in Nevada to locate the body of an alien recovered from a crash site several years prior. Unknown to Indiana, the body contains a Crystal Skull which is of high importance to the Soviets due to the skull's ability to bestow boundless knowledge. After locating the body, Indiana escapes into the Nevada desert, only to be caught in a nuclear blast.

He is then sought out by Mutt, who asks for his help in finding his mother, "Mary," and Indiana's old friend Harold Oxley, who have also been kidnapped by Soviets. Much like in *Crusade*, Indiana is drawn to this quest initially to find people, not objects. But once the people are located, the object once again takes hold, and Indiana assists the Soviets in returning the Crystal Skull from the alien corpse back to Akator. The crystal skulls, once they are reunited, trigger the ignition of a long-dormant interdimensional craft, and Indiana, with his son, friend, and estranged lover Marion at his side, watches as the craft vanishes into another dimension. Relationships have been repaired, or in Mutt's case, established, but the object has once again escaped Indiana's hands.

If ever Indiana Jones actually sees a call to adventure through to the glass case of a museum, we will know for certain the curtains have closed on the character's arc. But the objects themselves are not the ultimate goal of Indiana's adventures; his ability to evolve as a person in response to his quests are what make the franchise so meaningful and memorable to audiences across generations. Indiana begins as a selfish man, seeking diamonds and fortune and glory (to follow the timeline of the films), but he learns that money is not the ultimate meaning of life. He seeks the Ark and instead of capturing it, rekindles a romance with a woman he thought was out of his life forever. He seeks his father, and finds not only the man, but the missing relationship. He ventures out for the safety of a woman he believes to be a stranger, and a man he hasn't spoken to in years, and returns with a wife and a son. As Professor Frederick Turner writes in his conclusion, "[a]s humans our deepest pleasures, thanks to our evolution ... are in just such transformations of ourselves," and this is the reason that Indiana Jones will continue to be kept alive through memes, forever punching Nazis.

Works Cited

Campbell, Joseph. *The Hero with a Thousand Faces*. Princeton University Press, 1973.
Cohen-Cole, Jamie. *The Open Mind: Cold War Politics and the Sciences of Human Nature*. University of Chicago Press, 2014.
Girard, René. *Deceit, Desire, and the Novel*. Johns Hopkins University Press, 1966.
Jung, Carl. *Man and His Symbols*. Dell Publishing, 1964.
Merrill, Samuel. "Punching Nazis: what would Indiana Jones do?" *The Conversation*, 19 May 2019, https://theconversation.com/punching-nazis-what-would-indiana-jones-do-71756.
Turner, Frederick. *Epic: Form, Content, and History*. Transaction Publishers, 2012.

"It belongs in a museum," or Does It?
Indiana Jones, Artifactology and the Afterlives of Objects

Kerry Dodd

The Indiana Jones franchise has fostered an instantly recognizable image of the archaeologist in popular media. With his trademark bullwhip, fedora hat, and rogue-like charm, Indiana Jones epitomizes the action adventurer who brought the wonder of "fortune and glory" to mainstream audiences, offering moviegoers a portal to exoticized lands and magical objects. Certainly, while such depictions are quite divorced from real-world applications of archaeology, the popularity and pervasiveness of such representations influence public perceptions of archaeological excavation. Authors such as Cornelius Holtorf in *Archaeology Is a Brand!* have highlighted the unique recognition that the field has garnered and argued that archaeology's popularity is something to embrace and utilize, rather than to dismiss on account of the factual inaccuracies that popular representations of archaeology often propagate. But it is not only the role of Indiana Jones within these tales that merits examination. The framing and representation of the movies' central artifacts also provide a crucial opportunity to appreciate cultural perceptions of materiality, non-human ontology, and notions of object "belonging." For while Indy may suggest in *Indiana Jones and the Last Crusade* that these relics "belong in a museum," poignantly, very few of Indy's sought-after objects actually end up there. The question of material ownership is undeniably steeped in a particularly colonial mode of appropriation. Beyond this political aspect of the films, however, the franchise also emblematizes a particular framing of the non-human world, one which deploys a host of subconscious visual framings to elicit a recognition from the audience of what constitutes an artifact. Thus, the film series offers a compelling occasion to reflect on how filmmakers and audiences perceive the non-human, and, ultimately, to examine the possibility of a more nuanced appreciation of the world of objects.

Such an endeavor necessitates an exploration of how an artifact is defined or indeed recognized—a process, which I term "artifactology," that will run throughout this essay. Michael Shanks and Mike Pearson in *Theatre/Archaeology* (2001) argue that artifacts are a fundamental resource for understanding human ontology and thus offer a framework of "interpretative archaeology" according to which, they contend, "society is inconceivable without artefacts" (90). Certainly, excavation often points toward the human *absent presences* that are projected to be "behind" materiality, a process that Bjørnar Olsen in *In Defense of Things* (2010) summarizes: "[t]hings were studied primarily as a means to reveal something else, something more important—the societies and cultures, women and men, *behind* the artefact" (25, original emphasis). Both identifications approach a "post-processualist" outlook where the artifact becomes a form of text, and where material signifiers are read to deduce the existence of the people that encountered, shaped, and utilized the item. Such a perspective, however, pays little attention to the materiality of the artifact itself or indeed how this very category has become instantly recognizable. For, as I will argue presently, it is through the subliminal visual framings perpetuated by archaeological media, which also align with the taxonomic schemas of the museum, that viewers have been trained to differentiate the singular artifact from the object collective.

If an artifact thus reflects upon the cultural perception of materiality, how do we approach a recognition of the non-human itself? Graham Harman in *Tool-Being—Heidegger and the Metaphysics of Objects* (2002) draws on Martin Heidegger's differentiation of "ready-to-hand" and "present-to-hand" in *Being and Time* (1927) as a process that "gives birth to an ontology of *objects themselves*" (1, original emphasis). Heidegger proposes that a frequently operated tool lapses into subconscious utilization by a subject as it is "ready-to-hand" until a change in its status forces an immediate recognition, causing it to become "present-at-hand." For example, a human subject only becomes consciously aware of engaging with a door-handle once it has broken. This dissonance arises through a shift in material labels, where the handle is other than we expect it to be. Harman's Object-Orientated Ontology seeks to understand the object, or non-human in-itself, proposing that "[t]he true chasm of ontology lies not between humans and the world, but between *objects and relations*" and "if this reserve cannot be *located* in any of these relations, then it must exist somewhere else" (2, 230, original emphasis). Harman's analysis identifies the entrapment that characterizes anthropocentric thought, and his perspective is one I will query through an examination of the "afterlives" of artifacts, specifically their poignant fate beyond the Indiana Jones films themselves. By focusing on the golden idol at the beginning of *Raiders of the Lost Ark*, the Holy Grail in *Last Crusade*, and the Crystal Skull in *Indiana Jones and the Kingdom of the Crystal Skull* in relation to artifact framing, object ontology, and material futurities, I contend that the Indiana Jones series offers a crucial touchstone to better appreciating interactions with the non-human world.

Raiders *of the Golden Idol*

Throughout the majority of *Raiders*, Indy strives to locate the Ark of the Covenant and prevent it from "belonging" to his rival René Belloq and the Nazi antagonists he works for. Yet the start of the film is essentially its own microcosmic encapsulation of the artifact trope tale. Opening in Peru, Indy races against Belloq to locate a golden idol—the identity or significance of which is never confirmed within the film itself and indeed is not brought up again outside of this instance. The recognition of the artifact is first foregrounded through its situational exclusivity, as the adventurers must gain access to the secluded and hermetic space—often a tomb or temple—to locate the object they are seeking. Unlike realistic excavations, where a multitude of recovered items would be expected, the archaeological quest foregrounds the importance of the singular artifact. Thus, while Indy may interact with objects such as maps, traps, keys, or puzzles, ultimately, these are transitory catalyst components, and the encounter with the final artifact sets it aside as something non-quotidian.

Locating an overgrown temple with his local guides, Indy penetrates to its deepest recesses to find the golden idol. The dangers of pitfalls, spike traps, and pressure-plated puzzles cultivates the audience's sense of expectation, building a sense of aura and bestowing it upon the artifact at the center. Although Indy passes multiple objects—including some quite overt relics—it is clearly the singular idol that he is questing for.

This differentiation between the individual and collective is one that resurfaces throughout framings of artifact ontology and is equally mirrored in Indy being the only person who actually reaches the "heart" of the temple itself, designating a sense of exclusivity. Although there is no diegetic explanation of what the object actually is, the cinematic framing of the golden idol makes its artifactual status overt from its very first scenic presence. Situated in the center of the shot, the slow zoom of the camera trains the audience's focus to reflect that of the archaeologist, to mirror his gaze. Raised on a pedestal and diegetically centralized, this very enshrining of the object implies that it is something unique, something to be differentiated from the ordinary. Thus, while there are other *objects* in the room, it is quite evident that this is the single *artifact* that both Indy and the audience are seeking. Roger Luckhurst in *The Mummy's Curse* (2012) identifies how location is a prime constituent in appreciating artifact ontology. Commenting on the opening of the Tomb of Tutankhamen, he remarks that "the materials dug out of the ground of Egypt become artifacts only within the frame of the museum" (145). Thus, whether it is museum or tomb, recognition of artifact ontology is guided both by an expectation of where such items should be found and by their taxonomical proximity to surrounding examples. The critical and commercial success of the Indiana Jones franchise has helped to catalyze this iconic representation of the central artifact, as the golden idol is immediately recognizable without any oral confirmation of its projected material "identity."

Once Indy reaches the artifact, he must navigate the final puzzle of the weight-sensitive pedestal upon which the golden idol rests. To claim the artifact, the archaeologist attempts to switch the idol with a bag of sand, the inference being that by replicating the weight, the two can be exchanged. However, while this may seem like a compelling solution to the problem, within a wider anthropocentric frame, such a prospect cannot be upheld. For by exchanging the two objects, Indy necessarily equates their evident worth— that a bag of sand may indeed stand in for the golden idol. The cinematic presentation of the artifact up to this point has emphasized a sense of exclusivity, that it is quite clearly an item of great value. Thus, if the collective multitude of the grains of sand may replace the singular artifact, wider materialist notions of worth would be disrupted. As such, the only possible conclusion is that the trap must be set off and the temple destroyed—a retribution that reinforces the designated "belonging" of the artifact and preserves the exclusivity of the archaeological adventure. Crucially, this scene demonstrates that designations of value emerge from human perception, where the extraordinary artifact cannot be replaced with the commonplace item. Although this exchange arguably adheres to an Object-Orientated perspective where each item can only be appreciated in its own terms, the activation of the trap rather underscores the emphasis placed on preserving the materialist differentiation at the heart of anthropocentric and taxonomic pursuits. Matthew Johnson in *Archaeological Theory: An Introduction* comments on the inability of artifacts to reflect upon the past: "This love of artefacts, in itself, has nothing to do with archaeology in the strict sense as the study of the past. Artifacts tell us nothing about the past in themselves" (12). Thus, while anthropocentric framings will often seek to elicit the object's compliance in narrating its own history—most evidently denoted by museal descriptive labels—artifacts do not actually convey narratives about history but bear material traces of their temporal experiences.

From an Object-Oriented perspective, it may occur to us to ask, what happens to the bag of sand beyond the film? Evidently, for the audience, the golden idol is foregrounded as the "prime" object to be concerned about. The exchange of idol and sand, however, emphasizes the importance of considering the "afterlives" of objects, to think about their existence beyond their encounter with humanity. The destruction of the temple cannot help but perpetuate a rather anthropocentric arrogance, that it is humanity's interference which will cause chaos for the non-human. Projects like garbology—the archaeology of garbage—have been pioneered by archaeologists such as William Rathje and Cullen Murphy, who, in *Rubbish! The Archaeology of Garbage*, contend, "To an archaeologist, ancient garbage pits or garbage mounds ... are always among the happiest of finds, for they contain in concentrated form the artifacts and comestibles and remnants of behavior of the people who used them" (10). The consequences of Indy's actions thus curate another form of "mound" to be excavated, one which archaeologists themselves are notionally implicated with. The bag of sand in *Raiders* elicits a vital rumination on the implications of these archaeological framings; thus, the franchise overall highlights the anthropocentric structures from which artifact ontology emerges and is a prime opportunity to instigate alternative engagements with the non-human. Even at the end of the film, the fate of the golden idol is necessarily unknown. Although Indy may succeed in escaping the temple with both his life and the artifact, ultimately, it is Belloq who claims this emphatic colonial "loot"—as he has convinced the local indigenous people that he is prospectively helping them defend their heritage. Undeniably, the filmic franchise is tied to dubious representations of colonial appropriation. The self-reflexive awareness of this contention is even mapped by the seemingly pedagogical nature of the filmic timeline as Indy develops from wishing for "fortune and glory," to arguing that objects "belong in a museum," and finally works to return these items to where they "belong." The cinematic framing of the idol within *Raiders*, therefore, lays the foundation for an iconic and archetypal depiction of the artifact, one that reflects upon the particularly Western processes that project notions of value and identity as inherent within the non-human world and that suggest that these designations are revealed through human encounters with the non-human.

The Last Crusade *for the Holy Grail*

Unlike *Raiders*, *Indiana Jones and the Last Crusade* emphasizes its mythic narrative from the very start, portraying the pursuit of the glorified and legendary Holy Grail as a magical or supernatural tool. As such, the film stands in a long tradition of Grail quest narratives and draws upon an archaeological imagination that bestows vitalism to the non-human, where—in this case—an object can grant the human desire for eternal life. For materiality to be a conduit for such perpetuity is both an apt and ironic metaphor, especially given the brief attention given to the very consequential "afterlives" of objects within these narratives. Although the Grail is the central artifact of the film, like many archaeological relics, its presence is retained for the film's concluding moments, as its exclusivity must be maintained not only within wider taxonomic systems but also within the diegetic framing of the film itself. Due to this imperative, Indy's Grail quest is guided by his father's journal, a narrativized object which becomes a form of legitimization for the quest—a materialization of an otherwise intangible and immaterial pursuit. Akin to *Raiders*, the multiple objects utilized become catalysts or gateways to the final artifact, a process that underscores and reinforces the perception of a material hierarchy—an "order of things" that emerges from the non-human. Thus, while Indy is eventually forced—once again—by the Nazi antagonists to guide them to the relic, crucially, only a select few make it to the final chamber where the Grail resides.

Navigating three trials to prove his worth, Indy emerges into a room that houses not only a singular Grail but a multiplicity. Indy, along with the film's principal antagonists, Walter Donovan and Elsa Schneider, encounter the knight who guards the resting place of the Grail. Unlike the elevated enshrinement of the artifact in *Raiders*, here the desired object is obscured within the collective, and it must be identified to obtain its splendor. As the knight proclaims, "You must choose. Choose wisely, for while the true Grail will bring you life, the false Grail will take it from you." The very inference that there exists a "true" and "false" Grail is an overtly anthropocentric formulation, as notionally it is through the *encounter* with humanity that such a designation may arise. Indeed, it is only within a human frame that such a differentiation is both required and sustainable. The notion that one object will grant life while another will grant death presents a powerful mediation on materialist utilization, as incorrect use is revealed to have drastic consequences. This inscription of vitalism, however, cannot escape the inference that the non-human aspects of the artifact will "activate" in response to human contact, itself a reinforcement of anthropocentric exceptionalism. Similar to *Raiders*, *Last Crusade* represents the idea that artifact ontology emerges within human perception while further highlighting that the projection of mythic narratives causes a dangerous, and at times fatal, attraction that all participants ultimately suffer from.

The encounter with the Grail fundamentally returns to the necessity of separating the individual from the collective, to hierarchize the one over the many. Appropriately, then, Donovan proclaims that he has "no idea what [the Grail] looks like," despite his persistent pursuit of the object up until this point. This lacuna between a recognition of what an object *is* and what it *does* returns us to the tool utilization of human ontology and its dependence on taxonomic structures. Elliot Colla, for instance, in *Conflicted Antiquities: Egyptology, Egyptomania, Egyptian Modernity*, suggests that such materialist recognition arises from a network of similarity and difference: "As a consequence, an artefact was not considered as a unique piece, but rather as part of a class of objects arranged within an emerging taxonomical grid" (9). Thus, the perpetuation of museal structures that imply a certain "order of things" as emergent from the non-human is shattered when observers can no longer depend on textual descriptions to explain what they are viewing. Locating the Grail, then, depends on specific historical knowledge, despite the apparent lack of knowing what the item should "look like." Consequently, this identification falls upon archetypal framings of artifact ontology, recalling the structures that evoke an instant recognition that the golden idol in *Raiders* is notionally non-quotidian. Elsa's selection of an ostentatious Grail for Donovan is interpreted by the latter as a valid choice precisely because it *conforms* to his recognition of what an artifact *should* look like. The apparent subversion of this trope culminates in the antagonist's accelerated bodily deterioration, his elision from subject to object as he joins that which remains.

Indy's choice, meanwhile, is represented as more considered. Although the camera may linger with a deep-focus shot once again on grails that have a more spectacular appearance, notionally he looks beyond the surface to select the most unassuming object—the Carpenter's Cup—behind them. Even this very designation cannot help but reference the person who is interpreted to be behind the object, signifying an interaction with the human past rather than the non-human present. Through this process of selection, Indy also once again conforms to the prioritization of the individual over the collective—that while all the items may be grails, evidently a *specific* Grail is required. Eugenio Donato in "The Museum's Furnace: Notes towards a Contextual Reading of *Bouvard* and *Péuchet*" underscores the importance of the artifact's individualism, noting that "archaeological origins are important in two ways: each archaeological artefact has to be an original artefact, and these original artefacts must in turn explain the 'meaning' of a subsequent larger history" (*Textual Strategies* 220). Within taxonomic structures, each artifact must exhibit a sense of individualism—an exclusivity—which underscores the wondrous nature of its spectacle, while also being situated within a matrix of similarity and difference. Thus, each object must be unique enough that it stands apart from the collective while being recognizable enough to act as a micro-fragment within a macro-narrative. *Last Crusade* demonstrates that it is the understanding of this "history" that guides Indy's correct choice, a narrative legitimization of the materialist-structured hierarchies. For the artifact to retain its wondrous aura, however, a sense of exclusivity must be maintained. Thus, the Guardian warns that "the Grail cannot pass beyond the great seal," implying a very overt notion of "belonging" for the relic. This warning is unsurprisingly ignored, as Elsa becomes an embodiment for the wider human greed that is attracted to such individuality and thus attempts to transgress this containment. The resulting destruction of the temple is an appropriate echo of *Raiders*, where the artifact must almost inevitably be "lost"—as its attempted integration into economic modes of circulation would prospectively be so paradigm-rupturing that the very system of object worth would be challenged. While the "afterlife" of the Grail may appear to represent a non-human exteriority—finally outside the grasp of humanity—*Last Crusade*'s conclusion underscores a reinforcement of the taxonomic arrangement; indeed, it is the wonder and fascination with absent presences within exhibitionary collections that only further perpetuates their projected individual exceptionalism.

Returning the Crystal Skull

Unlike the three theatrical films that precede it, *Indiana Jones and the Kingdom of the Crystal Skull* is rather motivated by the quest to put the artifact *back* where it notionally "belongs." Here, Indy searches for the lost city of Akator to uncover the secrets behind the apparent "aliens" from an alternate dimension before the Soviet Union army. Drawing on Ancient Astronaut theories and Earth mysteries, *Crystal Skull*—as in Indy's search for the Holy Grail—seeks out deeper mysteries to uncover, secrets that are revealed through human contact with non-human objects and that offer some affirmation to the place of humanity within the wider cosmos. To facilitate this, the film once again draws on a central artifact—the Crystal Skull—which deploys the non-human as a material canvas upon which humanity can etch their own desires. Yet, unlike the previous examples, the skull seemingly destabilizes the distinction between subject and object—as its later reunion with the rest of the "alien" body raises new ethical questions about the processes employed in its original pillaging. This contentious boundary has a much longer tradition in archaeological studies, particularly through the moral and ethical implications of staging human remains in exhibitionary or museal settings. Thus, while the films arguably serve a pedagogical function—where Indy transitions from seeking "fortune and glory" to reversing appropriative processes—the Crystal Skull as an object provides an evocative opportunity to consider the implications of the artifact's gaze and the vital potential of confronting perceptions of aberrant materiality.

The Crystal Skull itself is located by Indy and Mutt in the secluded tomb of a Conquistador grave in Peru. Once again, the archaeological adventurer must cross into an excluded space, where topographical proximity encourages a recognition of artifact ontology. Like the Grail in *Last Crusade*, the Crystal Skull is not elevated on a pedestal or seemingly differentiated from the collective. Instead its presence is betrayed by other objects which are physically drawn to it; even materials which are not conventionally magnetic are still attracted. The prime artifact is eventually separated from the collective, as, while there are many other objects of value and wonder within the tomb, they are ultimately disregarded by Indy and Mutt. The overt visual signification of these latter artifacts being centripetally attracted to the Crystal Skull thus acts as a metaphor for the wider taxonomical systems that conventionally draw colonial "loot" from Western-designated peripheries to the imperial hub for exhibition. Unlike in *Raiders*, where the camera frames the artifact and Indy against each other, in *Crystal Skull* the archaeologist's wonder is situated *alongside* the item—for he has no frame of reference from which its provenance can be deduced. His subsequent comment that the object bears "no tool marks" not only emphasizes the materiality of the anomalous artifact but demonstrates how—in a very Heideggerian manner—Indy experiences an immediate encounter, rather than subconscious engagement, with this seeming aberration. This emphasis on the production of the object—the very *artificiality* of artifacts—is echoed also by Colla, who suggests that the term refers to "on the one hand the human rather than natural origin of an object; and on the other, its status as the product of an act of making" (9). Although Indy originally suggests that the item is a piece of seamless quartz, his wondrous reaction is compounded by the seeming abnormality of the artifact's material composition. Although *Crystal Skull* may posit that its central object is something altogether non-quotidian, these "unknown" qualities do not preclude its recognition as an artifact. Indeed, while the anthropocentric paradigm is slightly disrupted, ultimately, the Crystal Skull follows the structure of the individualized and elevated item identified thus far and is not so "alien" that it truly sits outside materialist interpretation.

The suggested subversion of the artifact is equally implied by its transition from a vehicle of wonder to one of horror. Following their recovery of the Crystal Skull, Indy and Mutt are captured by the Russian agent Spalko who forces the archaeologist to "observe" the artifact so that he may be influenced by its apparent psychic properties. Placed on another form of pedestal and returning to the oppositional framing identified in *Raiders*, here the artifact is rather something to fear—as Indy cannot look away from the wider non-human consequences of the visual structures that underpin artifactology. Walter Benjamin in "The Work of Art in the Age of Mechanical Reproduction" (1935) highlights how the veneration projected upon objects curates a form of aura, one where "[t]o perceive the aura of an object we look at means to invest it with the ability to look at us in return" (*Illuminations* 190). Cer-

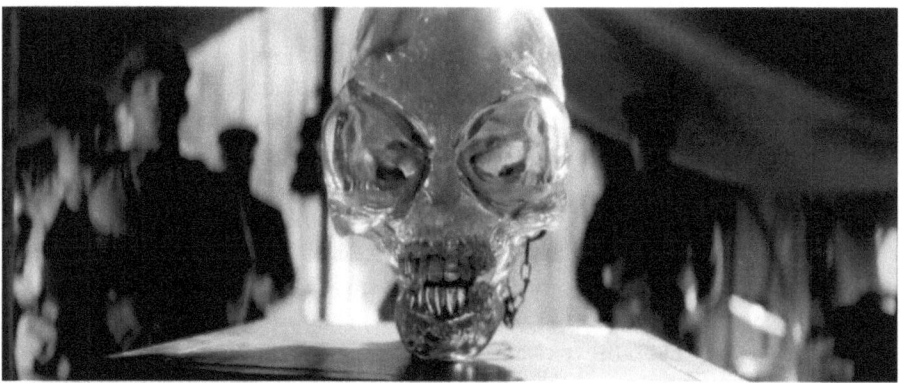

Gazing at the Crystal Skull, a moment of wonder becomes a moment of horror in *Indiana Jones and the Kingdom of the Crystal Skull* (2008).

tainly, it is the textual aura projected upon the Crystal Skull that is rather reciprocated upon the archaeologist. However, such notions cannot—once again—help but reinforce the anthropocentrism that can only appreciate or engage with the non-human when it is configured within human terms. For Spalko, the Crystal Skull represents the fulfillment of Soviet fascist ideology, the ability to control the macro (public consciousness and reason) through the curation of the micro (the "tool"). Akin to the differentiation of artifact from collective, Spalko seeks to use the very same bridging process through the utilization of this notional "order of things" to impose a form of indoctrination. Shawn Malley in *Excavating the Future* contends that Spalko "transforms the heretofore colonial artefact into an SF icon of the Cold War cinema, an object of burgeoning American global hegemony mirrored in fears of Soviet mind control" (107). While certainly a compelling reflection on the geopolitical implications of artifact utilization and recognition, neither Malley nor *Crystal Skull* pay attention to the anomalous materiality of its central item. Although human thought is by its definition anthropocentric, a notion that undercuts the possibility of fundamentally understanding an Object-Orientated Ontology, *Crystal Skull* gestures to an anomalous materiality but ultimately rather depicts an entrenchment of artifactual framing.

Although the true artifactual encounter occurs, unsurprisingly, at the conclusion of the film, in this instance *Crystal Skull* is compelled to follow such an archetypical schema to preserve the mystique of the "alien" and to avoid a prolonged engagement with an incommensurable non-human otherness. Indeed, the gravitas of this encounter is so monumental that Indy and his group pass through a room full of artifacts on their way to the final chamber, as even these once-revered and individual items are relegated to the status of collated objects, beheld by none. Further, while Indy's is ostensibly a quest to put the artifact back where it "belongs," the final confrontation—as in *Raiders* and *Last Crusade*—is represented as a form of exchange, one in which Spalko seeks to "know everything" and fulfill her desire of totalitarian control. Such a system implores the non-human to validate and affirm a human wish, although one which overwhelms the antagonist with the sheer unknowability of the non-human. The return of the artifact, the film suggests, provides a sense of completion, a wholeness in which the multitude of alien bodies are collapsed into a singular instance and their ship departs to an alternate dimension. Unsurprisingly, the temple is destroyed as a result of this departure, flattened by the ship's centripetal motion, which erases any previous material boundaries and horizontalizes all that remains. Pushed to an even further extreme, the Crystal Skull is thus so far out of humanity's possession that it quite aptly inhabits another dimension entirely.

"It belongs in a museum"

The Indiana Jones films have become a fundamental cornerstone for the public perception of archaeology and the visual structures that encourage a recognition of artifact ontology. For both Indy and audience, this is a realization that emerges from the contact with the non-human, one situated within human perception and not emergent from the object itself. As such, it is not only crucial to understand these very framings to confront the implications of projecting a materialist differentiation upon the non-human, but also to explore and expose the consequences of such an outlook. In *Raiders*, *Last Crusade*, and *Crystal Skull*, each of the sought-after artifacts remains outside of humanity's ownership by the conclusion, implying—despite Indy's claim that these items "belong in a museum"—that their "belonging" is elsewhere, beyond our grasp. However, a more compelling response emerges through the recognition that these objects are affected by human contact but still, in some form, persist beyond it. Indeed, if the temple at the beginning of *Raiders* had not been destroyed, it is curious to consider whether another subsequent explorer would venerate the bag of sand as an artifact due to its very overt taxonomical framing. The "false" Grails in *Last Crusade* are equally objects of wonder—and most likely value—yet their fate is also unknown. Indeed, even the relics of Akator are seemingly "lost" once again. While each of these questions are left unanswered by the conclusion, as an affirmation of the taxonomical system, it is through the implications and gaps that arise from such artifactual framing that materialist attitudes can be challenged. The Indiana Jones franchise is itself an integral cultural artifact, one which has dramatically influenced perceptions of artifact and material ontology; thus, it is also a text that allows us to confront these very structures so that a more nuanced engagement with the non-human may be conceptualized.

WORKS CITED

Benjamin, Walter. *Illuminations*. Trans. Harry Arendt. Fortana/Collins, 1982.
Colla, Elliot. *Conflicted Antiquities: Egyptology, Egyptomania, Egyptian Modernity*. Duke University Press, 2008. ProQuest Ebook Central, http://ebookcentral.proquest.com.ezproxy.lancs.ac.uk/lib/lancaster/detail.action?docID=1170470, accessed 10 October 2016.
Donato, Eugenio. "The Museum's Furnace: Notes Towards a Contextual Reading of *Bouvard and Péuchet*" in *Textual Strategies*. Ed. Josué V. Harari. Methuen & Co., 1979.
Harman, Graham. *Tool-Being—Heidegger and the Metaphysics of Objects*. Open Court, 2002.
Heidegger, Martin. *Being and Time*. Trans. John Macquarrie and Edward Robinson. Blackwell Publishing, 1962.
Holtorf, Cornelius. *Archaeology Is a Brand! The Meaning of Archaeology in Contemporary Popular Culture*. Archaeopress, 2007.
Johnson, Matthew. *Archaeological Theory: An Introduction*. Blackwell Publishers, 1999.
Luckhurst, Roger. *The Mummy's Curse: The True History of a Dark Fantastic*. Oxford University Press, 2012.
Malley, Shawn. *Excavating the Future: Archaeology and Geopolitics in Contemporary North American Science Fiction Film and Television*. Liverpool University Press, 2018.
Olsen, Bjørnar. *In Defense of Things: Archaeology and the Ontology of Objects*. AltaMira Press, 2010.
Pearson, Mike, and Michael Shanks, *Theatre/Archaeology*. Routledge, 2001.
Rathje, William, and Cullen Murphy. *Rubbish! The Archaeology of Garbage*. University of Arizona Press, 2001.

Extended Franchise

Raiders of the Lost Longbox
Rediscovering The Further Adventures of Indiana Jones

Joseph S. Walker

Raiders of the Lost Ark, the film in which director Steven Spielberg introduced the world to the swashbuckling archaeologist Indiana Jones, contributed numerous iconic images to popular culture. Among them, certainly, is the warehouse seen at the movie's ending, a gargantuan space in which the crated Ark is placed alongside innumerable other boxes of various shapes and sizes, containing unknown treasures and wonders. That warehouse finds its real-world counterparts in unnumbered basements, closets, storage units, and comic shop back rooms across America, spaces filled with comic book collections sorted, reverently bagged, and filed away in the hobby's ubiquitous longboxes. Indiana Jones is motivated (sometimes problematically, as we shall see) by his obsessive desire to reclaim the lost cultural riches of the past, restoring them to the light of scholarly attention. Following in his footsteps, we can carry out our own quest, digging into the dusty storehouses of recent pop culture to ask if there is anything worth reclaiming there. Specifically, we can turn our attention to one of the more obscure artifacts of the transmedia franchise *Raiders* spawned: the 1983–1986 Marvel comic book series *The Further Adventures of Indiana Jones*.

Today, the publication of such a series would be taken for granted as part of a coordinated strategy of franchise development encompassing film, television, novels, comics, video games, and assorted other media forms. The transmedia franchise has become, in many ways, the dominant cultural form of our historical moment, and an object of almost obsessive interest both for fans and for the academics who study the behavior of those fans. As defined by Henry Jenkins, "transmedia storytelling represents a process where integral elements of a fiction get dispersed systematically across multiple delivery channels for the purpose of creating a unified and coordinated entertainment experience." In recent decades, media conglomerates have become increasingly sophisticated and ambitious in their creation of such fictions, fans have become increasingly active in consuming and responding to them, and scholars of both popular culture and fandom have become increasingly concerned with them as a frequent locus of examination. While the study of transmedia franchises initially focused on contemporary examples which have been carefully and strategically planned across multiple platforms from the start (for example, the *Matrix* franchise or the Marvel Cinematic Universe), Fast and Örnebring point out that there has been growing attention to the history of the development of such characters and fictive worlds, for many of which any element of transmedial coordination has been "emergent (i.e., unplanned, contingent, organic)" (637). Alongside this, there has been a recognition of "the many disjunctions and contradictions that almost inevitably follow when extending/transferring/adapting transmedia worlds across/between media" (637). These disjunctions and contradictions are particularly visible in franchise texts created prior to the turn of the twenty-first century, "*before* they become entrenched in discourses of media franchising" (Benson 23).

The Further Adventures of Indiana Jones (hereafter *FA*) is certainly an example of emergent, rather than planned, transmedia storytelling, and elements of it are, in light of the better-known Indiana Jones stories, rather jarring. In part, of course, this is because few at the time, among either the creators or the readers of the series, would have likely thought of the comics as constituting part of a complex "transmedia" textual experience, as opposed to being a straightforward expansion—or exploitation—of a single film.[1] Most of the 34-issue run of the title came out prior to the 1984 release of *Indiana Jones and the Temple of Doom*, meaning that only *Raiders* could be drawn upon by the writers and artists as inspiration. Even when the second film was released, it had virtually no impact on the comic, aside from a two-page appearance by Short Round in issue 26.[2] *FA* did not follow *Doom* in shifting to an earlier period in Indy's life, instead sticking to a 1936/37 time frame for its remaining issues and continuing deliberate callbacks to the events and characters of *Raiders* through almost to the end (René Belloq is briefly mentioned in issue 33, for example). Here, then, is one reason why this seemingly ephemeral piece of pop history might be worth examining: as an indication of how Indiana Jones was perceived by creators and fans prior to the "official" expansion of his character in subsequent films. As we will see, elements of his characterization were very much a point of tension for the series.

Finding such points of interest is important, because there is an understandable impulse to dismiss *FA* as being so fleeting and inconsequential that its proper fate is to be simply forgotten. As Nicolas Pillai has noted, "Licensed comics are ontologically impure, dismissed as distant echoes of their parent media" (103). Here, suspicion of this particular artifact arises not because the character of Indiana Jones is inherently unsuited to the comic book form; quite the opposite is the case. Although the primary inspiration for *Raiders* was clearly the Saturday-morning B-movie serial, it also manifestly draws inspiration from adventure-based comic strips like Milton Caniff's *Terry and the Pirates* and, as George Lucas and Steven Spielberg have frequently acknowledged, the Donald Duck and Uncle Scrooge comic books by Carl Barks, in which the ducks were depicted as globe-trotting adventurers frequently on the hunt for fabulous lost treasures.[3] Putting Indy in comic books (a medium which itself dates almost precisely from the time period in which *Raiders* is set) is in many ways returning the character to his roots, liberating the scope of his adventures from such concerns as stunt doubles and special effects budgets.

Nor was the fact that *FA* was a licensed title necessarily a predictor of low quality, creative limitations, or a brief existence. Indeed, by the time the title was created, Marvel had had considerable success, both creatively and commercially, with similar titles. Beginning in 1970, for example, the company published licensed comic books based on Robert E. Howard's Conan the Barbarian which were among the most popular and critically praised comic books of the decade. The example of Star Wars is perhaps more directly relevant to *FA*. Marvel published a six-issue adaptation of the first Star Wars film upon its release[4] and then, beginning in issue 7, began telling original stories about the characters in a series which ultimately lasted 107 issues, ending only several years after the release of *Return of the Jedi*. Both the *Conan* and *Star Wars* Marvel comics of these years remain popular enough with fans that they have recently been collected into expensive, oversized omnibus editions featuring high-quality binding and paper. Even licensed titles based on far more obscure sources were published successfully. In 1979, for example, the toy company Parker Brothers asked Marvel to create a backstory and comic promoting their new action figure, the vaguely robotic Rom. The toy itself was an immediate commercial failure, but the resulting comic, *Rom: Spaceknight*, written by Bill Mantlo, ran for 75 issues, with Rom and his allies and enemies regularly interacting with characters from Marvel's main universe, such as the X-Men. Marvel saw similar success with comics based on toys such as the Micronauts (59 issues), the Transformers (80 issues), and G.I. Joe (155 issues), all of which remain hugely popular with comics fans disinterested in the toys themselves, though complicated rights issues have generally prevented the publication of high-end collections.

The mere fact that *The Further Adventures of Indiana Jones* lasted only 34 issues is the most obvious sign that it never achieved this kind of critical or commercial success. It is probably impossible, more than thirty years later, to determine whether the core cause of the title's lackluster performance was fan disinterest or confusion on Marvel's part over exactly how to best exploit the enormously popular character. There are certainly some indications that the publisher was not fully committed to making *FA* a top-tier title. Unlike many debut issues of the time, *FA* 1 carries no text page introducing the character or creators in an effort to promote fan engagement and, ultimately, sales; it wasn't until the fourth issue that so much as a letters page,[5] "Readers of the Lost Ark," appeared, and even after this debut, many issues neglected to include the "Readers" feature. Beginning with issue 30, the title shifted from a monthly schedule to bimonthly, almost invariably an indication of low sales. The final issue, 34, carries no text page, no announcement of the title's cancellation, and no promise that Indy will be seen again; it simply terminates the current storyline.

Perhaps most importantly, the creative team for the title was rarely stable for more than a few months at a time, an indication that assigning the writing and art duties was a relatively low priority for the company.[6] While popular perception of comic books focuses on characters such as Batman and Spider-Man, within the world of comics fandom, extended runs by specific creators, allowing for the development of a specific style and prolonged narratives, are vital to establishing and building a reliable readership. The long-term success of the *G.I. Joe* title, for example, can be traced almost entirely to the efforts of writer Larry Hama, who used elements of his own military experience and knowledge to balance the more fantastic elements of the franchise. *FA* never benefited from this kind of long-term attention from a distinctive creative voice. There is also no evidence, across the totality of the title's run, of any direct involvement by Spielberg, Lucas, or anyone else involved in the production of the films. As in other failed efforts at expanding various franchises, in other words, *FA* lacked "one central person who understood the property and its fan base" and whose presence might have "acted as an assurance to the fan base of a certain level of quality" (Benson 26).

That said, some high-profile creators did work on the title at various times. The first issue was written and drawn by John Byrne, at the time one of the company's most popular creators due to his work on titles such as *The Uncanny X-Men* and *Fantastic Four*; this in itself is a signal that Marvel was at least trying to launch the book in a high-profile way. Beginning with issue 4, writing duties were assumed by David Michelinie, who would eventually write or co-write 20 of the 34 issues of the comic. Again, Michelinie was a popular and well-regarded writer and, having already written many issues of Marvel's *Star Wars*, was familiar with the demands of licensed titles. However, eight of the final ten issues of the series were written by Linda Grant, who was primarily an editor for the company and had few other writing credits—another suggestion that the title was, at least by this late point in its run, not seen as a priority. Oddly, however, several of these final issues did feature artwork by undoubtedly the most famous creator to work on *FA*, Steve Ditko, revered by comics fans for his role in the creation of Spider-Man and his many other accomplishments in a storied career. While Ditko was famous, however, he was also known to be difficult to work with, which may account for his relegation to what was clearly, by this time, a lower-tier title.

These are all external aspects of the comic pointing to elements of its troubled history. An examination of the actual content of the full run of *FA* suggests another, which may ultimately have been decisive: the struggle to find a consistent way to depict Indy and to provide him with the kind of expansive world and supporting cast that characterize successful transmedia properties. *Star Wars*, to look at the most obvious comparison franchise of the time, had several engaging central characters (all of whom, save Obi-Wan Kenobi, survived the first film) and an entire galaxy of potential settings and conflicts. By contrast, *Raiders* offered only a handful of clearly identified characters, with Indiana Jones himself taking the lion's share of the screen time. The antagonists are all dead at the end of the film, meaning that *FA* cannot build fan excitement by presenting further clashes with Belloq or Toht (though one arc, in issues 9 and 10, does feature Toht's sister as the primary antagonist). Sallah, Jock (the pilot from the opening scene in *Raiders*), and Captain Katanga (captain of the ship which briefly carries the Ark) all make what amount to cameo appearances in *FA*, but none is made a regular supporting character, and for the most part the effort to use them at all feels rote. Short Round's appearance in issue 26 is representative of the dismissive treatment given these figures: he rescues Indy from some menacing opponents, only to have Indy tell him that he'll be going back to boarding school as soon as they return to the U.S. The issue then shifts to the main storyline, and Short Round is never seen or heard from again.

There are occasional efforts over the course of the series to provide Indy with new continuing antagonists, such as the rival Scottish archaeologist McIver and the unscrupulous collector Ben Ali Ayoob, but none appear more than two or three times or develop significant characteristics encouraging fan interest; *FA* has no equivalent to Darth Vader or the Joker. In the closing issues of the series, new writer Linda Grant makes a rather forced effort to begin fleshing out the cast of the book, introducing Alec Sutherland, a bumbling but enthusiastic student of Indy's, and Dr. Tavistock, a university trustee who disapproves of Indy's freewheeling adventures, though neither character makes much of an impression. The end result is that over the entire run of *FA*, only two characters, aside from Indy himself, make regular appearances, and both are taken from *Raiders*: Marcus Brody and Marion Ravenwood.

A reader of the comic who skipped over word balloons and captions might not realize that the two characters appear so regularly, since their physical appearances are anything but consistent. This is a problem which goes well beyond the variation that might be expected in a book that uses several different art teams. Even Indy, in most issues, bears only a passing resemblance to Harrison Ford, more usually being drawn as a rather generic white man, but at least he can usually be identified by his whip, fedora, and leather jacket. Indeed, it's notable that in the image of Indy which appears in the upper left corner of the cover of every issue (a design feature of all Marvel titles of the time), the face is in shadow, our recognition of the character assumed from the distinctive costume and prominently held revolver.[7] The appearance of Marcus and Marion is considerably more variable, and it is, again, unclear if this is due to a lack of reference materials or simple disinterest on the part of the artists. Marcus is sometimes drawn as though he is in his seventies or eighties, with a fringe of white hair around a bald dome; he is sometimes trim, and at other times approaches morbidly obese.

Marion, meanwhile, is often depicted as a freckled redhead, but her character presents an even greater challenge than her appearance. It is clear from the letters pages that did appear in *FA* that readers were interested in Marion and wanted to see more of her in the book (the letters column in issue 8 features seven consecutive letters making this demand), but the creators seemed to struggle to decide how she would fit into the narrative. The end of *Raiders* can be taken as presenting Indy and Marion as an established romantic couple, but she is entirely absent from the first issues of the comic, perhaps because either Marvel's creators or the studio controlling the property thought such a relationship would be too restrictive for the hero.

When Marion finally makes her first appearance, in issue 6, she is preparing to open a nightclub in Manhattan, but by the end of the issue it has burned down and is never mentioned again. In the very next issue she has, without explanation, become a reporter tagging along to write about Indy's search for a lost tribe from Atlantis. This eventually evolves into a job handling PR for Indy's employer, Marshall College, and its National Museum. During his run, writer Michelinie presents Indy and Marion as strong-willed people who frequently clash but essentially trust each other, and who are gradually establishing a romantic coupling. The relationship, however, is terminated abruptly and awkwardly. At the end of issue 23 (written by Herb Trimpe), Marion sees Indy being kissed by another woman, grateful after their shared adventure, and walks away in anger. She is next seen in issue 25 (Linda Grant's first issue as writer), where she is waiting to introduce Indy for a lecture at the college and is enraged to learn that he is in Peru. At the end of this issue, Indy returns and finds a letter from her: "Mr. Jones, I've got to get away. Don't you dare come looking for me." Assured by Marcus that Marion was not forced to write the letter, Indy simply says, "Then ... she's really gone. Goodbye, Marion!" and the character disappears for the remaining run of *FA*. It is perhaps not coincidental that this issue came out shortly after the release of *Temple of Doom*, which suggested that Indy, like James Bond, was to have a different romantic interest in every adventure. Whatever the case, the letters from fans in the remaining issues continued to request Marion's return, and in issue 32 the editors actually promised that she would be back in issue 35. In the event, of course, that issue was never published.

FA thus suffered from a lack of cohesion and momentum in terms of both its creative team and its presentation of a convincingly populated world for its hero to inhabit. Ultimately, however, it is the inconsistent, and sometimes unappealing, presentation of that hero which is perhaps the book's most fatal flaw. Since the character of Indiana Jones is, across the entire franchise, "the true driving force of the narrative" (Hernández-Pérez and Rodriguez 28), a suspect treatment of that character cannot be sustained. A brief examination of the first storyline in *FA*, spanning the initial two issues,[8] is illustrative. We first see Indy, on the splash page of the first issue, in front of his classroom, where he is using his bullwhip to knock a cigarette from the mouth of a female student because, he tells Marcus, he needed the practice and the student got extra credit. Told by a horrified Marcus that he could have injured the student and gone to jail, Indy responds that "without risks, there isn't much point to it all. Or much fun, either."[9] Already we can see that Indy has been stripped of the element of weary resignation which made Harrison Ford so charming in the role; this version of the character is brash, cocky and motivated by adventure rather than scholarship. Indy is visited by a former student, Charlie Dunne, who excitedly claims that he and his sister Edith have learned the location of the "Ikons of Ikammanen," legendary golden statues which can become "living avengers." Indy scoffs at the claim, but before Charlie can convince him, he is murdered by a knife thrown from outside the office window. Indy tells Marcus to "call the police and play their games" while he, shedding his glasses and producing his fedora from nowhere, will be taking a leave of absence.

Indy travels to Africa and finds Edith Dunne in the fictional city of Krikambo, where the two of them are abducted and forced to cooperate with the gangster Solomon Black in his own pursuit of the Ikons. They travel by boat to a previously unknown island off "the northwest coast" of Africa, where they find the Ikons in a huge tower and learn that they are not statues, but people who were lowered into molten gold by the previously unknown natives of the island. The natives capture Indy and Edith and attempt to kill them in this way, but are interrupted and ultimately slaughtered by Black and his men. Black has the Ikons crated and taken aboard his ship, but a Nazi submarine later sinks it, leaving only Indy, Edith, and a single remaining crate. Since America and Germany are not yet at war, Indy persuades the submarine's captain to spend a month giving them a ride to New York City.

There, the two of them, along with the crate, board a small plane to fly to an unidentified museum where Edith will receive the glory she feels she is due. Indy reveals that he has figured out that Edith, hungry for all the credit, was behind her brother's murder, which was carried out by Jerry, a previously unknown accomplice now revealed to be piloting the plane. The two of them attempt to force Indy to jump out, but he has translated the inscription found with the Ikons, and he speaks the words which bring the remaining Ikon to life to "bring vengeance to the wicked." As the golden figure lurches toward a terrified Edith and Jerry, Indy sets the plane to crash into the Atlantic, takes a parachute, and jumps.

The fact that much of this sounds absurd in summary is not a great concern; much of *Raiders* would seem equally outlandish if stripped to its most basic elements. What is troubling is the actions and attitudes manifested by Indy during this adventure, and the ways in which the presentation of the story frames those choices. Throughout, Indy appears to relish not only risk, as he tells Marcus at the start, but violence itself. This is evident in the sadistic pleasure he takes in abandoning Edith to her fate; it is at its most problematic when he joins Black and his men in viciously gunning down the natives of the island, apparently killing the entire tribe. After the slaughter has ended, Indy, drawn with a smile on his face, proclaims, "That's that! Another triumph for decency, culture, civilization, and automatic weapons." The comment might be taken as sarcastic, but there is no indication at any point that Indy is bothered by what has happened. The representation of the natives themselves is equally problematic; none is individualized, and they are drawn wearing elaborate robes and headgear which prevent even a clear identification of their racial identity. Essentially, they are ciphers to be eliminated, the fact that they are being murdered and robbed given no consideration at all. *FA* will continue to be troubling in its representation of minority figures throughout its run, both in terms of how they are presented and how casually the presumed hero of the title dismisses them. Issue 11, for example, opens with Indy battling a "tribe of aborigines" in the Australian outback after he has taken a significant artifact from them. The aborigines are drawn as primitive, almost demonic figures wearing only loincloths and carrying spears, and Indy again does not hesitate to gun them down. For the most part, the book seems to endorse his views. Issues 9 and 10 depict his clashes with a group of South American tribesmen seeking to reclaim the idol from the opening sequence of *Raiders*; despite the fact that much of the story is set in Manhattan, the tribesmen continue to wear only flimsy loincloths and arm themselves with darts and arrows. When their leader falls to his death following a struggle with Indy on a biplane, a narrative text box describes this as being "at long last, justice."

Of course, the colonialism and racism apparent in these sequences is,

Raiders of the Lost Longbox (Walker) 159

In a scene from the second issue of *The Further Advntures of Indiana Jones*, Indy shows no remorse as he joins a criminal gang in gunning down a previously unknown tribe.

to some degree, visible in most of the Indiana Jones stories; the character's repeated line of "this belongs in a museum" inherently privileges Western acquisition. It could be argued, too, that the lust for violence Indy exhibits in much of *FA* is not greatly different from his casual gunning down of the swordsman in a famous sequence from *Raiders*. To judge from the letter pages, however, the difference was a significant one; several issues feature letters from readers protesting Indy's apparent enjoyment of violence and saying it was inconsistent with the film. Responding to one such letter, in issue 26, the editors claimed that Indy, in calling one particular fight fun, "was speaking as a man used to fighting of necessity, not necessarily as one who revels in it" but thanked the reader for "keep[ing] us on our creative toes."

To return to the story of the Ikons, the ending of the story not only once again portrays Indy as a man who revels in violence, but also uncovers another central tension within his character: he is, insistently, a man of science, and yet he lives in a world in which the supernatural is regularly shown to be real. When Charlie Dunne initially mentions the Ikons, Indy scoffs at the idea of them existing, let alone coming to life. By the end of the second issue, however, he is staking his life on their ability to do so; the narrative makes it clear that he boards the plane knowing Edith to be a murderer and relying upon the Ikon to save his own life. No explanation for this shift of attitude is given, but it is a pattern which is repeated throughout the series: no matter how many times he sees events that can only be explained through the supernatural, Indy is skeptical of them until the moment when he suddenly, conveniently, is not.

In the final analysis, it should be said that *The Further Adventures of Indiana Jones*, as a cultural artifact, is not without merit; some of the individual stories are exciting and engaging, particularly those which come near the end of David Michelinie's extended run on the title. However, the same elements that seem to have contributed to its early cancellation (frequent changes to the creative team, an inability to establish a coherent sustained narrative or cast of characters, and the troubling aspects of Indy's representation) continue to make it a curiosity today, as opposed to a vital part of the character's transmedial text. It's worth noting that when another company, Dark Horse Comics, began producing Indiana Jones comics in the 1990s, they took the form not of an ongoing series but rather of a succession of self-contained miniseries, thus avoiding the central problem that *FA* did not solve: how to build an entire world around a single character.

Appendix: Creator Credits for The Further Adventures of Indiana Jones

Issue	Cover Date	Story Title	Writer(s)	Principal Artist(s)
1	Jan. 1983	The Further Adventures of Indiana Jones	John Byrne	John Byrne Terry Austin
2	Feb. 1983	22-Karat Doom!	Denny O'Neil	John Byrne Terry Austin
3	March 1983	The Devil's Cradle	Denny O'Neil	Gene Day Richard Howell Mel Candido Danny Bulanadi
4	April 1983	Gateway to Infinity	David Michelinie	Ron Frenz Danny Bulanadi
5	May 1983	The Harbingers	David Michelinie	Ron Frenz Danny Bulanadi
6	June 1983	Club Nightmare!	Archie Goodwin David Michelinie	Howard Chaykin Terry Austin
7	July 1983	Africa Screams	David Michelinie	Kerry Gammill Sam de la Rosa
8	Aug. 1983	Crystal Death	David Michelinie	Kerry Gammill Sam de la Rosa

Issue	Cover Date	Story Title	Writer(s)	Principal Artist(s)
9	Sept. 1983	The Gold Goddess	Archie Goodwin David Michelinie	Dan Reed Danny Bulanadi
10	Oct. 1983	Amazon Death-Ride	Archie Goodwin David Michelinie	Dan Reed Danny Bulanadi
11	Nov. 1983	The Fourth Nail Chapter 1: Blood and Sand!	David Michelinie	Kerry Gammill Sam de la Rosa
12	Dec. 1983	The Fourth Nail Chapter 2: Swords and Spikes!	David Michelinie	Kerry Gammill Luke McDonnell Mel Candido
13	Jan. 1984	Deadly Rock!	David Michelinie Archie Goodwin	Ricardo Villamonte Sam de la Rosa
14	Feb. 1984	Demons	David Michelinie	David Mazzacchelli The Saint
15	March 1984	The Sea Butchers Chapter 1: Island of Peril	David Michelinie	Herb Trimpe Vince Colletta
16	April 1984	Death on Dark Waters	David Michelinie	Herb Trimpe Vince Colletta
17	May 1984	The Grecian Earn	David Michelinie	Herb Trimpe Vince Colletta
18	June 1984	The City of Yesterday's Forever!	David Michelinie	Herb Trimpe Vince Colletta
19	July 1984	Dragon by the Tail!	Larry Lieber	Larry Lieber Vince Colletta
20	Aug. 1984	The Cuban Connection	David Michelinie Christopher Priest	Luke McDonnell Danny Bulanadi
21	Sept. 1984	Beyond the Lucifer Chamber	David Michelinie Christopher Priest	Steve Ditko
22	Oct. 1984	End Run	David Michelinie Christopher Priest	Joe Brozowski Mel Candido
23	Nov. 1984	The Secret of the Deep	Herb Trimpe	Herb Trimpe
24	Dec. 1984	Revenge of the Ancients	Herb Trimpe	Herb Trimpe Danny Bulanadi
25	Jan. 1985	Good as Gold	Linda Grant	Steve Ditko Danny Bulanadi
26	Feb. 1985	Trail of the Golden Guns	Ron Fortier David Michelinie	Steve Ditko Danny Bulanadi
27	March 1985	Trail of the Golden Guns Chapter 2	Ron Fortier David Michelinie	Steve Ditko Danny Bulanadi
28	April 1985	Tower of Tears	Linda Grant	Steve Ditko Danny Bulanadi
29	May 1985	Shot by Both Sides	Linda Grant	Ricardo Villamonte Danny Bulanadi
30	July 1985	Fireworks!	Linda Grant	Ricardo Villamonte Danny Bulanadi
31	Sept. 1985	Will Indy Survive—The Summit Meeting?	Linda Grant	Ricardo Villamonte Danny Bulanadi

continued on page 162

Issue	Cover Date	Story Title	Writer(s)	Principal Artist(s)
32	Nov. 1985	Double Play!	Linda Grant	Steve Ditko Danny Bulanadi
33	Jan. 1986	Magic, Murder and the Weather	Linda Grant	Steve Ditko Danny Bulanadi
34	March 1986	Something's Gone Wrong Again!	Linda Grant	Steve Ditko Danny Bulanadi

Notes

1. Said film being, significantly, accessible only via memory for most of the audience. It may be difficult for fans and critics today to fully appreciate the implications of a time when, once a film had left the local cinema, there could be no certainty of when it could be seen again, and the experience of doing so had to be sublimated through such secondary sources as magazines, novelizations, and comics.

2. In the letter column of *FA* 31, the editors claim that "both Willie Scott and Short Round have appeared here recently, and they will be popping up again according to new scripter Linda Grant." A close reading of the entire series, however, fails to turn up any use of the Willie Scott character, or any appearances of Short Round aside from issue 26. Had the title not ended with issue 34, of course, Grant's plans might have been carried out.

3. See, for example, George Lucas's introduction to the collection *Uncle Scrooge McDuck: His Life and Times* by Carl Barks.

4. Marvel also published a two-issue adaptation of *Raiders of the Lost Ark*, sales of which were evidently strong enough to encourage the creation of *FA*. Unlike with *Star Wars*, however, the numbering was not continued into the new stories, which were treated as a separate title. Adaptations of *Temple of Doom* and, well after the cancellation of *FA*, *The Last Crusade* were also published, but again as stand-alone titles; by contrast, the adaptation of *The Empire Strikes Back* appeared as issues 39–44 of the regular *Star Wars* title, indicating a conscious effort to at least present the appearance of a unified narrative.

5. Letter pages rarely appear in comics today, having been supplanted by Internet commentary and direct interaction between fans and creators. For much of the history of comics fandom, however, they have been vitally important as a point of contact between publishers and consumers. This was particularly the case at Marvel, where Stan Lee had established a style of chatty enthusiasm on letter and editorial pages as an effective way of promoting fan identification and engagement. For a title of this period to regularly lack a letters page is an indication either that fans are not responding to the publication, or that editors lack the time and interest to compile it, or possibly both.

6. See a table of the main creator credits in the appendix to this essay.

7. It could be argued that this is appropriate for a comic-book version of the character. We recognize Superman by his costume, not his facial features.

8. Although there are some one-issue stories, most of *FA* is structured around two-issue adventures, the better to permit one of the central tropes associated with the character: the mid-story cliffhanger.

9. Page numbers in comics of this period are given sporadically, and not always accurately.

Works Cited

Benson, Nicholas. "Apes on TV: Medium Specificity and Considerations of Continuity in Early Transmedia Storytelling." *Critical Studies in Television*, vol. 14, no. 1, 2019, pp. 22–39.

Fast, Karin, and Henrik Örnebring. "Transmedia World-Building: *The Shadow* (1931–Present) and *Transformers* (1984–Present)." *International Journal of Cultural Studies*, vol. 20, no. 6, 2017, pp. 636–652.

Hernández-Pérez, Manuel, and José Gabriel Ferreras Rodriguez. "Serial Narrative, Intertextuality, and the Role of Audiences in the Creation of a Franchise: An Analysis of the

Indiana Jones Saga from a Cross-Media Perspective." *Mass Communication and Society*, vol. 17, no. 1, 2014, pp. 26–53.

Jenkins, Henry. "Transmedia Storytelling 101." *Confessions of an Aca-Fan* (22 Mar. 2007). http://henryjenkins.org/2007/03. Accessed 7 Aug. 2019.

Lucas, George. "Prologue." *Uncle Scrooge McDuck: His Life and Times by Carl Barks*. Ed. Edward Summer. Berkeley: Celestial Arts, 1987.

Pillai, Nicolas. "'What am I looking at, Mulder?': Licensed Comics and the Freedoms of Transmedia Storytelling." *Science Fiction Films and Television*, vol. 6, no. 1, 2013, pp. 101–117.

The Shadow of the Archaeologist
Archetypes of Evil in Marvel's The Further Adventures of Indiana Jones

Brian A. Dixon

In the tense opening moments of *Raiders of the Lost Ark*, deep in the primal jungles of Peru, we are confronted by a shadowy figure. Initially defined only by the visuals of his distinctive accouterments—the dark fedora, worn leather jacket, and coiled bullwhip—he is a figure at once mysterious and commanding, rugged and uncompromising. Stepping into a shaft of bright sunlight that filters through the jungle canopy, he is revealed to be Harrison Ford as Indiana Jones. This classic shot, with its tantalizing interplay between light and shadow, introduced audiences to one of cinema's most beloved and iconic heroes. In the thrilling and unforgettable film that follows, a film that blends the narrative cues of classic Hollywood film serials with the archetypes of mythological lore, we come to know this remarkable character—archaeologist, adventurer, academic, and hero.

In mythic narratives, a hero is defined by his villains, and Indiana Jones is no exception. In *Raiders of the Lost Ark* and the many stories that it would inspire, the daring archaeologist faces hateful antagonists who serve to reflect or explicate his own fascinating character. Noteworthy examples can be found in the colorful rogues encountered in the comic books published by Marvel Comics in the years following the film's debut. It is these stories that represent the first original adventures featuring Indiana Jones in a new medium. *The Further Adventures of Indiana Jones* (1983–86) offers a unique example of cross-media adaptation as the hero's quest seen in the first Indiana Jones film is developed by a talented roster of comic book scribes into a storytelling formula for sequential art. Examining the narratives of Marvel's *Further Adventures*, with their inventive plots and archetypal villains, invites a greater scrutiny of the role that Jungian archetypes play in the Indiana Jones mythos, particularly in the relationship between hero and villain. In repeatedly enacting a confrontation between Dr. Jones and his own shadow, Marvel's *Further Adventures* established an enduring narrative formula, one that initiated an expansive transmedia franchise that continues to this day.

Raiders of the Lost Ark was an unqualified box office success. It was the top-grossing film of 1981, earning $389 million worldwide during its initial theatrical run, and it remains one of the highest grossing films of all time, adjusted for ticket price inflation. From the start, Lucas conceived of the film as the first in a series. Collaborating with Spielberg, he created a hero capable of carrying a franchise. That hero was an amalgamation of various cultural influences, most notably the heroes of the film serials of the 1930s. Other influences can be traced to "pulp magazine proto-heroes like Doc Savage, H. Rider Haggard's safari hunter Allan Quatermain, Ian Fleming's superspy James Bond, and even real-life adventurers such as Hiram Bingham and T.E. Lawrence" (DiFruscio 59). Significantly, both Lucas and Spielberg were also inspired by comic book narratives, with such unlikely sources as Carl Barks's *Walt Disney's Uncle Scrooge* comics providing the basis for key set pieces in the blockbuster film (Blum).[1] The success of *Raiders of the Lost Ark* established an instant demand for new stories featuring heroic archaeologist Indiana Jones and provided the impetus for an expansive transmedia franchise. The character would go on to star in video games, original novels, roleplaying games, theme park attractions, a television series, and comic books of his own.

The first hint of the expanded universe to be built around the iconic Indiana Jones is found in the first cross-media adaptation of the film, a licensed comic book published by Marvel Comics. Lucasfilm had already established a working relationship with Marvel through the development of their successful *Star Wars* series, which began in 1977. A screening of footage from *Raiders of the Lost Ark* inspired Marvel Editor-in-Chief Jim Shooter to commission a comic book adaptation of Indiana Jones's debut, published concurrently in *Marvel Super Special* #18 (September 1981) and *Raiders of the Lost Ark* #1–3 (September–November 1981). The adaptation was produced by some of the publisher's top talents, including writer Walt Simonson and artist John Buscema, with covers from Howard Chaykin, James T. Sherman, and Walt Simonson.

The comic adaptation of *Raiders of the Lost Ark* brings all of the heroes and villains, trials and triumphs, adventure and intrigue of the hit film to the comic book page. Its vivid action and serialized storytelling inspired editor Jim Salicrup to recommend that Marvel further capitalize on their licensing arrangement with Lucasfilm. In Indiana Jones, the two companies had a hero who could carry his own ongoing series of adventure comics. *The Further Adventures of Indiana Jones* launched with issue number one in January of

1983. Despite "a routine of instability and creative turnover on the book," the series would run for a further thirty-three issues, ending in March of 1986 (DiFruscio 60). Once again, it was the talent involved in the comic that convinced Lucasfilm of its potential (Cronin). *The Further Adventures* made the most of Marvel's roster, spotlighting the work of legendary comic creators such as John Byrne, Denny O'Neil, David Michelinie, Archie Goodwin, Herb Trimpe, Jackson "Butch" Guice, and Steve Ditko.

The challenge associated with an ongoing series such as *The Further Adventures of Indiana Jones* reflects the challenge inherent to the process of transmedia adaptation itself. The telling of "further adventures" featuring Indiana Jones, Marcus Brody, and Marion Ravenwood necessitated a storytelling formula, one that could provide the framework for twelve regular issues a year.[2] It would have to be based on the content of a single film—*Raiders of the Lost Ark*—and remain true to the spirit of what had come before. Just as significantly, however, it would have to consistently provide the audience with something new.

In pitching original comic book adventures for Indiana Jones, writers such as Byrne and Michelinie adapted the narrative of the blockbuster film into a reliable formula, one heavily dependent upon mythic elements. The sequential storytelling of Marvel's *Further Adventures*, like the narrative of the Spielberg film, lends itself to mythological criticism. Such an approach is appropriate considering the pivotal role that mythic elements play in the narratives of George Lucas. Much has been written about Lucas's use of the monomyth studied by Joseph Campbell, particularly in *Star Wars* (Gordon, et al.). Archetypes are the cornerstones of such narratives. In *Raiders of the Lost Ark*, we recognize the explorer, the mentor, the lover, or the stoic, just as the object-quest that provides the plot itself follows in the footsteps of the hero's journey, from departure through initiation to return. Character archetypes—particularly those associated with heroism and villainy—would also prove to be an important element in the sequential storytelling of Marvel's *The Further Adventures of Indiana Jones*.

For stories built around a mythic hero such as Indiana Jones, villains provide an essential opposition. *Raiders of the Lost Ark* features a spectrum of villainy. In Toht, the Gestapo agent, we sense the horror of sadism. In Oberst Dietrich, we witness the cruelty and efficiency of the Nazi war machine. Satipo establishes the threat of betrayal, and the one-eyed Monkey Man, with his devious trained capuchin, embodies the vast network of spies and assassins who seek to bring an untimely end to the hero's quest.

The most complex villain of the film is René Belloq. Belloq is a French archaeologist—like Jones, a seeker of antiquities. Both are mercenaries in search of mythic relics. Instead of acting on behalf of a museum or other legitimate academic institution in the quest for the Ark of the Covenant, however, Belloq's activities are controlled by Nazi masters who aspire to world domination. Brilliant but also misguided, Belloq serves as the film's central antagonist. His role as the hero's nemesis is established during the film's captivating opening sequence, in which he relieves Dr. Jones of the golden Pachamama fertility idol outside of the Temple of the Chachapoyan Warriors in Peru. The scene is succinct but revealing. At once, we sense the longstanding rivalry between these two fortune hunters, and we understand the depth of the conflict between them. In Marvel's comic adaptation, based on early drafts of the film's script, Dietrich expresses admiration for the animosity between them: "The purity of your hatred, gentlemen, is an inspiration to us all" (Simonson 74).

The character of Belloq was developed during a story conference between George Lucas, Steven Spielberg, and screenwriter Lawrence Kasdan held in January of 1978, a conference that provided the basis for the original screenplay for *Raiders of the Lost Ark* (Keefe). During these lengthy brainstorming sessions, Belloq was conceived of as Jones's "arch-rival," a character who would serve as a villainous counterpart to the archaeologist hero. Lucas introduces the idea early in the story conference: "He's the corrupt version of our guy. He's the one who really goes in and rapes the temples, and steals all that stuff, and sends it off to private collectors, and takes antiquities, and breaks them into small pieces, and sells each piece for the price of the original" (12). Though Kasdan offers a number of suggestions for story elements that would have established a personal vendetta between the two characters—suggestions that include setting up Belloq as a man who has lashed out at Indy's family or lover—Lucas insists that theirs must be a professional or "friendly" rivalry, deadly though it may be. "They hate each other, they have tried to kill each other, and all that stuff, so it's sort of a friendly animosity," Lucas describes. "They respect each other and, sooner or later, one of them is going to kill the other. It's Moriarty and Sherlock Holmes" (13).

This concept for the character remains unchanged in the finished film, in which Belloq's role as "the corrupt version of our guy" is refined into a distinct and compelling figure. In one of *Raiders of the Lost Ark*'s more contemplative scenes, Jones sits in a bar in Cairo, mourning the apparent loss of Marion and grappling with the guilt that he associates with that loss. It is at this moment that he is confronted by a self-righteous Belloq, who expounds on the truth of their relationship:

> How odd, that it should end this way for us, after so many stimulating encounters. I almost regret it. Where shall I find a new adversary, so close to my own level?... You and I are very much alike. Archaeology is our religion, yet we have both fallen from the pure faith. Our methods have not differed as much as you pretend. I am a shadowy reflection of you. And it would take only a nudge to make you like me, to push you out of the light.

Notably, the action described in Kasdan's screenplay elaborates on Jones's reaction to this assertion: "There is a certain amount of truth to this; the recognition of it flickers across Indy's bleary eyes. Belloq sees it there" (50).[3] Spielberg's careful use of light and shadow in this scene, analyzed by media critic John Kenneth Muir, places the hero "half-in and half-out of the shadows." This furthers our understanding of the character dynamics at play, serving to "pinpoint a morally uncertain Indiana Jones perched half-way between good and evil."[4] Here, Belloq's efficacy as an arch-villain is elucidated for the audience, his function in the mythic narrative made clear. He is openly established as a shadow archetype, the "shadowy reflection" of the hero.

As defined by Carl Jung, the shadow represents those aspects of consciousness and personality that the conscious ego does not identify in itself. The shadow encapsulates qualities and impulses that an individual "denies in himself but can plainly see in other people—such things as egotism, mental laziness, and sloppiness; unreal fantasies, schemes, and plots; carelessness and cowardice; inordinate love of money and possessions" (von Franz 174). The shadow is typically recognized only in projection, in individuals who mirror our own personalities but for those transgressions or sins that we deny in ourselves. Throughout his writings on analytical psychology, Jung demonstrates that the shadow is a motif "well known to mythology" (Jung, *Aion* 10) and encourages its study, acknowledging "that side of psychic experience which expresses itself in superstition and mythology... this aspect of psychic life is not to be undervalued" (Jung, *Modern Man* 196). For the protagonist in a spiritually transformative narrative, as for the individual undergoing psychoanalysis, confronting the shadow and recognizing the dark aspects of the personality as real and affecting "is the essential condition for any kind of self-knowledge" (Jung, *Aion* 8).

For Indiana Jones, confronted with a man who is his shadowy reflection, a rival archaeologist who embodies the temerity and greed and moral corruption that he denies in himself, the conflict with René Belloq is decisive.[5] Not only does it inspire a crucial renewal of his faith during the Biblical final act of *Raiders of the Lost Ark*, it provided the base template for the stories told in Marvel's *Further Adventures*.

Though licensed comic books are often wrongly regarded as "ontologically impure, dismissed as distant echoes of either of their parent media" with nothing to contribute to the fictional universes established by films or to the field of comic book publishing, these new adventures were both inventive and influential (Pillai 103). They would, in turn, initiate the development of an expansive transmedia franchise. Archaeologists serve as the dominant villains in stories featuring Indiana Jones, and this is a pattern that first becomes apparent in the *Further Adventures*. With Belloq as a foundational figure, others would follow. The use of archaeologist shadow figures as villains lends Indy's battles a mythic quality. The result is the kind of storytelling that inspires the reader "to express the difference between higher and lower values and the depth of emotional experiences" (Jones 54). Such antagonists elevate those four-color conflicts of the comic book page to the level of mythological struggle.

The covers for *The Further Adventures of Indiana Jones* #4–5 bear an eye-catching notice that advertises that this is a comic "featuring the hero of *Raiders of the Lost Ark!*" The announcement is a reminder that the advent of further adventures featuring the iconic hero of Spielberg's film demanded careful attention to the balance between novelty and nostalgia. Certain expectations accompany this promise of adventure. Readers picking up a comic book after viewing the hit film had reason to expect that key elements of the screen story would reoccur in the sequential art, but there was also an understanding that the quest for the Ark of the Covenant represented but one of Dr. Jones's many thrilling adventures, each of them with their own distinct villains, allies, exotic locales, and legendary relics. Some comic stories follow the formula while others defy it.[6]

Throughout his tenure at Marvel, in his quests for the Crystal Cylinder of Stonehenge and the Crown of Rurick and even Bigfoot, Indiana Jones would face a veritable rogues gallery. Some of the villains are to be expected in an adventure comic modeled on a film inspired by the action serials of the 1930s.[7] American gangster Busby Giles ("Deadly Rock!," *Further Adventures* #13), whose scheme to build a criminal hideaway amid the protected ruins of a Hopi cave city is inspired by tales of Butch Cassidy and the Sundance Kid, bears all the hallmarks of a Hollywood caricature. He would not be out of place in a book featuring Dick Tracy. Esmeralda Vasques ("The Sea Butchers," *Further Adventures* #15–16), a pirate as bloodthirsty as she is greedy, plunders an ancient Chinese temple for its treasures in a plot that evokes *Treasure Island* or Milton Caniff's *Terry and the Pirates*. Other villains, such as the enigmatic Elizabethan immortal known only as Prospero ("The Devil's Cradle," *Further Adventures* #3), are utterly unique. Naturally, Jones battles a never-ending succession of Nazis, including Emil Loeb ("Gateway to Infinity!," *Further Adventures* #4–5), Curt Vogel ("Africa Screams!," *Further Adventures* #7–8), Ilsa Toht ("The Gold Goddess," *Further Adventures* #9–10), and Hans Degen ("The Cuban Connection!," *Further Adventures* #20–22). In later stories, he even runs afoul of Chinese Tongs and the Irish Republican Army ("Shot by Both Sides!," *Further Adventures* #29–30). Whether these villains are motivated by politics or greed, conquest or revenge, Jones's heroism is reinforced through his opposition to them in a dynamic that echoes *Raiders of the Lost Ark*.[8] During the harrowing climax of "Africa Screams!," when Indy is held captive along with a contingent of Nazi troops and contemplates his options for escape, he vows that he would never join them: "I'd rather face a pitful of cobras than deal with Vogel's bunch!" (Michelinie, "Africa Screams!" 258). To an audience deeply familiar with Jones's phobia, the strength of the rebuke is clear at once.

More common in these comic book stories are villains that are in some way associated with Dr. Jones's own anthropological interests. The sometimes-colorful narratives of the *Further Adventures* regularly remind us that "Indiana Jones is an archaeologist, a seeker after history.... Doctor Jones is indeed a man who reveres the past" (Michelinie, "The Fourth Nail" 345). Many of the comic book villains who oppose him reflect these sensibilities, even if they are not trained archaeologists. The artifact smuggling at the heart of "Club Nightmare!" (*Further Adventures* #6), for instance, is the work of Jamal, a crooked antiquities dealer whose scheming threatens to sabotage the opening of Marion Ravenwood's New York nightclub. Bitter resentment drives National Museum archivist Harvey Pondexter to embrace the demonic influence of ancient bones in "Demons" (*Further Adventures* #14). The corrupt Flaggart, who plays an important role in deciphering the deadly mysteries of "Revenge of the Ancients" (*Further Adventures* #24), is recognized by Jones as an epigrapher, "that member of an archaeological team who deciphers, interprets, and classifies ancient inscriptions" (Trimpe 345). Each of these villains reflects the hero's focus on history and his passion for preserving the past, as well as those excesses or faults that he must strive to overcome.

Most significant among the archeological aficionados presented in the pages of the comic book is Ben Ali Ayoob. One of only two villains to feature in more than one story during the *Further Adventures*, Ayoob is described in his second appearance as Indiana Jones's "arch nemesis." A wealthy Arab collector, Ayoob is obsessed with historical artifacts. Introducing himself to Jones, he confesses, "That is my one weakness, I'm afraid—whenever I hear of a unique find, I simply *must* have it" (Michelinie, "The Fourth Nail" 329). In Jones's response to Ayoob's unabashed and selfish greed, he employs what will become a character-defining refrain: "An artifact that important belongs to the world!" (360). Ayoob is an obsessive, driven by his insatiable greed to possesses ancient wonders such as the fabled Fourth Nail of Christ's crucifixion, and he is willing to steal or counterfeit such artifacts in a ruthless effort to undermine opponents such as Jones. Though their relationship begins with an offer of partnership from Ayoob, an overture that emphasizes their shared interests, Jones is repulsed by the villain and rejects him outright, for he embodies a degree of avarice that suggests but ultimately eclipses the hero's own mercenary tendencies. Ayoob's villainy serves to demonstrate by contrast the importance of the archaeologist's role as a guardian of cultural heritage and the public interest.

The most dominant and memorable villains of the *Further Adventures* are, like René Belloq before them, trained archaeologists who serve as shadow figures, mirroring the comic's protagonist in attributes, expertise, or origin. Sigfried Klexx stands as a prime example. A German archaeologist of imposing stature, Klexx's background and styling instantly evoke the Nazi villains of previous stories. He is the embodiment of the initial conception of the arch-rival of *Raiders of the Lost Ark*, described by Lucas as a "German version" of Jones (12). In "Revenge of the Ancients"—written by Herb Trimpe, with art by Trimpe and Danny Bulanadi—Klexx seeks to plunder the wealth and treasures of a South American temple constructed by "a people that predated known civilization" (Trimpe 358). Again, rampant greed serves as a defining trait, as does Klexx's arrogance and his opposition to the established order. Klexx boasts, "I am the world's greatest archaeologist.... I don't play by the rules. I play to win.... The way is now clear for us. In a few days, we will have in our possession unlimited wealth ... and power!" (355). Encountering the infamous villain, Jones recognizes him at once, explaining to his companion, Julia Valdez, that Klexx has "busted every rule off [sic] the International Treaty for the Protection of Antiquities ... and he's wanted in a dozen countries for everything from petty theft to murder" (355). It is Klexx's utter disregard for human life that Jones finds most offensive, leading to a descriptive exchange. As Klexx regards a captive Indiana Jones, who will soon be forced to bear witness to the human sacrifice necessary to unlock the ancient temple, he remarks on the disapproving hero's character. "Ah, Jones, Jones, Jones. You're so... so clean." Jones's retort is swift: "Next to you, a sewer rat is clean" (359).

The resolution of "Revenge of the Ancients" is also noteworthy, as it offers Indiana Jones a unique opportunity to counter the villain's immorality and reassert a reverence for the past and, perhaps, indigenous peoples. With Klexx consumed by the titular revenge of the ancients in the form of a "roaring, scorching tidal wave of fire"—a supernatural force "bigger than even his greed-driven mind could imagine"—Jones escapes with Valdez, who is a "direct descendent" of the indigenous tribe that once inhabited the region (360–65). Valdez reflects on the events that led her to become embroiled in this unfortunate affair: "I'm a student at Berkeley. I was thinking of dropping out. My folks need help at home. I'm on a scholarship, but you know, with the Depression and all.... I wanted to be an archaeologist, believe it or not. But now I'm not so sure." In a moment that reminds us of his role as an educator and as a guardian of the past, Jones seizes this opportunity to balance the destruction that Klexx has wrought and insists, "Quitting would be a mistake" (366). Even as the story ends with the ominous implication that the "raw, unbridled, raging evil" of Klexx has survived incineration, we are left with the hope that Valdez will one day become an archaeologist in her own right, one whose studies of history and culture are motivated by the righteousness she has witnessed in Jones. The evil of Klexx is undying, but it has inspired an awakening or spiritual renewal in both teacher and student.

A more complex shadow figure can be found in the very first of the *Further Adventures*, "22-Karat Doom!" (also known as "The Ikons of Ikammanen"; *Further Adventures* #1–2)—written by John Byrne and Denny O'Neil, with art by Byrne and Terry Austin. At the center of this multi-faceted tale, part murder mystery and part action-adventure, is young Edith Dunne, a student of archaeology who studied under Dr. Jones himself at Marshall College. Researching in conjunction with her brother Charlie, Edith learns of the location of the Ikons of Ikammanen, corpses encased in gold that are reputed to be "capable of becoming living avengers" (Byrne 83). Charlie's sudden murder leads Jones and Edith to misadventure on the west coast of Africa, where they discover the terrifying origin of the legend. Jones is clever enough to discern the true motives directing these events. At the story's climax, he confronts Edith with the truth: she murdered her brother in an effort to seize credit for the discovery. As an archaeologist, she is concerned only with glory and self-promotion. She fantasizes about appearing on the cover of *Life* magazine and in movie newsreels. More significantly, she hopes to supplant the very legend of archaeology who mentored her: "I want the high and mighty Doctor Indiana Jones to die" (123). Though Professor Jones, "the most popular archaeology teacher on the faculty" at Marshall College, has sought to instill in students such as Edith Dunne a respect and appreciation for the principles of archaeology, she is moved to betrayal and murder based on a warped impression of the man's popularity and fame (82). Jones serves as a mentor archetype for Edith. In turn, she serves as his shadow. Her crimes reflect not only the excesses of Indiana Jones's own character but also the risk inherent in conflating archaeology with celebrity.

Perhaps the most memorable of the archaeologist villains depicted in Marvel's *Further Adventures* is Ian McIver. Introduced in "Africa Screams!" as a key player in a ring of international artifact thieves, McIver is a burly Scotsman distinguished by his bold spirit and blazing red beard. It is made clear to us that he and Jones are longtime competitors, positioning him as a further iteration of the arch-rival conceived by Lucas, Spielberg, and Kasdan. "He's a mercenary. He's for hire.... [He's] the other great guy in the world who does this sort of thing" (Lucas 14). In the two stories that feature him as an antagonist, "Africa Screams!" and "The Search for Abner" (*Further Adventures* #17–18), McIver and Jones clash repeatedly. As they are evenly matched, the action sequences that follow are exciting and memorable. Their first skirmish, set against the backdrop of the Mere d'Amitié Monastery in the hillside vineyards of France, ends with Jones's retreat and a vow from McIver that epitomizes their relationship: "G'wan, Indiana, take yer prize—but take me word with it! Because I swear that soon.... Perhaps vera soon.... We will meet again!" (Michelinie, "Africa Screams!" 231). McIver, more than any of the other shadows seen in the comics, seems for a time to be inescapable. The

Scottish archaeologist is distinguished from his American counterpart through his greed and, like Belloq, through his willingness to collaborate with Nazis. Their alliance is a happy one, for the Nazis believe that in matters of archaeology, "motivations do not matter—it is results that count" (252). The nature of the medium omits performance, but Kerry Gammill and Sam de la Rosa's vivid and characterful artwork, in particular, conveys much of McIver's persona. Here is an appropriately "rough and tumble" rival, a shadow who matches the cunning, training, rugged temperament, and sly wit of Indiana Jones. Though Ian McIver's appearances in the *Further Adventures* are brief, they are memorable, leaving a lasting impression. He stands as a comic book counterpart to *Raiders of the Lost Ark*'s Belloq, a "shadowy reflection" of the adventurer archaeologist hero.

The repetition of this dominant archetype across three years of licensed comic book stories is a testament to its efficacy in narratives featuring Indiana Jones. The *Further Adventures* take the iconic hero from the Aleutian Islands to the Himalayas to the Amazon rainforest. He encounters vengeful gods and demonic spirits and living dragons. Jones's many allies—including Marion Ravenwood, Marcus Brody, Short Round, Sallah, and Julia Valdez—provide material and moral support. Through it all, in every variation of the quest narrative, the shadow remains inescapable, delineating the hero's defining idiosyncrasies as well as the demands of his profession. It marks a cycle or sequence that analytical psychology recognizes as an essential determinant in individuation, the process through which aspects of personality and experience are integrated in the development of the self. Indiana Jones's repeat encounters with the shadow archetype are integral to his persona as a mythic hero. As Jung posits, such a hero "constantly needs the renewal that begins with a descent into his own darkness, an immersion in his own depths, and with a reminder that he is related by blood to his adversary" (Jung, *Mysterium Coniunctionis* 334). Without such renewal, there can be no individuation, no transformation, no resolution to the cycle of the monomyth.

The use of archaeologists as villains in cultural narratives such as these also has noteworthy implications for the field of archaeology. When archaeologist Jessie Hale meets our hero in the comic story "Good as Gold" (*Further Adventures* #25), her reaction to him coveys a familiar objection: "You may be a wonderful archaeologist, but you're also an adventurer. You don't take our work seriously!" (Grant 10). The Indiana Jones films and their comic book counterparts offer no pretense or apology for their depiction of archaeology and archaeologists, nor should they; these are dramatic narratives, not an attempt to offer a realistic, scientific representation of archaeological pursuits. In these narratives featuring characters who are both archaeologists and adventurers, the quest for ancient and mystical artifacts provides the basis for thrilling action and engaging drama. Nevertheless, the archetypal figures presented to the audience in such stories have an impact on the public's perception of an important field of scientific inquiry, as Kevin McGeough has argued in *Near Eastern Archaeology*: "While popular audiences may not take away messages from films about scientific techniques and excavation strategies, they are likely to take away important messages about who archaeologists are, why they do what they do, and how relationships to the past are constituted" (174). When we consider both the defining characteristics and the narrative function of characters such as Indiana Jones and Ian McIver, we begin to develop a greater understanding of the cultural resonance and widespread appeal of these stories. These characters are not merely depicted as archaeologists, as heroes or villains, they are depicted as intelligent, educated, canny individuals.

It is crucial that Lucas's conception of Indiana Jones's arch-rival, his shadow, was "also very intelligent ... like Moriarty," not least because it serves to reflect or mirror the traits that we associate with the hero (Lucas 12). Jones is not only an adventurer, he is also an academic; he is not only a mercenary, he is also a scholar. This defining character opposition is central to Lucas's conception of the character and to the character's continuing popularity with audiences. Lucas defines Indiana Jones as "an archaeologist and an anthropologist. A Ph.D. He's a doctor. He's a college professor" (3). In *Raiders of the Lost Ark* and the *Further Adventures*, his mental prowess is repeatedly emphasized for the audience, even as fight scenes and actions sequences demonstrate his strength and bravery. McGeough identifies these talents as integral to distinguishing him from other, similar heroes: "His skill with languages is apparent in his ability not only to sight-read ancient inscriptions, but also to speak numerous languages fluently. Other characters refer to him as Dr. Jones or Professor Jones, and acknowledge his various intellectual achievements, rather than focusing on his physical prowess" (177). Indiana Jones is a hero and an intellectual. That intellectualism—his academic affiliation, his guardianship of the past, his desire to teach and to educate—conveys a message as important as his relationship to the shadow, for "the authority of the archaeologist (in the public eye) is tied up in the archaeologist's heroic persona" (185).

For the Indiana Jones franchise, just as significant is the legacy of the shadow archetypes encountered in *The Further Adventures of Indiana Jones*, a legacy that transcends textual boundaries. The formulaic stories told in the pages of the comic book from 1983 to 1986 prefigured what was to come in future installments of the series—in books, videogames, and landmark films. Most noteworthy in this instance is *Indiana Jones and the Last Crusade* (1989)—adapted by Marvel Comics in *Indiana Jones and the Last Crusade* #1-4 (October-November 1989), written by David Michelinie, with art and covers by Bret Blevins. In the film's memorable opening, thirteen-year-old

Henry Jones, Jr., confronts a sinister figure at Arches National Park in Utah. Clad in a leather jacket and a distinctive hat, the man—referred to in the film's script and credits only as "Fedora"—is a grave robber who seeks to profit from the discovery of the Cross of Coronado, a jewel-encrusted golden crucifix. Young Jones, imbued with a passion for history by his learned father, recognizes the object at once. He also recognizes the moral implications of its theft: "That cross is an important artifact! It belongs in a museum!" For Jones, the encounter with this shadow figure is formative, his recognition of the sins that it represents defining. In the memorable sequence that follows, we witness the origin of the hero known to us as Indiana Jones, his development complete when that dark fedora is taken from the grave robber's head and placed atop his own. Here, at the very genesis of the saga, we witness the promise of individuation with the culmination of all those mythic struggles against shadow archetypes depicted in the panels of the comic book.

An era in which Hollywood relies on comic books to provide its inspiration and to further develop its fictional universes should inspire a reevaluation of these formative sequential narratives. Marvel's *The Further Adventures of Indiana Jones* represents the first attempt to establish an enduring narrative formula that would serve the hero created by George Lucas and Steven Spielberg for *Raiders of the Lost Ark*, a hero motivated by "the familiar rush of wonder, the hunger to illuminate dark corners of history that had first drawn him to archaeology over a decade before; the overwhelming, narcotic awe of having a dream turn tangible!" (Michelinie, "The Sea Butchers" 75). The comic's colorful villains, shadows of the archaeologist hero himself, contribute a mythic dimension to these innovative adventure stories and serve to further illuminate the character of an iconic cultural figure.

NOTES

1. The comic industry also played a more active role in the development of Indiana Jones, as comic artist Jim Steranko was instrumental in establishing the visual style of *Raiders of the Lost Ark*. Early in the film's development, Steranko was commissioned by George Lucas to create four paintings of hero Indiana Jones, paintings that capture the atmosphere of the finished film (Rinzler 34). Steranko has commented on the effectiveness of his paintings in communicating Lucas's vision: "The paintings were used to set the tone of the film.... When the paintings were commissioned, the film had not yet been cast. Indy's facial characteristics were left to me, and I went for a rough, rugged visage, weather beaten and strong.... The result was apparently not too far from what Steven and George were looking for, because Harrison Ford appears almost exactly like the figure in the painting" (Walentis 66, 69).

2. Much of the turmoil that had such an impact on the development of the *Further Adventures* was the result of conflict with Lucasfilm. The licensor resisted innovation, particularly as it related to the development of existing characters. Marvel editor Eliot R. Brown explains, "It was hard working with Lucasfilm, getting scripts to them with time enough for changes, and they didn't want anything of theirs changed or even suggested at—situations, but especially if it involved their characters" (qtd. in DiFruscio 61). This presented an obstacle, particularly, as writer David Michelinie observes, when the "one element that stood out when coming up with new stories evolving from what was established in the movie was the

characters. Indiana Jones was terrific, an irresistible combination of heroism and human foibles.... And with such a solid supporting cast as Marion Ravenwood, Marcus Brody, Sallah, and so many others, the possibilities for character-driven stories was enormous" (qtd. in DiFruscio 62). Lucasfilm's policies demanded an investment in original characters, such as the villains examined here.

3. Belloq further compares himself to Jones during the film's climax. When Indy confronts the contingent of Nazis carrying the Ark of the Covenant to the altar that has been prepared for its unsealing, threatening to destroy the artifact with an anti-tank rocket rather than allow his nemeses to possess it, Belloq's exasperated response reminds us the two are in the same line of work: "You are going to give mercenaries a bad name" (Kasdan 92).

4. John Kenneth Muir considers the appearance of Jones's literal shadow throughout the film, including its appearance during his dramatic entrance at the Raven tavern in Nepal: "Indiana Jones is ... a colossal shadow looming over Marion's life and her decisions. When she first sees him again, after all these years ... that's precisely as Indy appears in the frame, as an over-sized shadow dwarfing her body. He is as large and imposing as she has made him in her memory." Most noteworthy in an examination of the relationship between Jones and Belloq is the scene that takes place between the two characters at the bar in Cairo. "Indy is seen in the foreground of the frame, under a cloak of shadows that echoes his cloak of mourning.... It is here that Belloq refers to Indy as his "mirror," and he discusses with him how they are both men without faith, and thus very much alike.... Indy slips into shadow in this composition because he very much fears that Belloq's words are accurate."

5. During the story conference, George Lucas introduces the concept of Indiana Jones as a "rough and tumble" archaeologist, establishing these vices as inherent features in a complexly constructed hero. "He got involved in going in and getting antiquities. Sort of searching out antiquities. And it became a very lucrative profession so he, rather than be an archaeologist, he became sort of an outlaw archaeologist. He really started being a grave robber for hire, is what it really came down to. And the museums would hire him to steal things out of tombs and stuff" (3).

6. The earliest of the *Further Adventures* are among the most imaginative, offering thrilling narratives that deliver the anticipated blend of exotic discovery and occult possibilities. Later installments, particularly those written by Linda Grant, are more grounded, their drama rooted in political tensions and criminal escapades rather than mythology or legend. Stories such as "Shot by Both Sides!" (*Further Adventures* #29–30), in which Jones partners with an I.R.A. operative to take on a gunrunner in China, and "Big Game" (*Further Adventures* #31), in which accusations of espionage lead to unrest in an Alaskan village, are notably absent of arcane elements and eschew the mythic dynamics that typically serve to distinguish Indiana Jones's adventures.

7. The debt that George Lucas and Steven Spielberg owe to the Hollywood film serials of the 1930s—and that the *Further Adventures* owe to their newspaper strip counterparts—is cleverly acknowledged in a visual reference seen in "The Secret of the Deep" (*Further Adventures* #23), written and drawn by Herb Trimpe. As Indy and Marion argue outside of the Metro Theater, having walked out on a movie, they are standing before a film poster promoting *Ace Drummond*, a thirteen-chapter serial. Aviator Ace Drummond was the hero of a comic strip distributed by King Features Syndicate from 1933 to 1939. In 1936, the comic was adapted as a film serial for Universal Pictures, starring John King as Ace Drummond.

8. An adaptation of *Indiana Jones and the Temple of Doom* (1984) was published by Marvel Comics as a three-issue limited series following the film's release. *Indiana Jones and the Temple of Doom* #1–3 (September–November 1984)—written by David Michelinie, with art by Jackson "Butch" Guice—was published concurrently with *The Further Adventures of Indiana Jones* #21–23. The limited series had an impact on the continuing series, providing the inspiration for an expansion of the storytelling possibilities associated with Indiana Jones.

Works Cited

Blum, Geoffrey. "Wind from a Dead Galleon." *Geoffrey Blum: Writer*. Geoffrey Blum, 1996. Web. 29 May 2019.

Byrne, John, et al. "22-Karat Doom!" *Indiana Jones Omnibus: The Further Adventures: Volume 1.* Milwaukie, OR: Dark Horse, 2009, 79–126. Print.
Cronin, Brian. "Comic Legends: Did Lucasfilm Originally Pass on Marvel's Indiana Jones?" *Comic Book Resources.* CBR.com, 11 June 2018. Web. 23 May 2019.
DiFruscio, Mark. "When Adventure Had a Name: Exploring Marvel Comics' *The Further Adventures of Indiana Jones.*" *Back Issue* 1, no. 55 (April 2012): 59–67. Print.
Gordon, Andrew. "*Star Wars*: A Myth for Our Time." *Literature/Film Quarterly* 6, no. 4 (Fall 1978): 314–26. Print.
Grant, Linda, et al. "Good as Gold." *Indiana Jones Omnibus: The Further Adventures: Volume 3.* Milwaukie, OR: Dark Horse, 2009, 7–30. Print.
Jones, Katte. "An Exploration of Personality Development through Mythic Narratives." *Advanced Developmental Journal* 14 (2014): 42–58. Print.
Jung, C.G. *Aion: Researches into the Phenomenology of the Self.* 2nd ed. Trans. R.F.C. Hull. New York: Routledge, 2014. Print.
_____. *The Archetypes and the Collective Unconscious.* 2nd ed. Trans. R.F.C. Hull. New York: Routledge, 2014. Print.
_____. *Mysterium Coniunctionis.* 2nd ed. Trans. R.F.C. Hull. New York: Routledge, 2014. Print.
Kasdan, Lawrence. *Raiders of the Lost Ark* (Revised Third Draft). August 1979. Screenplay.
Keefe, Patrick Radden. "Spitballing Indy." *The New Yorker*, 25 March 2013. Web. 23 May 2019.
Lucas, George, Steven Spielberg, and Larry Kasdan. "*Raiders of the Lost Ark* Story Conference Transcript." 23-28 January 1978. Web. 24 May 2019.
McGeough, Kevin. "Heroes, Mummies, and Treasure: Near Eastern Archaeology in the Movies." *Near Eastern Archaeology* 69, no. 3/4 (September–December 2006): 174–185. Print.
Michelinie, David, et al. "Africa Screams!" *Indiana Jones Omnibus: The Further Adventures: Volume 1.* Milwaukie, OR: Dark Horse, 2009, 223–270. Print.
_____. "The Cuban Connection!" *Indiana Jones Omnibus: The Further Adventures: Volume 2.* Milwaukie, OR: Dark Horse, 2009, 175–246. Print.
_____. "The Fourth Nail." *Indiana Jones Omnibus: The Further Adventures: Volume 1.* Milwaukie, OR: Dark Horse, 2009, 319–366. Print.
_____. "The Sea Butchers." *Indiana Jones Omnibus: The Further Adventures: Volume 2.* Milwaukie, OR: Dark Horse, 2009, 57–104. Print.
Muir, John Kenneth. "*Raiders of the Lost Ark* (1981)." *Reflections on Film and Television.* John K. Muir, 24 August 2014. Web. 23 May 2019.
Pillai, Nicolas. "'What am I looking at, Mulder?' Licensed Comics and the Freedoms of Transmedia Storytelling." *Science Fiction Film and Television* 6, no. 1 (2013): 101–117. Print.
Rinzler, J.W. *The Complete Making of Indiana Jones.* New York: Del Rey, 2008. Print.
Simonson, Walt, et al. "Raiders of the Lost Ark." *Indiana Jones Omnibus: The Further Adventures: Volume 1.* Milwaukie, OR: Dark Horse, 2009, 7–78. Print.
Trimpe, Herb, et al. "Revenge of the Ancients." *Indiana Jones Omnibus: The Further Adventures: Volume 2.* Milwaukie, OR: Dark Horse, 2009, 344–366. Print.
von Franz, M.-L. "The Process of Individuation." *Man and His Symbols.* Eds. Carl G. Jung and M.-L. von Franz. New York: Dell, 1964. 157–254. Print.
Walentis, Al. "Steranko Art Helped Sell *Raiders.*" *Reading Eagle.* 14 June 1981: 66, 69. Print.

"We'll always have Iceland, Indy"

Indiana Jones and His Adventures in Video Games

CARL WILSON

Founded by George Lucas in 1971, Lucasfilm is the production company that famously originated the Indiana Jones and Star Wars movie franchises. Following the successes of Lucasfilm, a wider industrial remit was established. In 1975, Lucas created Industrial Light & Magic (ILM) to specialize in groundbreaking digital visual effects. Moving beyond the technological limitations he experienced while making *Star Wars: Episode IV—A New Hope* (1977), Lucas went on to form the Lucasfilm Computer Division in 1979 (Smith 11). Given that, by 1981, the "once-paltry home videogame market had grown to a respectable $1.2 billion" (Montfort 122), Lucasfilm Games was created to be a natural fit within the Computer Division (Smith 12). Founded in 1982, Lucasfilm Games was renamed LucasArts in 1990; for the purposes of clarity, this essay shall refer to this group as LucasArts throughout.

Compared to the attention, contracts, and plaudits that ILM was gaining in Hollywood, LucasArts was created with modest expectations, since "George was not convinced; he thought it might be a distraction" (Rubin 297). According to LucasArts designer David Fox, "Lucasfilm Games was actually set up so that the parent company could avoid the massive tax penalties it incurred due to the vast amount of revenue generated by the Star Wars and Indiana Jones franchises" (Rignall). Lucas's own perspective is that he was "captivated by the idea of interactive technology as a new and different way to tell stories" (Smith 7), but nevertheless, he still insisted that the newly formed division "be the best, stay small, and don't lose any money" (Schreier).

In a venture described at the time as "the first of its kind between a videogame and home computer maker like Atari and a movie company" (Rubin 298), Atari, Inc., the dominant videogame publisher of the era, gave Lucasfilm "about $1 million," with a target to "see what you can make," provided that they had "first right of refusal on manufacturing and distributing" (Smith 12). Yet, despite being financed by the profits of their movies, as LucasArts designer Noah Falstein recalls, "we were actually unable to do games based on Star Wars and Indiana Jones for the first several years of our existence because of pre-existing licensing agreements with other companies," such as Atari (Batchelor).

Atari

Released at the same time that LucasArts was created in 1982, the first Indiana Jones game, *Raiders of the Lost Ark*, was a movie tie-in developed and published by Atari for their home console, the Atari 2600. The game is significant in that *Raiders* is the first example of a movie-licensed video game. Notably, while the Indy films were distributed by Paramount Pictures, Atari was owned by Warner Communications, parent company of Warner Bros. Pictures. The box art is adapted from Richard Amsel's movie poster; the music is a compressed version of John Williams's "The Raider's March"; and while there are whips, snakes, and a fedora, the game is presented as a top-down puzzle-adventure, requiring exploration and experimentation (unusually, Indy was controlled by the player two stick). Created by Howard Scott Warshaw, *Raiders* was followed by *E.T. the Extra-Terrestrial*, another Steven Spielberg adaptation. However, where *Raiders* had "nearly nine months of development time" (Seppala), Atari had taken so long to acquire the $22–25 million license that "by the time the deal was made, Warshaw had just five weeks to get the game finished in time for its release at Christmas in 1982" (Lamble, *Atari*). Overshadowing *Raiders*, while also being tied to it, *E.T.* was unfairly blamed for the collapse of both Atari and the early video game industry.

Following the crash of 1983, where "profits from home console games" fell "by a staggering 97 per cent" (Lamble, *1983*), publisher Mindscape released their first licensed game, *Indiana Jones in the Lost Kingdom* (1985), for the Commodore 64 home computer. Advertising that "nobody told Indiana Jones the rules. And no one will tell you," *Lost Kingdom* is another abstract adventure-puzzle game, this time featuring snow/sand caves, castles, and alien creatures, all untethered to any movie. *Lost Kingdom* is noteworthy in that it created the "Indiana Jones Quotient" (IJQ), a scoring system that rewards the player for overcoming challenges in a manner befitting Indy himself.

In 1985, a reformulated Atari Games also released *Indiana Jones and the Temple of Doom* for the arcades. The game features sound bites, levels, and promotional artwork from the actual film, to benefit from being released close to the 1984 movie. Based on this cross-marketing success, *Temple of Doom* was ported to a number of home platforms, but as Mike French defines the moment, "there were quite a number of adaptations made off the original Atari game. Some were made by Mindscape, some were made by U.S. Gold. [...] All of them are disappointing [...] flimsy adaptations" (French, *Console Version*).

Mindscape followed with *Indiana Jones and the Revenge of the Ancients* (1987). In stark contrast with Atari's visually and aurally sophisticated tie-in to *Temple of Doom*, Mindscape's game is a pc-based text adventure: the game world is explored purely through onscreen text. More significantly, in foreshadowing *Indiana Jones and the Kingdom of the Crystal Skull* (2008), *Revenge of the Ancients* features the return of Marion Ravenwood, with the plot climaxing at a mystical pyramid in Mexico.

The last of the Atari/Mindscape Indy releases form a bookend in early video game licensing case studies. In 1984 Atari had split into two separate entities, with Atari Games creating Tengen in 1987 to continue to release their arcade games on home consoles. After Mindscape had released their officially licensed adaptation of *Temple of Doom* in 1988, Tengen followed with their unlicensed, yet identical, version in 1989. After more unlicensed releases and a series of $100 million lawsuits between Tengen (Atari) and Nintendo, it wasn't until 1994 when they "jointly announced that they had settled all litigation between them concerning alleged patent and copyright infringements and antitrust violations" (Current).

Founding LucasArts employee David Langston describes the period: "We could watch what Atari was doing with licensed things and say 'this isn't good enough,' but we didn't have to do that work ourselves" (McWhertor). With Lucasfilm's *Indiana Jones and the Last Crusade* on the horizon, a decision was made in the September of 1988 that they were to take their marquee games in-house to LucasArts and exert greater control over their outsourced licenses (Bevan 94). With Indiana Jones, LucasArts finally had a chance to adapt their first Lucasfilm property.

LucasArts

There is more than one video game version of *Indiana Jones and the Last Crusade*. There is *Last Crusade: The Action Game*, and *Last Crusade: The Graphic Adventure*, both published in 1989 to coincide with the theatrical release of the movie. In the "platforming" genre that was prevalent at the time, *The Action Game* received a wide release, being outsourced in development and distribution, and ported to every major platform in a steady slew every year from 1989 through to 1993. They are also subpar-quality games, echoing Langston's issues with games being developed as licensed mass-products.

The Graphic Adventure, on the other hand, was developed and produced entirely in-house by LucasArts. Falstein's concept document shows that he was originally planning an ambitious "hybrid of computer arcade game and book paragraph puzzle game" (Bevan 95). However, with a tight turnaround required, Ron Gilbert and David Fox were drafted in to help make a graphic adventure. Without the Indiana Jones or Star Wars licenses in the late '80s, LucasArts had built a reputation for their classic graphic adventures, such as *Maniac Mansion* (1987) and *Zak McKracken and the Alien Mind Benders* (1988). Utilizing Gilbert's SCUMM game-engine from these earlier projects, *The Graphic Adventure* is a more mature example of a LucasArts adventure game. The Indiana Jones game uses the IQ (Indy Quotient), a return to the IJQ system from Mindscape's *Lost Kingdom*, as puzzles and objectives could be solved in a multitude of ways, leading to different game endings. LucasArts had house-ruled that players would not die in their games, but through the intervention of the designers, players could now "choose poorly" and enjoy the graphic consequences unfolding onscreen (French, *Interviews*).

The Graphic Adventure is based on the original script for the movie, and several scenes that are omitted from the film appear within the game, such as the college boxing ring and zeppelin radio room, making it something of an alternative cut. Discussing the animated-games genre, Hal Barwood says: "What it really resembles is theatre. Plays," relying upon dialogue and setting more than action (Maher). The sequel, *Indiana Jones and the Fate of Atlantis: The Graphic Adventure*, recorded 8000 lines of scripted dialogue for their CD-ROM "talkies" release (Lamberton), while the theatrical backdrops to both games are visually analogous to the staged presentations of Elliot Scott's set-design illustrations for the actual movies (see: Vaz 183), or the matte painting backdrops used within the film frames themselves.

Moving beyond Lucas's original remit, by 1990 LucasArts was "the largest game company in the world at that point" (Bevan 94), and they scaled their ambitions to match. Despite being given a rejected Chris Columbus script for *Indiana Jones and the Monkey King* to adapt (Smith 69), where Lucasfilm went with *Last Crusade*, co-designers Hal Barwood and Noah Falstein opted to create an original story. Discarding early plans for an Arthurian quest for Excalibur, and heavily influenced by research in the Skywalker Ranch library, the same way that Lucasfilm movies are developed, the duo settled on the Lost City of Atlantis with new locations such as Iceland and Monte Carlo (Falstein).

Indy can't tell Reich from wrong at the end of *Indiana Jones and the Fate of Atlantis: The Graphic Adventure* (1992).

Barwood, the principle designer and project leader of the game, had worked with Lucas before. They were film students together, and Barwood had worked on Lucas's *THX-1138*. Barwood had also worked closely with Indiana Jones director, Steven Spielberg, in the past, selling him his script for *Sugarland Express* and carrying out uncredited rewrites on *Close Encounters of the Third Kind* (Pellegrom). Prior to *Fate of Atlantis*, Barwood and Falstein had collaborated on an early version of graphic adventure game, *The Dig* (1995), which Spielberg had taken to LucasArts to develop (Woodward 286). As a common refrain throughout all the Indy games, when asked, "Did George Lucas have any direct involvement in the production of Fate of Atlantis?" Barwood's response is "No, he didn't. He's pretty much always been an avuncular presence at the game company. A steadfast supporter, but always in the background" (Mishan). Likewise, "Steven [Spielberg] was not involved" (Bevan 205).

Designing *Fate of Atlantis*, LucasArts reincorporated the IQ system but added three paths to the game: "Fists," "Wits," and "Team," allowing the player to choose their own version of an Indiana Jones narrative. The "Team" path prominently features new Jones sparring-partner and fellow lecturer of archaeology, Sophia Hapgood. To utilize the character effectively, Barwood explains that Hapgood is "more of a driver of action than any of the film heroines" (French, *Interviews*), and Falstein believes he is "proudest of the

Team path because it brought a record number of women players into the game, letting them control Sophia as a character before female lead characters were common in games" (Wallett). Before Lara Croft, there was Sophia Hapgood, who would return in the 1999 game, *Indiana Jones and the Infernal Machine*.

As with adaptations of *The Last Crusade*, there was also a multi-platform release of the inferior isometric action game *Fate of Atlantis: The Action Game*, but, with their focus being on *The Graphic Adventure* as "the best-selling adventure game the company ever made" (Wallett), LucasArts began work on a further sequel. Initially called *Indiana Jones and the Philosopher's Stone*, the team settled on *Indiana Jones and the Iron Phoenix* (*Lost Sequel*). LucasArts stalwart Aric Wilmunder was brought in after they "ran into difficulties," but found that when his "new game design was complete, there were no resources, so we were asked to try to develop this game with a team outside the U.S.," in Canada, where "the work would not meet our high standards" (Hall). Other "difficulties" were equally problematic. With Barwood working as a story consultant on the game, the plot followed post-war Nazis hiding in Bolivia who would find an artifact enabling them to resurrect Hitler. Fifteen months into production, as Barwood explains it, "they were told that selling a game depicting post-war Nazi revival, no matter how negatively, would be illegal in Germany" (Mishan). The German market has always been the largest consumer of LucasArts adventure games, so this issue was catastrophic to development and the game was cancelled (Falstein). LucasArts eventually shifted focus onto *Indiana Jones and the Spear of Destiny*, again "due to be developed by an external studio" (Smith 71), but there is little evidence of how far they actually got with this project (*Lost Sequel*).

With *Iron Phoenix* and *Spear of Destiny* cancelled, they became official Indy comic books. Dark Horse Comics published *Iron Phoenix* as a four-part series from December 1994 to March 1995, which was followed by *Spear of Destiny* in April to July 1995. These comics were the sixth and seventh collected volumes in their series, the first being an adaptation of *Fate of Atlantis*. Like the relationship between *The Last Crusade* movie and game adaptations, *Fate of Atlantis* features scenes in the comic book that were actually dropped from the video game (*Secret History*).

Side Quests

With no new Hollywood movies to adapt or graphic adventures to successfully launch, few Indiana Jones games were released between 1992 and 1998. Two of them are based on the television property, *The Young Indiana Jones Chronicles* (1992–1996). Both *The Young Indiana Jones Chronicles* (1992) for the Nintendo NES and *Instruments of Chaos: Starring … Young Indiana Jones* (1994) for the Sega Genesis are, again, outsourced action-platform games, this time published externally by Jaleco USA, Inc. and SEGA, respectively. While these games are generic tie-ins that offer nothing new to the franchise, genre, or platforms on which they were released, they were not the only Young Indy projects in development at the time. Designed in-house with Lucasfilm Learning (an educational subsidiary set up by Lucas in 1987), developer Brian Moriarty was working on an educational adventure game, *Young Indiana Jones at the World's Fair* (García), but "The show didn't succeed and in the end it got cancelled, and the game I had been working on for about a year got cancelled" (Bevan 320).

Indiana Jones and His Desktop Adventures (1996) is equally interesting for its divergent approach to the license. As another project helmed by Barwood, *Desktop Adventures* was designed to be in competition with short-play home computer games such as *Solitaire*. It was only when the "LucasArts salespeople couldn't figure out how to sell the idea" that the Indy license was applied to the top-down adventure game. According to Barwood, *Desktop Adventures* was the first video game to create infinitely reconfigurable quests that also used re-playable storylines, but the game "barely sold" (Mishan). One might expect *Desktop Adventures* to be more successful if launched today on social media platforms or mobile devices under a casual games banner.

The Indy games that do fall under these headings have been released without LucasArts being the developer or publisher. In 2001, THQ Inc. published *Infernal Machine* as a pseudo–3D *Desktop Adventures*–style game for the Game Boy Color, but in 2008, subsidiary THQ Wireless released platformer-game *LEGO Indiana Jones Mobile Adventure* (a cheap-looking adaptation of the console game from TT Games), then followed it up with *Indiana Jones and the Lost Puzzles* (2009), a game in the "match-3" genre, with Indy reliving the "Name of God" crumbling-floor trap from *The Last Crusade*, to win *Raiders of the Lost Ark*–styled idols.

In 2008, THQ Wireless also released the graphically superior but more cumbersome platformer, *Kingdom of the Crystal Skull*, to coincide with the launch of the film. It was one of only two official tie-ins for the movie; the second *Crystal Skull* game was released on LeapFrog's niche handheld console, the DIDJ Custom Gaming System. Combining platform elements with mathematical puzzles designed to explore the school curricula, the DIDJ game shares its roots with the cancelled *World's Fair* as an educational game to come from Lucasfilm/Arts Learning. Given the history of the game franchise, it may seem incredible that these are the only two tie-ins to the movie, but at the time, LucasArts was developing an untitled flagship Indy game in-house, not related to *Crystal Skull*, which was also cancelled.

As with *Desktop Adventures*, Zynga's Facebook game *Adventure World* did not start out as an Indiana Jones product when it was released in September 2011, but became relaunched as *Adventure World: An Indiana Jones Game* a month later, again with Barwood being credited for Narrative Design (Barwood). Across chapters such as *Indiana Jones and the Calendar of the Sun*, "nine million users a month, according to Facebook's internal stat-tracking" (Totilo), could click and whip through isometrically presented jungles and tombs to solve puzzles for free; although, they couldn't actually play as Indy, because the goal "was to allow [players] to interact with Indiana Jones like in a social experience" (Szalai). That is, until the experience was shut down in January 2013, three months after Disney's acquisition of Lucasfilm. This makes *Adventure World: An Indiana Jones Game* all the more significant: it is the last Indiana Jones video game to be released, over eight years ago, which also marks the longest period (2011–) without a new Indy game being released in any form. Since Disney bought LucasArts, they have licensed Electronic Arts to exclusively make all of their Star Wars games for over a period of 10 years, but no new Indy games have been announced (Friedman).

Star Wars

Starting with Harrison Ford, the interplay between the Star Wars and Indiana Jones franchises begins with the films themselves; with the video games, the connections start as early as the formation of LucasArts. In September 1982, David Fox noted that "it seems appropriate to take a look at what Lucasfilm is famous for: its *films* [...] we need more escapist fantasy which the player can really embrace, a la *Raiders* or *Star Wars*" (Smith 14). Yet, while they couldn't use the licenses in 1982, the skew within LucasArts was eventually towards the Star Wars franchise.

Working with German co-developers, Factor 5, who later adapted the N64 version of *Infernal Machine* (2000), *Indiana Jones' Greatest Adventures* (1994) for the Super Nintendo is notable for being a compilation game spanning the movie franchise and in that it uses the same engine as previous games *Super Star Wars* (1992), *Super Empire Strikes Back* (1993) and *Super Return of the Jedi* (1994). As publisher JVC had bought the licensing rights from Lucasfilm, LucasArts found themselves being advanced "$80,000 to $100,000 per title" by JVC in a six-game deal to make their Lucasfilm-adapted games (Smith 74). There have been more recent examples of iterative development: *Infernal Machine* borrowed the game engine from *Star Wars: Jedi Knight* (Smith 128). Another example would be developer TT Games (who parallel early-Atari by being a subsidiary of Warner Bros. Interactive Entertainment). Their game, *LEGO Star Wars: The Complete Saga* (2007), has sold over 15 million units, making it the best-selling *Star Wars* video game

186 Extended Franchise

Weighty decisions to be made in *Indiana Jones: The Original Adventures* (2008).

(Guinness 109). Changing designs based on the physical LEGO Indy toys that were already available in shops, TT Games released *Indiana Jones: The Original Adventures* (2008) to match the release of *Crystal Skull*. Producer Nick Ricks knew that "what we had to do was strip it all back and look at what makes the Indy films different," so with added "exploration, solving puzzles and riddles" (Robinson), and with publisher Eidos Interactive already being behind the action-adventure *Tomb Raider* franchise, *The Original Adventures* (2008) is estimated to have sold 11 million copies, followed by 4 million copies of *LEGO Indiana Jones 2: The Adventure Continues* in 2009 (*VGChartz*).

Within LucasArts, internal staff were constantly being pulled from Indiana Jones projects to assist with their Star Wars titles. Artist Justin Chin left a mid-'90s "*Indiana Jones* adventure game" to work on *Star Wars: Dark Forces* in 1995 (Smith 89), while engineers were later pulled from an *Indiana Jones* development team to "optimize the code" for *Star Wars: Battlefront II* in 2005 (Smith 181). In 2008, the president of LucasArts, Jim Ward, acknowledged that they had neglected the Indiana Jones franchise as they insisted on "skinning *Star Wars* on every game genre," and planned to release a new Indy game each year (Smith 208). Yet, according to Peter Hirschmann, VP of Product Development, when LucasArts were working on *Star Wars: Force Unleashed* (2008), "*Star Wars* went from being the scrappy underdog [...] to having it all, and a lot of people from the *Indy* team had to stop work on that game to help out on *Star Wars*" (Smith 217).

Both *Force Unleashed* and an untitled Indy game from 2007 evolved from a tech demo set in Marion's bar from *Raiders*, but with Star Wars stormtroopers for enemies. Showing off the Euphoria engine, developed with NaturalMotion, alongside an agreement with Pixelux for their "digital molecular matter system," the demo was considered to be a breakthrough in adaptive environments and emergent game design (Smith 212). A further tech demo/trailer, shown to the press at E3 2006, had Indy brawling in the back alley of San Francisco's Chinatown. The untitled Indy game was set to be the first of the franchise to be made under the direction of Lucas, who was concurrently working on *Crystal Skull*, and the lighting system was being provided by ILM, working in collaboration with LucasArts for the first time (Castro). The game was in development for a new generation of consoles, Sony's PlayStation 3 and Microsoft's Xbox 360, and would have released alongside *Crystal Skull* in 2007. However, having been delayed until 2009, staff were allocated to other projects and the game was eventually cancelled (Ahearn).

Tomb Raider

While the untitled Indy game was delayed from a 2007 release, another 3D action-adventure franchise was launched to critical and financial success that same year. Developed by Naughty Dog, *Uncharted: Drake's Fortune* (2007) follows modern-day treasure-hunter Nathan Drake, who, with a familiar rugged charm, explores tropical islands and jungles through a series of Hollywood spectacle set-pieces in a search for the mythical city of El Dorado. Later games in the series see Drake successfully search other exotic locales for other lost cities. Yet, while the *Uncharted* games heavily borrow from the Indy franchise to the extent that they may have overshadowed or complicated the release of Indy games in the era of HD gaming, there have been other challengers.

The adventure games genre is saturated with dozens of Indy-influenced titles, such as *Adventure B: Inca Curse* (1982), *Heart of China* (1991), and *Flight of the Amazon Queen* (1995), which featured a crystal skull plotline decades before the Indy film. While the popularity of adventure games has waned, the platforming genre has had a different trajectory. Released just after *Raiders*, and heavily influenced by its jungle setting and artifact hunting, *Pitfall!* (1982) for the Atari 2600 was the best-selling video game of the year (Lendino). During the ascendancy of 2D side-scrolling platformers (not aided by the Indy tie-ins), developer Core Design released *Rick Dangerous* (1989), which recycles tombs, traps, hats, and the rolling boulder from *Raiders*. In 1996, with the fifth generation of home consoles encouraging the rise of 3D polygon gaming, Core Design went further, releasing 3D action-adventure platformer and cultural phenomenon *Tomb Raider*.

According to Jeremy Heath-Smith, founder of Core Design, when he was first shown the game "it was a male character. [...] He did look like Indiana Jones and I said, 'You must be insane, we'll get sued from here to kingdom come!'" (Anderson 239). Other accounts of Lara Croft's development differ, but *Tomb Raider*, and the following 17 games in the series—including a mature reboot in 2013, prompted by the success of *Uncharted* on seventh generation consoles—continue to follow the boulder-dodging antics of "Indiana Jane" (Meecham 162). Coming full-circle back to Indiana Jones, there are also three Tomb Raider movies, with the first two (2001 and 2003) being produced and distributed by Paramount Pictures (who released the Indy films), while the 2018 reboot movie was handled by Warner Bros. Pictures. Attached to an Uncharted movie, Director Shawn Levy already considers Indy to be history as he offers to give "an Indiana Jones–type franchise to an audience that didn't grow up on Indiana Jones" (Birch).

By comparison, since 1996 there have been only three Indy games to come directly from LucasArts: *Indiana Jones and the Infernal Machine* (1999), *Indiana Jones and the Emperor's Tomb* (2003), and *Indiana Jones and the Staff of Kings* (2009). *Infernal Machine* was designed to bring back "Pure Indy," as the box art proclaimed, which also featured artwork by Drew Struzan, who painted the international poster for the *Raiders* movie. For *Emperor's Tomb*, Struzan was again commissioned as his "style and taste is recognizable as the authentic Indy representation" (Struzan). Although Barwood was only involved in the early stages of *Emperor's Tomb*, he served as lead director, designer, and writer for *Infernal Machine* (Higgins). While the game also saw the return of the Indy Quotient and Sophia Hapgood in a new Soviet/Babylonian adventure, LucasArts had missed their window of opportunity to innovate. Playing catch-up after their cancelled graphic adventures, LucasArts started work on *Infernal Machine* when *Tomb Raider II* (1997) was out, and they finished when *Tomb Raider: The Last Revelation* (1999), the fourth game in the series, was on release. During production, *Infernal Machine* was also cancelled for the PlayStation (Kennedy), where Tomb Raider was making its name, and ported to the Nintendo N64 in a bizarrely exclusive rental/sale agreement with Blockbuster Video in the U.S (*Press Release*).

When *Infernal Machine* was adapted from the dated Sith engine, it caused difficulties in development (Smith 128); for *Emperor's Tomb*, LucasArts hired The Collective, asking them to modify their modern Slayer engine, which was used in *Buffy the Vampire Slayer* (2002). With a greater capacity for cinematic gameplay came the first use of Harrison Ford's likeness in an Indy game (Horton) and the first use of a full orchestra in a LucasArts game (Higgins). With the ability to quickly prototype ideas, Bob Donatucci, Senior Environment Artist, was able to engage with "a deep appreciation for old films and architecture," such as Xanadu from *Citizen Kane* (1941), while Brian

Horton, Lead Artist, found illustrator Howard Pyle and Classic Disney films to be an inspiration (Verschuere). *Emperor's Tomb* covers many Indy narrative tropes, ending in 1935 China to set up the beginning of *Temple of Doom*. *Emperor's Tomb* could have signaled the beginning of a modern Indy franchise in earnest, but with the cancellation of the in-house, next-gen untitled Indy game in 2009, the franchise leaned heavily on an outsourced side-project, *Staff of Kings*. Developed by Artificial Mind & Movement, specialists in unremarkable licensed tie-ins, *Staff of Kings* had already been delayed for years by this point, and despite early promises and expectations, the game was released only for last-gen consoles. Appearing like a franchise afterthought, Indy's quest for the Staff of Moses was poorly received.

Where Indy's main adventures end with *Staff of Kings* and a literal lack of Euphoria, the Indy-influenced Uncharted and Tomb Raider franchises have gone from strength to strength. Both series have enjoyed popular cycles, while the game technologies and trajectories of their protagonists have given scope for the games to mature and reflect upon the action-adventure genre itself. With the next generation of game consoles on the horizon and an Indiana Jones movie slated for a tentative, albeit already pushed-back, release in 2021, LucasArts has an opportunity to repeat history; entangled with the development of video games from the first licensed tie-in through to Bafta-winning imitators, Indiana Jones might choose to retire comfortably or he could continue in his search for "fortune and glory."

Works Cited

Ahearn, Nate. "Rumor: Next Indy Game Canned." *IGN*, 12 January 2009, uk.ign.com/articles/2009/01/12/rumor-next-indy-game-canned.

Anderson, Magnus, and Rebecca Levene. *Grand Thieves & Tomb Raiders: How British Video Games Conquered the World*. Aurum Press Ltd., 2012.

Barwood, Hal. "Credits." *Finite Arts LLC*, 2018, finitearts.com/Pages/creditpage.html.

Batchelor, James. "'Not making Star Wars games was a godsend': The early days of LucasArts, Part One." *MCV*, 10 December 2013, mcvuk.com/not-making-star-wars-games-was-a-godsend-the-early-days-of-lucasarts-part-one/.

Bevan, Mike, et al. *The Art of Point and Click Adventure Games*. Edited by Steve Jarratt. Bitmap Books, 2019.

Birch, Nathan. "'Uncharted' Director Is Aiming to Make a New Indiana Jones and Dodge Gaming Movie Pitfalls." ComicBook.com, 9 November 2017, comicbook.com/gaming/2017/08/20/uncharted-new-indiana-jones-avoid-video-game-movie-pitfalls/#2.

Castro, Juan. "E3 2006: Indiana Jones Eyes-on." *IGN*, 10 May 2006, uk.ign.com/articles/2006/05/10/e3-2006-indiana-jones-eyes-on?page=3.

Current, Michael. "A History of AT Games/Atari Games/Midway Games West." *Atari History Timelines*, 4 May 2019, https://mcurrent.name/atarihistory/at_games.html.

Falstein, Noah. "Ask Me Anything with Noah Falstein." *Reddit*, 9 May 2017, reddit.com/r/IAmA/comments/6a5v6m/im_noah_falstein_ive_been_making_games/.

French, Mike. "Indiana Jones and the Temple of Doom: The Console Version." *TheRaider.net*, date unknown, theraider.net/information/videogames/templeofdoom_console.php.

French, Mike. "Interviews: Hal Barwood." *TheRaider.net*, 15 December 2008, theraider.net/features/interviews/hal_barwood.php.

Friedman, Daniel. "Why Your Favorite Devs (Probably) Don't Want to Make a Star Wars

Game." *Polygon*, 30 January 2019, polygon.com/2019/1/30/18203484/star-wars-games-licensed-disney-cancelled-ea.

García, Paco. "Interview with Brian Moriarty." *Aventura y CÍA*, March 2006, aventuraycia.com/entrevistas/en/brian-moriarty/.

Guinness World Records: Gamer's Edition 2019. Edited by Mike Plant. Jim Pattison Group, 2018.

Hall, Charlie. "LucasArts' Indiana Jones and the Iron Phoenix design docs revealed 23 years later." *Polygon*, 26 July 2016, polygon.com/2016/7/26/12290090/lucasarts-indiana-jones-and-the-iron-phoenix-design-documents.

Higgins, Aaron. "Jim Tso interview." *TheRaider.net*, 8 October 2002, http://www.theraider.net/features/interviews/jim_tso.php.

Horton, Brian. "Indiana Jones and the Emperor's Tomb Development Report." *IGN*, 17 January 2003, archived at indianajones.de/games/emperor/texte/related_01.php.

"Indiana Jones and the Iron Phoenix: The Lost Sequel to Fate of Atlantis After Fate of Atlantis." *The International House of Mojo*, 12 July 2016, mixnmojo.com/features/sitefeatures/Indiana-Jones-and-the-Iron-Phoenix-The-Lost-Sequel-to-Fate-of-Atlantis/1.

Kennedy, Sam. "PlayStation Indiana Jones Cancelled." *GameSpot*, 27 April 2000, gamespot.com/articles/playstation-indiana-jones-cancelled/1100-2448523/.

Lamberton, Peter. "Indiana Jones and the Fate of Atlantis." *Adventure Classic Gaming*, 1 August 1998, adventureclassicgaming.com/index.php/site/reviews/78/.

Lamble, Ryan. "Atari: Game Over review." *Den of Geek*, 16 January 2015, denofgeek.com/movies/atari/33659/atari-game-over-review.

Lamble, Ryan. "The 1983 videogame crash: what went wrong, and could it happen again?" *Den of Geek*, 19 February 2013, denofgeek.com/games/24531/the-1983-videogame-crash-what-went-wrong-and-could-it-happen-again.

Lendino, Jamie. "Inside Atari's rise and fall." *TechCrunch*, 21 June 2018, techcrunch.com/2018/06/21/inside-ataris-rise-and-fall/.

"LucasArts' Secret History: Indiana Jones and the Fate of Atlantis Plato's Lost Trivia." *The International House of Mojo*, publication unknown, mixnmojo.com/features/sitefeatures/LucasArts-Secret-History-Indiana-Jones-and-the-Fate-of-Atlantis/5.

Maher, Jimmy. "Indiana Jones and the Fate of Atlantis (or, Of Movies and Games and Whether the Twain Shall Meet)." *The Digital Antiquarian*, 28 September 2018, filfre.net/2018/09/indiana-jones-and-the-fate-of-atlantis-or-of-movies-and-games-and-whether-the-twain-shall-meet/.

McWhertor, Michael. "Lucasfilm Games vets look back on the earliest days of George Lucas' game company." *Polygon*, 20 March 2014, polygon.com/2014/3/20/5530942/lucasfilm-games-vets-look-back-on-the-earliest-days-of-george-lucas.

Meecham, Pam and Julie Sheldon. *Modern Art: A Critical Introduction*. Routledge, 2013.

Mishan, Eddie. "Interview with Hal Barwood." *TheIndyExperience.com*, 10 October 2004, theindyexperience.com/interviews/hal_barwood_interview.php.

Montfort, Nick, and Ian Bogost. *Racing the Beam: The Atari Video Computer System*. MIT Press, 2009.

Pellegrom, Dennis. "Hal Barwood (LucasArts): Interview." StarWarsInterviews.com, August 2010, starwarsinterviews.com/various/lucasarts/hal-barwood-lucasarts/.

Press Release. "LEC/Blockbuster Link." *The International House of Mojo*, 31 October 2000, mixnmojo.com/news/LECBlockbuster-Link.

Rignall, Jaz. "'I actually was hunting Ewoks.' The Original Lucasfilm Games Team Talk About Life at Skywalker Ranch." *USG*, 26 December 2015, usgamer.net/articles/i-actually-was-hunting-ewoks-lucasfilm-games-the-early-years.

Robinson, Martin. "LEGO Indiana Jones Preview." *IGN*, 10 March 2008, uk.ign.com/articles/2008/03/10/lego-indiana-jones-preview.

Rubin, Michael. *Droidmaker: George Lucas and the Digital Revolution*. Triad Publishing Company, 2006.

Schreier, Jason. "How LucasArts Fell Apart." *Kotaku US*, 3 April 2015, kotaku.com/how-lucasarts-fell-apart-1401731043.

"Search: LEGO Indiana Jones." *VGChartz*, data collected 8 May 2019, vgchartz.com/gamedb/games.php?name=lego+indiana+jones.

Seppala, Timothy J. "The True Story of the Worst Video Game in History." *Engadget UK*, 5 January 2014, engadget.com/2014/05/01/true-story-et-atari/.
Smith, Rob. *Rogue Leaders: The Story of LucasArts*. Chronicle Books, 2008.
Struzan, Drew. "Interview with Cover Artist Drew Struzan." *LucasArts*, 28 November 2002, archived at indianajones.de/games/emperor/texte/interview_06.php.
Szalai, Georg. "Lucasfilm's Indiana Jones Ventures into Social Gaming with Zynga's Adventure World." *The Hollywood Reporter*, 28 November 2011, hollywoodreporter.com/news/lucasfilms-indiana-jones-ventures-social-266607.
Totilo, Stephen. "The New, Official Indiana Jones Prequel Isn't a Movie. It's a Zynga Facebook Game." *Kotaku US*, 28 November 2011, kotaku.com/the-new-official-indiana-jones-prequel-isnt-a-movie-i-5862715.
Vaz, Mark, and Shinji Hata. *From Star Wars to Indiana Jones: The Best of the Lucasfilm Archives*. Chronicle Books, 1994.
Verschuere, Gilles. "The Collective interview." *TheRaider.net*, 24 April 2003, theraider.net/features/interviews/collective_team.php.
Wallett, Adrian. "Noah Falstein (LucasArts)—Interview." *Arcade Attack*, 6 April 2018, arcadeattack.co.uk/noah-falstein/.
Woodward, Ryan, et al. *The Guide to Classic Graphic Adventures*. Edited by Kurt Kalata. Hardcoregaming101.net, 2011.

Indiana Jones and the Theme Park Adventure

SABRINA MITTERMEIER

Recent academic discussion of popular culture has placed particular focus on the role of franchising in the age of multi-conglomerates—from the Marvel Cinematic Universe to Star Wars to Star Trek. The Walt Disney Company's increasing monopoly in the media landscape has raised concerns about the direction that not only the American, but also what has long-since been an international, entertainment industry is taking. It is therefore curious that the Indiana Jones franchise has not been examined more frequently in these discussions, given how much it has been a key cog in the LucasArts machine ever since *Raiders of the Lost Ark* premiered to great success in 1981. Built on nostalgia for serial novels from the nineteenth century, film serials from the first half of the twentieth century, and 1950s low-budget adventure films or "jungle movies" (Hernández-Pérez & Ferreras Rodríguez 30–32), the Indiana Jones films constituted an inherently serialized narrative to begin with. They usually centered on "charismatic characters" (Hernández-Pérez & Ferreras Rodríguez 27) (such as Allan Quartermain), and Indiana Jones made this connection even more apparent when the second film, *Indiana Jones and the Temple of Doom*, now featuring the character's name in the title, premiered in 1984, and when *Indiana Jones and the Last Crusade* closed out the original trilogy in 1989. In many ways then, it was one of the first film series to profit from modern-day franchising, following in the footsteps of Lucas's own *Star Wars* (Hernández-Pérez & Ferreras Rodríguez 37). As communication scholars Manuel Hérnandez-Pérez and José Gabriel Ferreras Rodríguez argue, "the IJ [Indiana Jones] saga should be recognized as occupying a prominent position in the transition between franchises and transmedia storytelling" (49).

As an early case of this phenomenon, then, the movies were only one part of a wider constellation of multimedia productions bearing the likeness or name of Indiana Jones. The television film series *The Young Indiana Jones Chronicles* (1992–1993), later edited and re-released as *The Adventures of Young Indiana Jones*, which aired on ABC, is one popular example, but the franchise also yielded a number of books, comic books, video games, role-playing games, and merchandise products. Yet, one permanent presence of the franchise is often overlooked: the numerous attractions in Disney's theme parks worldwide that continued to promote the franchise and further establish it as a part of American popular culture. The first instance was the addition of the "Indiana Jones Epic Stunt Show Spectacular!" in 1989, as part of what was then called Disney MGM Studios (now Disney's Hollywood Studios) in Walt Disney World Resort, Florida. Ever since then, Indiana Jones and his adventures have become a mainstay in Disney's theme parks around the world—notably, long before Lucasfilm was acquired by the Walt Disney Company in 2012. In fact, Lucasfilm had collaborated on two other attractions in the 1980s, the 3D film *Captain Eo*, starring Michael Jackson, and the Star Wars-themed simulator ride, "Star Tours." It had only been a matter of time until Indiana Jones would follow. After the stunt show, "Indiana Jones and the Temple of Peril," a roller coaster, opened in the then-fledgling Disneyland Paris in 1993. Two years later, "Indiana Jones Adventure: Temple of the Forbidden Eye," an elaborate "E-Ticket" dark ride, was added to the original Disneyland's Adventureland section in 1995, and, since 2001, a variant of this ride, one of Tokyo DisneySea's opening day attractions, has been taking guests to the "Temple of the Crystal Skull." Finally, in 2015, "Jock Lindsey's Hangar Bar" opened at Walt Disney World's newly remodeled entertainment district, Disney Springs, adding a dining location to the roster.

Because, like theme parks overall, these attractions have so far not received much scholarly treatment, this essay analyzes these attractions as part of the larger franchise, examines what happens to Indiana Jones and his world when they are remediated into the three-dimensional, narrative space of the theme park, and investigates the sense in which the Indiana Jones property has been an almost perfect fit into this space to begin with.

Theme Park Cinema: Remediating Indiana Jones

To understand how Indiana Jones's stories are transformed to fit into the theme park narrative, one first has to understand how theme parks tell their stories. One key practice here is "remediation." According to media scholars Jay David Bolter and David Grusin, remediation refers to the process whereby one medium is transformed into another, such as when a film is turned into a theme park attraction, a practice that Disneyland first pioneered.

To effect this transformation, theme parks, as well as other immersive attractions such as themed restaurants, hotels, or shopping malls, make use of the strategies of theming, which Scott Lukas, one of the most prolific authors on theme parks, has defined as "the use of an overarching theme ... to create a holistic and integrated spatial organization of a consumer venue" (1). To theme a space, designers not only use architecture, but also other sensory stimuli such as music and other sounds, smells, costumed employees, food, and merchandising articles. Disney calls the practice of designing and building theme parks "Imagineering," a term coined by Walt Disney himself, meaning the "blending of creative imagination with technical know-how" (quoted in Sklar 10–11). Theming, then, is only one part of this larger process, which also encompasses several other technologies to tell a story; in addition to film and music, this can include audio-animatronics that simulate humans or animals, interactive information technology, vehicles for actual or simulated transport, and many more such tools, often state of the art. The purpose of all of these elements is the immersion of the guest into the story. The term immersion means being completely submerged into something, and thus implies "a transition, a 'passage' from one realm to another, from the immediate physical reality of tangible objects and direct sensory data to *somewhere else*" (Huhtamo 159; original emphasis). Joe Rohde, one of Disney's Imagineers, has also referred to this overarching design practice as "narrative placemaking," or "the building of ideas into physical objects," and highlights how the theme park is in and of itself a participatory storytelling medium. Consequently, then, as Abby Waysdorf and Stijn Reijnders argue, the theme park space provides "a spatial and embodied connection to a narrative world" (185).

While remediation is then only part of this larger practice of narrative placemaking, it has always been integral to the form: part of the enormous initial and continuous success of Disneyland has been the synergy it creates between the theme park space and other Disney products. In the park's early years, this synergy was reflected in, for instance, the ties between its Frontierland area and the enormously successful Davy Crockett films Disney had produced in connection to the Disneyland television show (Mittermeier 48–51). More recently, the remediation process has also been successfully reversed, as the classic Disneyland ride "Pirates of the Caribbean" has been transformed into an immensely popular film series, and consequently turned into a franchise in its own right, now inspiring a whole area based on the films at Shanghai Disneyland (Mittermeier 224–225). Theme parks have thus always been a vital part of both franchising as well as transmedia storytelling for the multi-conglomerates that own them, and they have become even more important in recent years.

Indiana Jones is remediated in many different ways into Disney's theme parks, always depending on the larger overarching theme it is set in. The "Indiana Jones Epic Stunt Show Spectacular!" is a stunt show that recreates action scenes from *Raiders of the Lost Ark*, including the famous temple scene that opened the movie and the street scenes set in Cairo, and, as a finale, the show features Indy and Marion trying to stop the Nazis from flying the Ark to Germany. The show premiered on August 25, 1989, only a few months after the opening of the Disney–MGM Studios theme park, and it is one of the only attractions that remain from its initial line up. Originally, the park had been themed to movie production, offering a behind-the-scenes look at the movie industry (similar to the Universal Studios theme park in Hollywood that grew out of an operational movie studio), and blended in with attractions more broadly themed to movies themselves. Yet this type of theme park, also termed the "postmodern style" (Younger 74), went out of fashion relatively quickly, and so the park was gradually remodeled and rethemed by removing the movie production facilities in the early 2000s, and, in 2008, the MGM licensing agreement was dissolved (MGM would declare bankruptcy in 2010). Ever since 2010, the theme park, now called Disney's Hollywood Studios, has received even more extensive overhauls and expansion, moving toward more immersive themed attractions representative of what has been called the "new traditional style" (Younger 76). The most notable example of this new style of theme park design is the Star Wars–themed Galaxy's Edge area, which opened in 2019.

The Indiana Jones–themed stunt show recreates recognizable scenes from the film, using locations and characters the audience is familiar with. This familiarity is a key element in theming, and it is one that is vital for making immersion work, as studies have shown that for theming to be successful, familiarity with the basis for the theme is important (Hofer and Wirth 167). Yet, while the first scene of the show is immersive, it breaks the fourth wall immediately after, and transitions into an explanation of how the stunt involving the famous huge boulder actually works. The show therefore remains something of an outlier in the current Hollywood Studios park—while it recreates scenes from the first film, it still makes use of fake camera props and the like to evoke the impression of an actual movie set. As film scholar Yvonne Tasker argues, here the "[m]ovie-making itself serves as an attraction (including the explosions that are so strongly associated with adventure cinema), just as … [the Indiana Jones] films acknowledge their pleasure in film history. The experiential qualities of action and adventure are thus incorporated into the theme park spectacle" (130). The stunt show's mixture of both the postmodern and new traditional styles is arguably what has kept it alive, along with the continued popularity of the Indiana Jones franchise. Yet it remains to be seen whether it will retain its staying power over the coming years, or if it will eventually vanish or be rethemed into a more immersive Indiana Jones attraction—especially given that Lucasfilm, now under Disney's roof, is currently producing a fifth film.

The second attraction themed to the franchise was "Indiana Jones and the Temple of Peril" ("Indiana Jones et le Temple du Péril" in French) that opened on July 30, 1993, as part of Disneyland Paris's Adventureland. The park was still called Euro Disneyland Park at this time, and it was experiencing major financial difficulties. While the attraction had been on the original drawing board for its opening in April 1992, it underwent significant changes for its final design. In a last-minute attempt to draw more guests with the inclusion of a much-needed thrill ride (Mittermeier 194), "Indiana Jones and the Temple of Peril" was scaled down from a much more immersive attraction to a simple looping coaster. The fact that the queue line features some of John Williams's score for the film is one of the only markers that ties this theming specifically to Indiana Jones, at least upon first look. Theming a roller coaster to an action adventure film is generally a common practice, but the temple setting combined with the mine car vehicles draws a visual connection to the mine car chase scene in *Indiana Jones and the Temple of Doom*. Writing on the film, Nigel Morris has fittingly described it as a "rollercoaster of sensation (literally in the climactic wagon chase)" (102). As Tasker has further argued, "it is by now commonplace to cite the analogy between action and adventure films and the ride—thrills, visceral effects and sweeping camerawork suggesting or simulating a rollercoaster experience" (129), and this scene from the second film remediates theme park experiences as much as the roller coaster eventually remediates the scene. Speaking to the prevalence of transmedia storytelling within these franchises, Tasker has fittingly termed modern adventure franchises like Indiana Jones and Pirates of the Caribbean "theme park cinema" (129).

The most elaborate and immersive theme park attraction based on Indiana Jones, however, is without a doubt "Indiana Jones Adventure: Temple of the Forbidden Eye," which opened in Disneyland's Adventureland on March 3, 1995, and Tokyo DisneySea's version of it, "Indiana Jones: Temple of the Crystal Skull," which premiered with the park on September 4, 2001. In California, the Temple's theming harkens back not only to the second film, as it is meant to be set in India, but also to the opening sequence of *Raiders*, and the attraction tells its own story—briefly related by John Rhys-Davies reprising his role as Sallah in a pre-show video. The ride itself uses so-called Enhanced Motion Vehicles (EMV), a ride system specifically built for the attraction, to transport guests through the ride and that makes sure no experience is ever the same twice, as the motions are randomized. They take riders through a number of elaborate show scenes based on the dangers Indy usually faces in the movies: booby traps, a rickety bridge, snakes (including a larger-than-life-sized cobra) and, at the finale, the famous giant boulder, which one barely dodges by diving under it. The ride at Tokyo DisneySea is largely the same, however the narrative is built on a different MacGuffin—the Crystal Skull, which, interestingly, had been part of this ride long before the release of *Indiana Jones and the Kingdom of the Crystal Skull* in 2008 and otherwise bears no relation to the film's story. The setting of the ride and the queue area is elaborately designed and, much like the rest of the Tokyo DisneySea theme park, is one of the most detailed and immersive works Imagineers have ever done. Guests are transported to the Lost River Delta: instead of a fictional Indian-inspired setting, the ride is housed inside an Aztec-style temple and small changes are made throughout, such as replacing the huge cobra audio-animatronic with one of the Mesoamerican deity Quetzalcoatl. Both versions of the ride also feature music by John Williams, adapted from the original film trilogy's scores.

In many ways, "Indiana Jones: Temple of the Crystal Skull" is the most effective remediation of the films into the theme park, and it shines a light on why Indiana Jones as a text is such a good fit for this kind of adaptation. As mentioned above, the Indiana Jones films are an homage to earlier serials on page and screen, but they are also "a more realistic, updated vision of the adventure serial genre" (Hernández-Pérez & Ferreras Rodríguez 32) in general. While they recreate a decidedly gaudy, B-movie aesthetic, they are "in fact benefit[ing] from a sizeable budget and the most sophisticated special effects of its time" (Hernández-Pérez & Ferreras Rodríguez 32). The ride similarly makes use of state-of-the-art technology and special effects while keeping this look intact, but it does more than just visually recreate Indiana Jones's style. As film scholar John Finlay Kerr has pointed out, the serials the Indy films are based on serve as a narrative concept of the films' inherent structure:

> We see all of the episodes of an old Republic Pictures adventure serial back to back (with all their cliffhangers). The dangers that arise—such as ancient temples, forbidden treasures, poisonous spiders, hissing snakes, sadistic Nazis, Thuggee cults, human sacrifices in molten lava, high-speed chases, brawls and booby traps—are all piled on, one after the other in rapid succession [15].

This technique is directly transferred to the Indiana Jones Adventures rides, where one is thrown from one danger to the next in a way that resembles one action sequence cutting into another action sequence. This somewhat disconnected form of storytelling is, however, not unique to the Indiana Jones rides; as Susan Aronstein has argued about Disney's dark rides, they "are effective only because the … narratives on which they are based are omnipresent; without the intertextual interpretive context provided by the films, these rides would be meaningless—a series of disconnected images" (67). The "Indiana Jones Adventure," then, does not only bank on previous knowledge of the franchise for its storytelling, it also makes effective use of a narrative structure already in place in the text it remediates. Kerr has further argued that the Indiana Jones films always engage the viewer "in medias res," as if one is "catching up on the latest instalment" (15) of a serial, as every one of them opens with an action scene not previously explained. While the Californian version of the Indiana Jones Adventure ride gives the guest some background info on the setting via the previously mentioned pre-show video, it does so only after one has traversed the temple already and therefore has already entered the story world "in medias res," dropped right into the action. The version in Tokyo meanwhile omits Sallah from the video and explains most of its story only through visual cues in the queue line—much like the implicit visual storytelling of the famous opening scene of *Raiders*.

As the storytelling of Indiana Jones, then, is in many ways disconnected, operating from cliffhanger to cliffhanger, it is important for the audience to have a focus, and that is the titular character. Much like the James Bond films that were also an important influence for Lucas and Spielberg (Hernández-Pérez & Ferreras Rodríguez 49; Biber 74), then, "the entire story revolves around the main character" (Hernández-Pérez & Ferreras Rodríguez 38), and it is thus no surprise that Indiana Jones makes an appearance at the end of the ride (in audio-animatronic form), saving the guests lost in the temple from harm.

It took until 2015 for Disney, three years after their acquisition of Lucasfilm, to include another attraction themed to Indiana Jones in one of their theme parks, and then only in a rather inconspicuous form. "Jock Lindsey's Hangar Bar" is a bar and dining venue that is part of Disney Springs, the entertainment district of Florida's Walt Disney World, and was established after a massive refurbishment of the older Downtown Disney area. The bar's connection to Indiana Jones is only apparent to the hardcore fan: the character of Jock Lindsey is Indy's pilot, who makes a brief appearance at the beginning of *Raiders*. The bar is themed to be his old airplane hangar and ties in with a backstory involving the fictional town of Disney Springs and a narrative surrounding the Society of Explorers and Adventurers that connects several attractions in Disney's parks around the world. It is the first time Indiana Jones is directly tied in with this larger story world, thus actively connecting it to pre-existing colonial narratives in their theme parks, a fact that invites closer analysis.

Indiana Jones, Disney and Armchair Colonialism

The Society of Explorers and Adventurers (S.E.A.) was created by Imagineers for the Tokyo DisneySea theme park to give backstory to a number of attractions housed there, such as the local version of the "Tower of Terror" or "Fortress Explorations." It connects several fictional characters of attractions with each other, among them Harrison Hightower III, the owner of Hightower Hotel (where the Tower ride is set), Lord Henry Mystic, owner of "Mystic Manor" (an attraction at Hong Kong Disneyland), Captain Mary Oceaneer (found at the Disney Magic cruise ship's kids club and Typhoon Lagoon water park in Florida), or Dr. Albert Falls, who harkens back to the original Disneyland's "Jungle Cruise" ride, and, more recently, to the Skipper Canteen restaurant at Walt Disney World's Magic Kingdom. The inspiration for this society and its characters goes back to the now-defunct "Adventurer's Club" night club, once part of Downtown Disney in Florida. The Society and its members are all portrayed as scientists, researchers, explorers, and adventurers, and they are all said to have lived around the turn of the century. Their mission is "to collect, conserve, and curate valuable cultural and artistic artifacts from around the world and make them available to the public in an artistically pleasing and sensitive manner" (Disney Wiki), a project that echoes Indiana Jones's repeated statement, "It belongs in a museum!" Much like Indy, the Society is framed as a benevolent collective of rich, educated white people who set out to preserve history by "equip[ping] and mount[ing] socio-cultural expeditions to discover, explore, chronicle and protect the artistic achievements of human society, past and present, exalted and forgotten" (Disney Wiki). As this mission statement makes clear, the underlying myth of Indiana Jones fits this framework perfectly, as they share much ideological common ground.

While S.E.A. is a rather new invention by Disney, another foray into transmedia storytelling that is meant to foster immersion for their fans, it is by far not the first instance of Disney turning towards such imagery. Carl Barks's comics surrounding Scrooge McDuck's explorer stories that were later remediated into the popular Disney animated show *DuckTales* (1987–1990; 2017–) harken back to the 1940s—and had themselves served as another inspiration for Lucas and Spielberg in making Indiana Jones (D23).

Disney's theme parks meanwhile have included such colonial narratives ever since the opening of Disneyland in 1955: Disneyland's Adventureland, an amalgamation of all places that a white middle-class American clientele in the 1950s would have considered exotic (Asia, Africa, South America, the Middle East) (Mittermeier, 41), had always been steeped in what Stephan Fjellman has called "'cute' colonial racism" (225), and what I have elsewhere termed "armchair colonialism" (Mittermeier 225). Both the theme parks' and Indiana Jones's depiction of the "exotic" locales feature "[t]emples, caves and passageways, along with inhospitable settings like jungles or exotic lands," that "fundamentally represent the forbidden and therefore the 'site of danger'" (Hernández-Pérez & Ferreras Rodríguez 42), but the draw for the audience in both cases is that they will not actually be put in danger. Disney's Adventureland and connected narratives like those of S.E.A. let the guest experience the "kick" of danger first-hand, but "without mosquitoes, monsoons or misadventure" (Fjellman, 226). While they are invited to step into the footsteps of Indiana Jones, they also know that they will always escape unharmed in the end.

The underlying fascination with the adventure genre's imagery, however, goes back to the roots of colonial literature itself, as well as to the World's Fairs and Expositions of the late nineteenth century, which are a direct predecessor of the theme park. As literary scholar Deborah Philips has argued, the colonial imagery that is common to both Indy and Disney (and for that matter, many other theme parks) promotes the same harmful stereotypes:

> The "norms" and the mapping imposed in the theme park are those of the masculine imperial explorer. The pith-helmeted adventurer is an unapologetically colonial figure who constantly reappears in the carnival site in a range of guises, most familiarly in the contemporary context as Indiana Jones. A parody of a parody, Indiana Jones traces his lineage back through Saturday morning cinema matinées, cartoon strips, radio and comic book serials, children's adventure stories and the novels of Kipling and Rider Haggard. Indiana Jones is a postmodern variant of the explorer hero. [144].

In perpetuating such stereotypes, these explorer stories "continue to give the West, and America in particular, the power to narrate" (Philips 163). In many ways, then, the popularity of Indiana Jones, also often not coincidentally connected back to a Reaganite masculinity (Biber), continues to perpetuate the myth of "the 'Empire Boys' genre: 'the adventure story which would take the boy into areas of history and geography that placed him at the top of the racial ladder and at the helm of all the world'" (Philips 146). While this genre remains largely gendered, it is telling that newer installments of it, such as Disney's S.E.A., try to include women in the narrative by featuring female explorer characters, yet they cannot escape the underlying racism of the genre. The racial "other" is too ingrained in all of these narratives—whether it's the depiction of "wild" tribesmen and troubling references to cannibalism in Disney's "Jungle Cruise," or Indiana Jones's depiction of people of color as uncivilized or villainous savages that spans across all the movies, most gratingly in *Temple of Doom*. As Ella Shoat and Robert Stam have argued, "[i]n the world of Indiana Jones, Third World cultures are synopsized as theme park clichés drawn from the orientalist repertoire" (124). It is more than telling that they refer back to the idea of the theme park to highlight this condensation of colonialist narratives that Indiana Jones builds on, proving again that Indy's story world had always been a perfect fit for Disney's theme park—after all, they share the same troubling colonialist ideology.

Conclusion

Indiana Jones is one of the earliest cases of modern-day efforts in franchising, and in turn, transmedia storytelling, even if it often is overlooked in favor of other texts, such as Lucasfilm's other major property, Star Wars. Based on a serial storytelling format long prevalent in the adventure genre it revived, the Indiana Jones property served as the perfect basis for many efforts in transmediality, and particularly for remediation into the narrative space of the theme park. Since 1989, Disney has built a variety of attractions based on the films, first as a mere licensing agreement with Lucasfilm, later as the parent company after their acquisition of the studio in 2012. The first foray into this collaboration, the stunt show at Disney–MGM Studios / Disney's Hollywood Studios perfectly showcased the spectacle of action-adventure filmmaking, what Yvonne Tasker has also fittingly called "theme park cinema," while the roller coaster in Euro Disneyland/Disneyland Paris has further banked on this shared thrill of experience. The "Indiana Jones Adventure" rides in both Anaheim's Disneyland and Tokyo DisneySea are some of the most immersive attractions in Disney's theme parks and remediate the cliffhanger-to-cliffhanger storytelling of the films perfectly. Finally, "Jock Lindsey's Hangar Bar" in Disney Springs is much more understated in its ties to the franchise, but it marks the franchise's important connections to pre-existing colonial narratives in Disney's theme parks. The adventure genre that underlies both Disneyland's Adventureland sections (and similar themed areas, such as Tokyo DisneySea's Lost River Delta) and the Indiana Jones franchise is steeped in colonial and thus racist imagery that neither text can escape, and this colonialist subtext is one of the elements that allows Indiana Jones's story world to tie in so seamlessly with the theme park space, as the ideological implications underlying both are the same. For better or for worse, then, Indiana Jones has found a perfect home with Disney's Society of the Explorers and Adventurers, as both texts continue to be two of the biggest purveyors of colonialist ideology in American popular culture—and beyond.

Works Cited

Aronstein, Susan. "Pilgrimage and Medieval Narrative Structures in Disney's Park." *The Disney Middle Ages: A Fairy-Tale and Fantasy Past*, edited by Susan Aronstein and Tison Pugh. Palgrave Macmillan, 2012, pp. 57–76.

Biber, Katherine. "The Emperor's New Clones: Indiana Jones and Masculinity in Reagan's America." *Australasian Journal of American Studies*, vol. 14, no. 2, 1995, pp. 67–86.

Bolter, Jay David, and Richard Grusin. *Remediation—Understanding New Media*. MIT Press, 2000.

Fjellman, Stephen. *Vinyl Leaves—Walt Disney World and America*. Westview Press, 1992.

Hernández-Pérez, Manuel, and José Gabriel Ferreras Rodríguez. "Serial Narrative, Intertextuality, and the Role of Audiences in the Creation of a Franchise: An Analysis of the Indiana Jones Saga from a Cross Media Perspective." *Mass Communication and Society*, vol. 17, 2014, pp. 26–53.

Hofer, Matthias, and W. Werner Wirth. "Präsenzerleben—Eine medienpsychologische Modellierung." *Montage A/V*, 2008, pp. 159–175.

Huhtamo, Erkki. "Encapsulated Bodies in Motion. Simulators and the Quest for Total Immersion." *Critical Issues in Electronic Media*, edited by Simon Penny. State University of New York Press, 1995, pp. 159–186.

Kerr, John Finlay. "Indiana Jones and the Readers of the Lost Art: Making the Kingdom of the Crystall Skull Educational." *Screen Education*, vol. 51, 2008, pp. 15–20.

Lukas, Scott. "The Themed Space: Locating Culture, Nation, and Self." *The Themed Space: Locating Culture, Nation, and Self*, edited by Scott Lukas. Lexington Books, 2007, pp. 1–22.

Mittermeier, Sabrina. *Middle Class Kingdoms: A Cultural History of Disneyland and Its Variations, 1955–2016*. 2017. LMU Munich, doctoral dissertation. [scheduled for publication with Intellect Books in 2020]

Morris, Nigel. *The Cinema of Steven Spielberg: Empire of Light*. De Gruyter, 2007.

Philips, Deborah. *Fairground Attractions: A Geneaology of the Pleasure Ground*. Bloomsbury Academic, 2012.

Rohde, Joe. "From Myth to Mountain: Insights into Virtual Placemaking." *ACM SIGGRAPH Computer Graphics*, vol. 47, no. 3, 2007, DOI: 10.1145/1281324.1281325.

Shoat, Elia, and Robert Stam. *Unthinking Eurocentrism: Multiculturalism and the Media*. Routledge, 1994.

Sklar, Marty. Introduction. *Walt Disney Imagineering: A Behind the Dreams Look at Making MORE Magic Real* by The Imagineers. Disney Editions, 2010, pp. 10–11.

"Society of Explorers and Adventurers." *The Disney Wiki*. Accessed June 1, 2019. https://disney.fandom.com/wiki/Society_of_Explorers_and_Adventurers.

Tasker, Yvonne. *The Hollywood Action and Adventure Film*. Wiley Blackwell, 2015.

"The Disney Afternoon Revisited." D23.com. Accessed June 24, 2017. https://d23.com/cue-the-disney-afternoon-theme-song/.

Waysdorf, Abby, and Stijn Rejinders. "Immersion, Authenticity and the Theme Park as Social Space: Experiencing the Wizarding World of Harry Potter." *International Journal of Cultural Studies*, vol. 2, 2018, pp. 173–188.

Younger, David. "Traditionally Postmodern: The Changing Styles of Theme Park Design." *Time and Temporality in Theme Parks*, edited by Filippo Carlà-Uhink et al. Wehrhahn, 2017, pp. 63–82.

About the Contributors

Andrew W. **Bell** is a Ph.D. candidate in the Department of History at Boston University. His research focuses on the relationship between archaeological fieldwork and American political and cultural engagements with the world in the late 19th and early 20th centuries. He will defend his dissertation—"Digging Deep: Archaeologists and American Foreign Relations in a World of Empire, 1880–1950"—in 2020.

Brian **Brems** is an associate professor of English at the College of DuPage. His academic work has focused on genre, with pieces on horror and westerns appearing in book-length edited collections. He is coediting a collection on the films of Paul Schrader for the ReFocus series. In addition, he publishes regularly in online film magazines and websites, including *Bright Wall/Dark Room*, *Vague Visages*, and *Film Inquiry*. He has also contributed to *Film School Rejects* and *Little White Lies*.

Jennifer **Crumley** is a Ph.D. candidate in humanities, studies in literature, at the University of Texas at Dallas. Her areas of focus are British modernism, post–World War II intellectual history, and American literature with an emphasis on vulgarity and the avant-garde. Her research interests center on the ability to connect the seemingly unconnected and to provide a scholarly anchor for the value of popular culture.

Brian A. **Dixon**, Ph.D., is an assistant professor of English at Goodwin University. His publications include studies on college writing centers, 19th-century American literature, detectives in film and fiction, ethnic humor in British sitcoms, the works of Ian Fleming, and the James Bond films. He was assistant editor of *ATQ: The American Transcendental Quarterly* and, with Adam Chamberlain edited *Columbia & Britannia* (2009) and *Back to Frank Black* (2012).

Kerry **Dodd** is a Ph.D. researcher at Lancaster University, UK, and acting head editor for *Fantastika Journal*. His thesis examines the intersection between archaeology and weird fiction, exploring how archaeological framings can offer a re-conceptualization of object ontology through the weird. He also works more widely in the fields of science fiction (particularly cosmic horror and cyberpunk), the Gothic, and glitch aesthetics.

About the Contributors

Mat **Hardy** is a senior lecturer in Middle East studies at Deakin University, Australia. He divides his publication efforts between exploring the use of role play technologies in delivering political science, teaching, and unpacking the way in which fantasy authors and filmmakers depict Middle Eastern cultures and geographies.

Kasey **Jones-Matrona** is a doctoral candidate and graduate teaching assistant in the literary and cultural studies English program at the University of Oklahoma. She studies Native American literature, Indigenous futurisms, and Indigenous feminisms. She previously attended two Maryland universities, Washington College and Salisbury University, where she received degrees in English.

Randy **Laist** is a professor of English at Goodwin University. He is the author of *The Twin Towers in Film* (2020), *Cinema of Simulation* (2015), and *Technology and Postmodern Subjectivity in Don DeLillo's Novels* (2010). He is also the editor of several books, including *Cinema U* (2018), *Plants and Literature* (2013), and *Looking for Lost* (2011).

Siobhan **Lyons** is a writer and scholar in media and cultural studies. Her books include *Death and the Machine* (2018), and *Ruin Porn and the Obsession with Decay* (2018). Her work has been included in *Understanding Nietzsche, Understanding Modernism* (2019), *Westworld and Philosophy* (2018), *Approaching Twin Peaks* (2017), and *Philosophical Approaches to the Devil* (2016) among others. She earned a Ph.D. from Macquarie University in 2017.

Sabrina **Mittermeier** is the author of a forthcoming cultural history of Disneyland, 1955–2016 (2020), as well as the coeditor of the *Routledge Handbook to Star Trek* (2021), *Fighting for the Future* (2020), and *Here You Leave Today* (2017). She has also published and taught on other diverse topics of American popular culture and history and is working on a postdoc project dealing with LGBT public history in the U.S. and Germany.

Debaditya **Mukhopadhyay** is an assistant professor of English at Manikchak College, affiliated with the University of Gourbanga, India. He is pursuing his Ph.D. on spy fiction from Rabindra Bharati University. Popular literature and films, myths, adaptations, and theater are his areas of interest. His research articles have been published in different peer-reviewed journals and edited anthologies. His recent chapter on Bill Condon's *Beauty and the Beast* has been published in the collection *Parenting Through Pop Culture*, edited by Joe Leeson-Schatz.

Tatiana **Prorokova** is a postdoctoral researcher at the Department of English and American Studies, University of Vienna, Austria. She holds a Ph.D. in American studies from the University of Marburg, Germany. She is the author of *Docu-Fictions of War* (2019) and a coeditor of *Cultures of War in Graphic Novels* (2018).

Ryan **Staude** holds a Ph.D. in history from the University at Albany, SUNY, where he wrote his dissertation on George Washington's political philosophy and the shaping of American national identity in the 1790s. In addition, he has published articles and presented papers on the intersection of film and history, specifically on Steven Spielberg's use of history in his movies. He is the chair of the history department at the O'Neal School in Pinehurst, North Carolina.

About the Contributors

Joseph S. **Walker** is an independent scholar, a cultural critic, and an active member of the Mystery Writers of America. His critical publications include essays on *Veronica Mars*, *Mystery Science Theater 3000*, and the Western film in the 21st century. His fiction has appeared in *Alfred Hitchcock Mystery Magazine*, *Mystery Weekly*, *Dark City*, and a variety of anthologies. Follow him on Twitter @JSWalkerAuthor and visit his website at https://jsw47408.wixsite.com/website.

Linda **Wight** is a senior lecturer of literature and screen studies in the School of Arts at Federation University, Australia. Her Ph.D. dissertation examined the depiction of masculinities in science fiction and she has published several articles and chapters analyzing men and masculinity in science fiction film and literature and the Daniel Craig James Bond films. She continues to research the way masculinities are portrayed and constructed in science fiction, fantasy, and other popular genres.

Carl **Wilson** is a contributing guest writer for the Eisner-nominated comic book publishers Fanbase Press and a former film editor for PopMatters.com. He has published work in over a dozen edited collections and has chapters forthcoming on the depowering of DC superheroes as they cross into video games and the representation and branding of women in Batman video games. His work can be found at carl-wilson.com.

Index

Adventure B: Inca Curse 187
Adventure World: An Indiana Jones Game 185
Akator 42, 43, 44, 45, 87–88, 92, 94–97, 128, 131, 135, 143, 146
Aladdin 64, 65
Albrecht, Michael 106
Aliens 105
Allen, Paula Gunn 93–94
Amsel, Richard 179
Ancient Society 88
Andrews, Roy Chapman 104, 109
Annals and Antiquities of Rajasthan 79
Archaeological Institute of America (AIA) 15–17, 19, 20, 22
Archaeological Theory: An Introduction 139
Archaeology Is a Brand! 136
Ark of the Covenant 2, 21, 33, 36, 42, 43, 44, 46, 51, 52, 53–55, 58–59, 60–61, 64, 68, 69, 74, 84, 104, 107, 109, 110, 111, 128, 131, 132–133, 135, 151, 166, 169, 195
Aronstein, Susan 197
Art and Archaeology 15–16
Austin, Terry 172
The Authenticity Hoax 107
Ayoob, Ben Ali (character) 155, 170

Back to the Future 105
Barks, Carl 153, 165, 199
Barranca (character) 30
Barwood, Hal 181–182, 183, 184, 185, 188
Baudrillard, Jean 112
Being and Time 137
Belloq, René (character) 2, 33, 35, 36, 42, 68, 77, 107, 111, 132, 138, 140, 152, 166–168, 170, 173
Belzoni, Giovanni 15
Benjamin, Walter 107, 144
Bergman, Ingrid 66
Biber, Katherine 84
Bieder, Robert E. 89
The Big Trail 29

Biggles series 71
Bingham, Hiram 15, 51, 165
Black, Solomon 157, 158
Blade Runner 105
Blegen, Carl W. 18
Blevins, Bret 174
Blumburtt, Captain (character) 80
Bly, Robert 115
Bogart, Humphry 66
Bolter, Jay David 193
The Book of the Thousand Nights and a Night 64, 65
Brantlinger, Patrick 82
Brass, Tom 60
Breasted, James Henry 17
Britton, Andrew 5
Brody, Marcus (character) 35, 43, 67, 110, 117, 118–119, 120, 127, 129, 132, 133, 155–156, 157, 158, 166, 173
Bruzzi, Stella 115
Buckland, Warren 26, 36
Buffy the Vampire Slayer 188
Bulanadi, Danny 171
Burton, Sir Richard 64, 65
Buscema, John 165
Byrne, John 166, 172

Calabrese, Omar 4
Campbell, Joseph 4, 127–128, 166
Caniff, Milton 153, 169
Captain America 126, 127
Captain Eo 193
Captain Katanga (character) 155
Carr, E.H. 40
Carroll, Noel 36
Carter, Howard 16
Casablanca 66
Catron, Evan 118, 121, 122
Chandra, Bipan 78
Charisma, James 6–7
Chaykin, Howard 165
Chin, Justin 186

207

208 Index

Citizen Kane 188
Close Encounters of the Third Kind 27, 182
Cohen-Cole, Jamie 130–131
Colla, Elliot 142, 144
Columbus, Chris 181
Conan the Barbarian 153
Conflicted Antiquities: Egyptology, Egytomania, and Egyptian Modernity 142
Croft, Lara (character) 183, 188
Cross of Coronado 1, 21, 41, 42, 89, 108, 115–116, 129, 134, 175
Cruise, Tom 27
Crum, Stephen 97–98
Crystal Skull 42, 44, 87–88, 89, 92–95, 123, 128, 131, 134, 135, 138, 143–146, 197
Curtiz, Michael 66

Davis, Wade 3
Deceit, Desire, and the Novel 128
Degan, Hans (character) 169
de la Rosa, Sam 173
Deloria, Vine 90
di Cesnola, Luigi 15
Dietrich, Herman (character) 166, 167
The Dig 182
Disney, Walt 194
Ditko, Steve 155, 166
Don Quixote 128
Donato, Eugenio 142
Donatucci, Bob 188
Donovan, Walter (character) 35, 43, 106, 107, 109–110, 111, 119, 141–142
DuckTales 199
Dunne, Charlie (character) 157, 159, 172
Dunne, Edith (character) 157–158, 160, 172

Ebert, Roger 3, 4
Eisele, John C. 66–68
The Empire Strikes Back 30, 104
Epic: Form, Content, and History 129–130
E.T. the Extra-Terrestrial (film) 105
E.T. the Extra-Terrestrial (video game) 179
Evans, Arthur 15
Excavating the Future 145
Eyman, Scott 27

Falstein, Noah 179, 181, 182–183
Fantastic Four 154
Fast, Karin 152
Fedora (character) 115–116, 129, 175
Fight Club 115
Fincher, David 115
Fine-Dare, Kathleen 90
Fjellman, Stephan 199–200
Flaggart (character) 170
Fleming, Ian 165
Flight of the Amazon Queen 187
Ford, Harrison 2, 4, 6, 28, 30–32, 104, 121, 124, 156, 157, 164, 185, 188
Ford, John 7, 25–36

Fort Apache 27
Fox, David 178, 181, 185
French, Mike 180
Friedman, Lester D. 114, 117–118, 119
The Further Adventures of Indiana Jones 8, 151–175

Gallagher, Tag 32, 34, 35
Gammill, Kerry 173
Gandhi, Mahatma 78
Gates, Philippa 121, 122
General Ross (character) 131
Germain, David 112
Ghostbusters 105
Ghostbusters franchise 7
G.I. Joe 154
Gilbert, Ron 181
Giles, Busby (character) 169
Girard, René 127, 128
Glueck, Nelson 22
Goodwin, Archie 166
The Goonies 103
Gopnik, Adam 103
Gordon, Andrew M. 115
Grandmothers of Light 93
Granger, Stephanie 91
Grant, Barry Keith 27
Grant, Linda 154, 155, 156
Grave Injustice 90
Great Depression 20, 21
Griffith, D.W. 29
Grusin, David 193
Guice, Jackson "Butch" 166
Gunga Din 27, 82

Haber, Alejandro 92
Haggard, H. Rider 56, 165, 200
Hale, Jessie (character) 173
Hama, Larry 154
Hamad, Hannah 121, 123
Handlin, Oscar 40
Hapgood, Sophia (character) 182–183, 188
Harman, Graham 137–138
Hart, Gary 108
Haskell, Molly 26, 29
Heart of China 187
Heath-Smith, Jeremy 188
Heidegger, Martin 137, 144
Helpern, David 26
Henderson, Joseph L. 131–132
Hérnandez-Pérez, Manuel 192
The Hero with a Thousand Faces 127–128
Himmler, Heinrich 76
Hirschmann, Peter 186
Hitchcock, Alfred 26
Hitler, Adolf 20, 183
Holtorf, Cornelius 105, 107, 136
Holy Grail 1, 33, 42, 43, 45, 46, 64, 68, 72, 84, 104, 106, 109–111, 114, 116–120, 127, 128, 131, 134, 138, 140–143, 144, 146

Index 209

Horton, Brian 188–189
Howard, Robert E. 153

Imam (character) 107
In Defense of Things 137
"Indiana Jones Adventure: Temple of the Crystal Skull" 193, 196–197
"Indiana Jones Adventure: Temple of the Forbidden Eye" 193, 196–197
Indiana Jones and His Desktop Adventures 184
Indiana Jones and the Adventure of Archaeology 2
Indiana Jones and the Emperor's Tomb 188–189
Indiana Jones and the Fate of Atlantis (comic book) 183
Indiana Jones and the Fate of Atlantis: The Action Game 183
Indiana Jones and the Fate of Atlantis: The Graphic Adventure 181–182, 183
Indiana Jones and the Infernal Machine 183, 184, 185, 188
Indiana Jones and the Iron Phoenix (comic book) 183
Indiana Jones and the Iron Phoenix (video game) 183
Indiana Jones and the Kingdom of the Crystal Skull (film) 1, 7, 8, 30, 31, 35, 41, 43, 45–46, 47, 87–98, 111, 114–115, 120–124, 128, 129, 130, 131, 134–135, 138, 143–146, 180, 184, 186, 187, 197
Indiana Jones and the Kingdom of the Crystal Skull (LeapFrog video game) 184
Indiana Jones and the Kingdom of the Crystal Skull (THQ Wirlesss video game) 184
Indiana Jones and the Last Crusade 1–2, 3, 8, 27, 30, 31, 33, 34–35, 41, 42, 43, 45, 47, 64–74, 81, 89, 104, 106, 107, 108–109, 109–111, 112, 114, 115–120, 121, 122, 124, 128, 129–130, 134, 135, 136, 138, 140–143, 144, 146, 174, 180, 183, 184, 192
Indiana Jones and the Lost Puzzles 184
Indiana Jones and the Monkey King 181
Indiana Jones and the Raiders of the Lost Ark 2, 3, 4–5, 6, 8, 26, 27, 28–29, 30–31, 33–34, 35, 39, 41, 42, 43, 44, 45, 47, 51–62, 64–74, 76, 77, 96, 103, 104, 107, 110, 111, 112, 114, 128, 132–133, 138–140, 141, 142, 143, 144, 146, 151, 152, 153, 155, 156, 158, 159, 164, 165, 166–168, 169, 171, 173, 174, 175, 184, 185, 187, 188, 192, 195, 196, 198
Indiana Jones and the Revenge of the Ancients 180
Indiana Jones and the Spear of Destiny (comic book) 183
Indiana Jones and the Spear of Destiny (video game) 183
Indiana Jones and the Staff of Kings 188–189
Indiana Jones and the Temple of Doom (film) 1, 2, 8, 27, 30, 31–32, 33, 34, 44–45, 47, 76–85, 108, 112, 114, 121, 123, 128–129, 133–134, 152, 157, 180, 189, 192, 196, 200
Indiana Jones and the Temple of Doom (video game) 180
"Indiana Jones and the Temple of Peril" 193, 196
"Indiana Jones Epic Stunt Show Spectacular!" 193, 195–196
Indiana Jones' Greatest Adventures 185
Indiana Jones in the Lost Kingdom 179, 181
Indiana Jones: The Original Adventures 186
The Informer 26
Instruments of Chaos: Starring ... Young Indiana Jones 184
Iron John 115

Jackson, Michael 193
Jacobs, Justin 13–14, 82, 84
Jamal (character) 170
Jaws 38
Jayne, Horace 20
Jayyusi, Lena 96
Jefferson, Thomas 14
Jenkins, Henry 151–152
"Jock Lindsay's Hangar Bar" 193, 198, 201
Johns, W.E. 71
Johnson, Matthew 139
Jolivette, Areyon 6
Jones, Henry, Sr. (character) 34–35, 47, 67, 68, 107, 108–109, 110–111, 114, 115–120, 122, 124, 127, 134, 135, 141
Joyce, Christopher 89
Jung, Carl 5, 131–132, 165, 168, 173
Jurassic Park 103, 111

Kabir, Ananya Jahanara 79
Kael, Pauline 3, 4
Kasdan, Lawrence, 1, 39, 167, 168, 172
Kaufman, Philip 82, 98
Kazim (character) 73, 107, 134
Kendrick, James 5
Kerr, John Findlay 197, 198
Kidder, A.V. 17
King Solomon's Mines 56
Kipling, Rudyard 60, 62, 82, 200
Klexx, Sigfried (character) 171
Knopp, David 98
Kunz, George 93
Kydd, Elspeth 56

Lal, Chattar (character) 80
Landrus, Mallicia Kumbera 81
Langston, David 180, 181
Lao Che (character) 77, 81, 133
Last Crusade: The Action Game 180–181
Last Crusade: The Graphic Adventure 180–181
Lawrence, T.E. 165
Lawrence of Arabia 27

Laycock, Joseph 93
Lean, David 27
LEGO Indiana Jones Mobil Adventure 184
LEGO Indiana Jones 2: The Adventure Continues 186
LEGO Star Wars: The Complete Saga 185–186
Levy, Shawn 188
Lewis, Nathaniel 106, 107
Lindsey, Jock (character) 155, 198
Live Free or Die Hard 121
Lowenthal, David 40
Lucas, George 3, 4, 26, 27, 28, 31, 38–39, 42, 46, 66, 67–68, 82, 98, 104, 108, 109, 111, 153, 154, 165, 166, 167, 171, 172, 174, 178, 182, 187, 198, 199
Luckhurst, Roger 139
Lukas, Scott 194

Mac (character) 35, 122
MacCannell, Dean 113
Macfie, Alexander Lyon 83
Madame Bovary 128
Magoffin, Ralph Van Deman 16–17, 18–19
Maharaja (character) 34, 77, 80
Malley, Shawn 145
Malone, David M. 85
The Man Who Shot Liberty Valance 28
Maniac Mansion 181
Marchetti, Gina 81
"The Mark of the Beast" 82
Marvel Cinematic Universe 152, 192
Matheson, Sue 26
Matrix franchise 152
McBride, Joseph 25–26, 29
McDougall, Walter 40–41
McGhee, Robert 91
McGeough 174
McGuire, Daniel 91
McIver, Ian (character) 172–173, 174
McKay, Alex 76
McNeill, William H. 40, 46
Merrill, Samuel 126–127
Merrill, Selah 15
Michelinie, David 154, 156, 160, 166, 174
Mitchum, Robert 30
Mola Ram (character) 2, 33, 44, 79, 80, 82
Monkey Man (character) 72–73, 166
Morgan, Henry Lewis 88–89
Moriarty, Brian 184
Morley, Sylvanus 17, 19
Morris, Nigel 5, 28–29, 30, 36, 54, 57, 196
Morton, Samuel 89
Muir, John Kenneth 168
Mukherjee, Rohan 85
The Mummy's Curse (book) 139
Murphy, Cullen 140

Nathanson, Jeff 98
Near Eastern Archaeology 174
Nelson, Nels 18

Nevins, Allan 40
Night Gallery 25
Night of the Hunter 30
1941 39

Office of Naval Intelligence 15
Office of Strategic Services 22
Olsen, Bjørnar 137
O'Neil, Denny 166, 172
The Open Mind 130–131
Orellanna, Francisco (character) 89–90, 94, 96
Orientalism 65
Örnebring, Henrik 152
Oxley, Harold (character) 43, 44, 87–88, 95–97, 123, 135

Panama Hat (character) 77, 129
Pattanaik, Devdutt 83–84
Peacock's Eye 133
Pearson, Mike 137
Petrie, Flinders 15
Philips, Deborah 200
Phoenix, River 31
Pillai, Nicholas 152–153, 168
"Pirates of the Caribbean" 194
Pirates of the Caribbean franchise 196
Pitfall! 187
Politis, Gustavo 91
Poltergeist 105
Pondexter, Harvey (character) 170
Potter, Andrew 107, 108, 109
Prakash, Ishwar 78
Predator 105
Prospero (character) 169
Pyle, Howard 189

"The Raider's March" 179
Raiders of the Lost Ark (film) *see Indiana Jones and the Raiders of the Lost Ark*
Raiders of the Lost Ark (video game) 179
Raiders of the Lost Ark: The Adaptation 6
Raiders: The Story of the Best Fan Film Ever Made 3
Rajghatta, Chidanand 85
Rathje, William 140
Ravenscroft, Trevor 109
Ravenwood, Abner 17, 43, 55, 114
Ravenwood, Marion (character) 6, 33–34, 35, 55, 57, 60, 61, 67–68, 77, 81, 105, 108, 114, 120, 122, 123, 132–133, 135, 155–157, 166, 167, 170, 173, 180, 187, 195
Reagan, Ronald 5, 29, 85, 104, 200
Red 122
Reijnders, Stijn 194
Relics of the Past 91
Return of the Jedi 153
Rhode, Joe 194
Rhys-Davies, John 196
Rice, Donna 108

Rick Dangerous 187
Ricks, Nick 186
Robinson, Edward 15
Rocky Balboa 121
Rocky franchise 7, 121
Rodríguez, José Gabriel Ferreras 192
Rom: Spaceknight 153
Roosevelt, Franklin D. 21
Rubbish! The Archaeology of Garbage 140

Said, Edward W. 53, 65, 84
Salicrup, Jim 165
Sallah (character) 70–72, 107, 110, 118, 155, 173, 196, 198
Sankara Stones 2, 32, 33, 42, 44, 77, 78, 80, 84, 112, 128, 131, 133
Satipo (character) 30, 107, 166
Schatz, Thomas 30–31
Schindler's List 104
Schleimann, Heinrich 15
Schneider, Elsa (character) 2, 34, 45, 68, 77, 81, 108, 109, 116, 141–142, 143
Scott, Elliot 181
Scott, Willie (character) 31, 33, 45, 76–77, 81, 84, 123, 133
The Searchers 26, 27, 35
Selleck, Tom 104
Serling, Rod 25
The Serpent and the Rainbow 3
Shanks, Michael 137
She 56
She Wore a Yellow Ribbon 27
Sherman, James T. 165
The Shining 105
Shohat, Ella 5, 55, 56, 57, 59, 200
Shooter, Jim 165
Short Round (character) 31, 34, 77, 82, 83, 114, 133, 155, 173
Simonson, Walt 165
Sleeman, William Henry 83
Smithsonian Museum 2–3, 14, 18, 93
Soderbergh, Steven 6
Spalko, Irene (character) 3, 35, 45–46, 87–88, 92, 93–95, 97, 123, 144–146
Spear of Destiny 109
Spencer, Richard 126
Spielberg, Steven 3, 4, 7, 25–36, 38–39, 42, 46, 51, 53, 59, 67–68, 85, 87, 98, 103, 104, 108, 109, 114, 115, 123, 127, 129, 131, 151, 153, 154, 165, 166, 167, 168, 169, 172, 175, 179, 182, 198, 199
Spinden, Herbert 16
Spivak, Gayatri Chakrovorty 53
Springer, Claudia 54, 55–56
Staff of Ra 4, 132
Stagecoach 27–28, 29–33
Stallone, Sylvester 121
Stam, Robert 5, 200
Stanforth, Charles (character) 120
Star Trek franchise 192

Star Wars 30, 38, 104, 111, 153, 166, 178, 192
Star Wars: Battlefront II 186
Star Wars: Dark Forces 186
Star Wars: Force Unleashed 186–187
Star Wars franchise 3, 7, 153, 155, 165, 178, 179, 181, 185–187, 192, 193, 195, 201
Star Wars: Jedi Knight 185
Stephens, Lloyd 15
Stevens, George 27, 82
Stillman, W.J. 15
Stone, Oliver 105
Strompolos, Chris 3, 4
Struzan, Drew 188
The Sugarland Express 38, 182
Sultan of Hatay (character) 70
Super Empire Strikes Back 185
Super Return of the Jedi 185
Super Star Wars 185
Sutherland, Alec (character) 155

Tambelini, Flavio 98
Tasker, Yvonne 195, 196, 201
Tavistock, Bradley (character) 155
Telotte, J.P. 29
The Terminator 105
Terry and the Pirates 153, 169
Tharoor, Shashi 80, 85
Theater/Archaeology 137
"Theme from Indiana Jones" 34
The Thief of Baghdad 65–66
THX-1138 182
Tobacco Road 26
Tod, James 79
Toht, Arnold (character) 54, 56, 107, 155, 166
Toht, Ilsa (character) 169
Tomb Raider franchise 186, 187–188, 189
Tomb Raider: The Last Revelation 188
Tomb Raider II 188
Tool-Being: Heidegger and the Metaphysics of Objects 137
Treasure Island 169
Trimpe, Herb 156, 166, 171
Trump, Donald 6, 126
Turner, Frederick 129–130, 135

Umland, Rebecca A. 110
Umland, Samuel J. 110
The Uncanny X-Men 154
Uncharted: Drake's Fortune 187, 188, 189, 189

Valdez, Julia (character) 171, 173
Vasquez, Esmeralda (character) 169
Vogel, Curt 169–170
von Ranke, Leopold 40

Wagner, Kim A. 83
Wall Street 105
Walsh, Raoul 29
Walt Disney theme parks 193–201

Walt Disney's Uncle Scrooge 165
War of the Worlds (2006) 27
Ward, Jim 186
Warner, Langdon 18, 22
Warshaw, Howard Scott 179
Wasser, Frederick 36
Wayne, John 27, 29–33
Waysdorf, Abby 194
Williams, John 34, 179, 196, 197
Williams, Mutt (character) 35, 41, 87, 89–90, 94, 95–97, 114–115, 120–124, 130, 134, 135, 143–144
Willis, Bruce 121
Wilmunder, Aric 183
Wood, Bryant 112
Wood, Robin 5, 36, 115
Wooley, Leonard 16
World War I 14, 15, 16, 17, 20
World War II 14, 20, 21, 27, 39, 57, 61, 127, 130
Wu Han (character) 77

The Young Indiana Jones Chronicles (television show) 6, 183–184, 193
The Young Indiana Jones Chronicles (video game) 183–184

Zak McKracken and the Alien Mind Benders 181
Žižek, Slavoj 113

www.ingramcontent.com/pod-product-compliance
Lightning Source LLC
Chambersburg PA
CBHW032043300426
44117CB00009B/1172